# Sustainability in the Oil and Gas Sector

Thomas Walker · Sergey Barabanov ·
Maya Michaeli · Victoria Kelly
Editors

# Sustainability in the Oil and Gas Sector

## Adaptation and Mitigation Strategies for Tackling Climate Change

palgrave
macmillan

*Editors*
Thomas Walker
Department of Finance
Concordia University
Montreal, QC, Canada

Sergey Barabanov
Department of Finance
University of St. Thomas-Minnesota
Saint Paul, MN, USA

Maya Michaeli
Emerging Risks Information Center
Montreal, QC, Canada

Victoria Kelly
Emerging Risks Information Center
Montreal, QC, Canada

ISBN 978-3-031-51585-9 ISBN 978-3-031-51586-6 (eBook)
https://doi.org/10.1007/978-3-031-51586-6



This Palgrave Macmillan imprint is published by the registered company Springer Nature Switzerland AG
The registered company address is: Gewerbestrasse 11, 6330 Cham, Switzerland

Paper in this product is recyclable.

# Acknowledgments

We acknowledge the financial support provided through the Jacques Ménard—BMO Centre for Capital Markets. We appreciate the invaluable copy-editing and editorial assistance we received from Charlotte Frank, as well as the assistance of Mauran Pavan and Meaghan Landrigan-Buttle.

# Contents

# Notes on Contributors

**Dayo Akindipe** is an energy transition specialist with technical, research, and consulting experience that cuts across CCUS, geothermal energy, and oil and gas. He currently leads projects on geothermal technoeconomic analysis and repurposing of oil and gas infrastructure for energy storage. He has a B.Sc. in Chemical Engineering from the University of Lagos, Nigeria, an M.Sc. in Petroleum (Reservoir) Engineering from the Norwegian University of Science and Technology (NTNU), Norway, and a Ph.D. in Petroleum Engineering (minor in Environment and Natural Resources) from the University of Wyoming, USA.

**Binny Bagga** is a vice president in Rystad Energy's Supply Chain team and is Product Manager of Service Market Solution. Her primary focus is supply and demand in the energy supply chain across energy sectors, sustainability, and financial benchmarking. She is a CFA charterholder from the CFA Institute, Charlottesville, USA, and has a Bachelor of Commerce degree from the University of Delhi. She has more than eleven years of experience and has previously worked at SeaBird Exploration and Ernst & Young.

**Sergey Barabanov** is an associate professor of finance at the Opus College of Business, University of Saint Thomas. He teaches graduate and undergraduate investments, corporate finance, fixed income, and financial management courses. He has also developed two "professor plus professional" courses, which professors teach alongside industry executives. His teaching innovation brings together academic knowledge with the latest hands-on investment experience for students. His research focuses on institutional investors, corporate governance, securities litigation, behavioral finance, and socially responsible investing. He has served as a CFO, controller, chief accounting officer, and business consultant for several international firms and government agencies.

**Steven Bryant** serves as Schulich School of Engineering Research Chair in Materials Engineering at the University of Calgary and, in his previous role, served as the university's first Canada Excellence Research Chair. He leads an interdisciplinary research program for energy and climate applications. Bringing together advances in fields such as nanotechnology, novel materials, and microbiology, the program re-imagines how society can benefit from hydrocarbon resources with reduced environmental impact. To date, this work has yielded more than two dozen inventions and five start-up companies. Previously, he directed the Geological $CO_2$ Storage Joint Industry Project and the Nanoparticles for Subsurface Engineering Industrial Affiliates Program at the University of Texas at Austin after working in industry research centers in Europe for a decade. He has published extensively on production and reservoir engineering, formation evaluation, and $CO_2$ storage and has trained 150+ graduate students and postdoctoral fellows. He is the proud recipient of the 2021 Society of Petroleum Engineers Sustainability and Stewardship in the Oil and Gas Industry Award.

**André Castro Carvalho** holds an LL.B., LL.M., and Ph.D. in Law from the University of São Paulo, where he received the "CAPES 2014 Thesis Award" for his Ph.D. thesis. He was a visiting postdoctoral researcher at the Massachusetts Institute of Technology (2016) and the University of São Paulo (2018). He is a professor of law at Ibmec-SP and Insper and vice president of the Brazilian Institute of Business Ethics.

**Juliano Ribeiro de Almeida** holds a Ph.D. in Finance from the Faculty of Business, Economics, and Accounting of the University of Sao Paulo (FEA/USP). He is a postdoctoral fellow in corporate finance and investments at FEA/USP. He worked for almost twenty years as a financial consultant and project coordinator at Fundacao Getulio Vargas, one of Brazil's most prominent think tanks. He has extensive experience in corporate finance, especially investment analysis and business valuation, and relevant experience with regulating public services.

**José Roberto Ferreira Savoia** has been a professor of finance at Faculdade de Economia, Administração, Contabilidade e Atuária da Universidade de São Paulo (FEA-USP) since 1998. In addition, he was an adjunct professor at the School of International and Public Affairs, Columbia University, New York, in 2007 and 2009, and a visiting professor at Open University, in the United Kingdom, in 2012. He is also the President of Previc—the National Authority for Pensions Funds Supervision. He is the founder and director of the Center for Studies in Regulation and Public Policies at Fundação Instituto de Administração (FIA). Additionally, he participated in the strategic plan "Paths to Brazil" (2020) to the Brazilian Congress, as well as the discussion regarding the impacts of the Brazilian Pension Reform with the Brazilian Congress (in 2019). He also contributed to regulating piped gas in São Paulo and to economic-financial models rebalancing road, water, and sewage concessions.

**Salim Ghettas** is an environmental health and safety professional with more than ten years of experience in the oil and gas sector. He worked for different private and multinational companies in the Middle East and North Africa region in mid-management and consulting positions. He holds a bachelor's degree in occupational health and safety from the University of Batna, Algeria, and a Master degree in environmental sustainability health and safety management from the Rochester Institute of Technology. He received multiple awards, grants, and scholarships such as the Fulbright Graduate Exchange Student Scholarship in 2013 from the US State Department Bureau of Educational and Cultural Affairs. His research interests are on process safety management, critical infrastructure protection, and sustainability in the oil and gas sector. He authored and co-authored technical reports and peer-reviewed journal articles with researchers from the Collaboratory for Resiliency and Recovery at the Rochester Institute of Technology, NY.

**Victoria Kelly** holds a B.Sc. in Biology with an additional major in Irish Studies. She has worked with the Emerging Risks Information Center at Concordia University since 2020, where she has been involved in numerous book projects and research papers in the area of sustainability, fintech, and climate change, and has assisted with the center's administration. She is pursuing a Master's degree in History at Concordia University, examining the 1832 Cholera epidemic in Montreal and its management on a social, urban, and economic level, drawing parallels with the recent COVID-19 pandemic.

**Maya Michaeli** is a research assistant in the Department of Finance at Concordia University, Montreal. She has a natural passion and enthusiasm for financial markets, which has led her to further pursue her studies in this field. She has worked on numerous book projects and research papers related to a sustainable future and responsible finance at the Emerging Risk Information Center (ERIC). Her research interests include risk management, speculative investing, derivatives trading, and sustainable investing.

**Dr. Øystein Noreng** is a professor emeritus in the Department of Leadership and Organizational Behavior at BI Norwegian Business School, Norway. Since 1990, he has been the Director of the M.Sc. Program in Energy Economics and Management at BI. Throughout his career, he assumed numerous consultancy roles for Norwegian, foreign, and international public and private organizations, including the governments of Norway, Denmark, and Sweden, the US Department of State, the US Internal Revenue Service, the United Nations, the World Bank, the International Monetary Fund, the International Energy Agency, and several oil and gas companies; all while being a member of the Supervisory Board of RWE DEA (Hamburg). Additionally, he has published a multitude of reports, articles, and books relating to energy, oil, international politics, and the political economy.

**Dandina N. Rao** is a distinguished professor in the Craft and Hawkins Department of Petroleum Engineering at Louisiana State University, Baton Rouge, USA. He previously worked as Principal Petroleum Engineer with TRW/BDM Petroleum Technologies (Formerly NIPER) in Bartlesville, Oklahoma; as Staff Research Engineer with the Petroleum Recovery Institute in Calgary; and as Research Engineer with Shell Canada. In addition to developing the Gas-Assisted Gravity Drainage (GAGD) process for enhanced oil recovery, he has invented the HydroFlame process for steam and flue gas generation for various industrial applications, the dual-drop dual-crystal technique for confident reservoir wettability characterization, and the vanishing interface technique (VIT) for quick and cost-effective gas-oil miscibility determination. He holds a B.Tech with Distinction from India, an M.Sc. from the University of Saskatchewan (Canada), and a Ph.D. from the University of

Calgary (Canada). He holds several patents in the USA and other countries in addition to publishing over 150 technical papers. He is a member of APEGA, SPE, and has served as Editor-in-Chief of the *Petroleum Science and Technology Journal*. In 2019, he was elected as senior member of the US National Academy of Inventors, for "producing technologies that have brought real impact on the welfare of society."

**Luiz Eduardo Ganem Rubião** is a partner responsible for Industry 4.0 practice within Deloitte's Financial Advisory | Infrastructure & Capital Projects group. He has over 35 years of experience in planning and implementing engineering and software projects in multinational companies in the oil and gas, chemical and petrochemical, pulp and paper, metals and mining, and power and utility markets, with professional education in chemical engineering (B.Sc.) and process control (M.Sc.). He has significant experience as an entrepreneur in innovative areas (having founded three high tech companies in Brazil) and within large companies (Exxon and Siemens). He has worked on several engineering projects related to the industrial gas market, including coke gas treatment, natural gas processing, biogas upgrading to biomethane, air separation units, and hydrogen and oxygen pressure swing adsorption.

**Dr. Bikash D. Saikia** is a postdoctoral research associate at Louisiana State University (LSU), with research interests in the area of enhanced oil recovery, fluid flow, rock-fluid interactions, and carbon sequestration. He has co-authored two patents on Single Well Gas-Assisted Gravity Drainage process that fosters sustainable oil production through concurrent $CO_2$ sequestration. He is pursuing yet another patent on the conversion of orphan wells, which pose both safety and environmental risk, into carbon neutral sustainable producers. He regularly serves as a reviewer in reputed journals including those of SPE, Elsevier, Springer, Taylor & Francis, and was the deputy editor of Petroleum Science and Technology (PST) journal from 2020 to 2021. He is the recipient of LSU's prestigious Economic Development Assistantship awarded to outstanding candidates for pursuing the Ph.D. program at LSU. He has over 7 years of oil-field experience, working in both offshore and onshore locations, in the areas of production optimization, artificial lift, reservoir management, process operations, and safety.

**Dr. Soheil Saraji** is an associate professor of energy and petroleum engineering and co-director of the Hydrocarbons Lab at the University of

Wyoming. He has a B.Sc., M.Sc., and Ph.D. in Petroleum Engineering. His expertise spans over the areas of subsurface energy storage and extraction, fluid-rock characterization, and application of digital technologies in the energy sector. His current research focuses on enabling technologies for energy transition including carbon and hydrogen geo-storage, carbon accounting using blockchain technology, and geothermal energy optimization.

**Dr. Siân Stephens** is a senior lecturer in International Business at Middlesex University Business School in London and a founding co-lead of the Business Ethics, Accountability and Governance Research Cluster. She has worked on issues relating to the extractive and energy sector for many years, with a focus on the relationship between companies and communities. More recently, she has turned her attention to the challenges facing alternative and renewable sources of energy and the impact of operations such as onshore wind farms on local communities.

**Thomas Walker** is a full professor of finance, the director and academic lead of the Emerging Risks Information Center (ERIC), the inaugural director of the Jacques Ménard/BMO Center for Capital Markets, and the Concordia University Research Chair in Emerging Risk Management (Tier 1) at Concordia University in Montreal, Canada. He previously served as associate dean, department chair, and director of Concordia's David O'Brien Centre for Sustainable Enterprise. Prior to his academic career, he worked for firms such as Mercedes Benz, KPMG, and Utility Consultants International. He has published over 80 journal articles and books.

# List of Figures

# List of Tables

PART I

# Introduction

CHAPTER 1

# Sustainability in the Oil and Gas Industry: An Introduction

*Thomas Walker, Sergey Barabanov, Maya Michaeli, and Victoria Kelly*

## Introduction

The push for sustainability in the oil and gas sector has taken center stage in both climate action debates and mitigation/adaptation efforts in the recent decades. Numerous publications, reports, books, and conventions have presented, analyzed, and compared the actions and strategies taken by governments, non-governmental organizations, and the private sector—all in hopes of curbing both the direct emissions linked to the

T. Walker
Department of Finance, Concordia University, Montreal, QC, Canada
e-mail: thomas.walker@concordia.ca

S. Barabanov
Department of Finance, Opus College of Business, University of St Thomas, Saint Paul, MN, USA
e-mail: ssbarabanov@stthomas.edu

M. Michaeli · V. Kelly (✉)
Emerging Risks Information Center, Montreal, QC, Canada
e-mail: victoria.kelly@concordia.ca



T. Walker et al. (eds.), *Sustainability in the Oil and Gas Sector*,
https://doi.org/10.1007/978-3-031-51586-6_1

exploration, production, transportation, and refining of carbon fuels as well as the emissions stemming from their eventual use. Extant reports and studies discuss specific scenarios tied to the oil and gas industry such as flaring, water usage, methane emissions, plastics waste and recycling, greenhouse gas emissions, and carbon reduction, and offer insights into substitute products including alternative sources of energy in, e.g., the utility and transportation sector.

The oil and gas industry has evolved dramatically in recent years, necessitating significant changes in the way it conducts business. Due to the increasing amount of energy consumers need to maintain their way of life, this industry, which is among the biggest in the world, continues to experience strong sales and remains one of the largest polluters. A majority of evaluations conducted to-date show that the industry is unprepared for the effects of climate change, at both the commercial and institutional levels, as companies and countries race toward a true net-zero emissions (Cox et al., 2022). Therefore, it is imperative to assess the development of environmental, health, safety (EHS) initiatives, and the development of sustainability in the oil and gas industry.

Because it is one of the biggest emitters of greenhouse gases, the oil and gas industry has long been a significant factor in the discussion of climate change (Yuan et al., 2018). There exist various possibilities for reducing those emissions and making businesses more environmentally conscious, including developing new technologies, increasing participation in international renewable energy projects, and tighter, more stringent regulatory measures.

The notion of what makes a sector and its activities sustainable, however, has long been debated. In its Brundtland Commission report in 1987, the United Nations initially defined the concept of sustainable development as "meeting the needs of the present without compromising the ability of future generations to meet their own needs" (p. 16). The challenge appears to be in reconciling economic success with the environmental implications and consequences inherent in the oil and gas sector. Although it has been demonstrated that sustainable economic growth is simple to achieve (Anis & Siddiqui, 2015), the industry's financial viability

M. Michaeli
e-mail: maya.michaeli@concordia.ca

is increasingly threatened by sustainability risks such as climate change, safety risks, and social pressures (Anis & Siddiqui, 2015).

Policymakers have increased their support for renewable technologies as pressures increase to adopt more sustainable energy practices. However, despite the benefits of using these energy sources in the oil and gas sector, they have not been widely implemented. For example, the United States (US) Department of Energy estimated in 2017 that the commercial viability of renewable energy sources in the US could reduce global warming by 0.8 degrees Celsius, but this has yet to be implemented (Dmitrieva & Romasheva, 2020).

In recent years, businesses have taken several measures that have benefited from market changes and efforts to use more environmentally conscious techniques. For example, companies may buy offsets from green energy projects when they develop new projects. Alternatively, companies may engage with communities and organizations involved in renewable energy efforts to take advantage of these incentives for their operations (Yuan et al., 2018). This improved involvement in the market's growing interest and realization of the advantages of renewable energy is expected to be a factor that stimulates the development and implementation of policies for the oil and gas sector. As the market continues to embrace net-zero carbon investment solutions, this shift will play a significant role in future investments.

In addition to becoming more environmentally friendly, companies must separate their business objectives from climate change impacts. For instance, an organization may be interested in seeking permission to construct a pipeline through a community or region to which it is not fully committed. However, in areas with vulnerable populations, this may contribute to social injustice or conflict, especially if such conflicts cause major changes in human livelihoods and access to resources (Gardas et al., 2019). Future generations will appreciate companies trying harder than they currently do to respect the rights of people affected by their activities. Their environmental performance can be improved by implementing more efficient and effective systems for monitoring and responding to project community impacts.

Key components must be addressed when discussing the sustainability of a sector: economic, environmental, and social sustainability—often referred to as the "Triple Bottom Line", or TBL. A TBL approach is frequently used when attempting to holistically evaluate a company's performance in light of its financial, environmental, and social impacts.

This concept was first applied to corporate America by John Elkington, who brought to the forefront the idea that a company's sustainability not only depended on its economic profit and its ability to continue its operations, but also on its environmental and social impacts (Slaper & Hall, 2011). These three dimensions of sustainable development are also commonly referred to as the 3Ps: people, planet, and profit. Following such events as the 1994 ratification of the United Nations Framework Convention on Climate Change (UNFCCC) and Shell's publication of its first sustainability report in 1997, the call for a 3P-oriented sustainability approach in the oil and gas industry has grown tremendously, with researchers, practitioners, and regulators focusing on how the sector can adapt to today's climate change realities and respond to public pressures for cleaner energies.

In today's globalized world, nations find themselves engaged in a race for progress and economic prosperity. The concept of degrowth, along with other visionary goals like steady-state economies and the circular economy, has gained attention for its potential to address sustainability challenges. However, the practicality of embracing such ideologies while keeping up with competing nations is a subject of debate. It is also important to acknowledge the hurdles involved in transitioning from fossil fuels to renewable energies, including material limitations for batteries and short-to-medium-term technological and infrastructure obstacles. While these visionary goals are undoubtedly crucial for a sustainable future, their implementation requires careful consideration of the present realities. As global trends shift toward a more sustainable future; we must find methods to integrate our sustainable efforts within the oil and gas industry, as it will certainly remain a necessary resource used across many sectors in the near future.

Although these societal pressures have affected the reputation of many companies in the industry and have led many firms to implement measures to ensure their compliance to environmental sustainability, research has shown that the reliability and verity of these implemented measures can be brought into question (Cherry & Sneirson, 2011; Scanlan, 2017; Stephenson et al., 2012). Studies have identified issues surrounding emissions, process safety, the protection of the environment and personnel, and sustainability, but highlight that these issues are not sufficiently addressed by many companies.

Many questions currently surround sustainability scholarship in the oil and gas industry. This edited book explores how societal pressures have induced new and continuous developments and how companies, governments, and individuals can act to impact the future of energy production. The book integrates the financial, political, social, and ethical fields of sustainability studies and applies them to several case studies in the oil and gas industry. The chapters we featured in this book offer practical solutions applicable to the industry within the short-to-medium term. Concurrently, we recognize the societal imperative of striving for more visionary goals in the long run. Among these aspirations, the circular economy emerges as the most promising for implementation in the shorter term. By clarifying this distinction, we aim to strike a balance between immediate practicality and the overarching pursuit of sustainable ideals.

## Overview of Content

**Section 1:** Fundamentals of Sustainable Development in the Oil & Gas Industry

This section is comprised of four chapters which examine the fundamental components of the oil and gas industry and how these relate to sustainability and an increase in environmentally and socially conscious behaviors. As the section progresses, a particular emphasis is put on an examination of alternative fuel sources, and the importance of the oil and gas industry in a progression to more sustainable energy sources.

The section begins with Chapter 2, "Structural Transitions in the Petroleum Industry", in which **Øystein Noreng** defines the fundamental structure of the oil and gas industry and explores the implications of the currently observed structural transition in the industry. As demand shifts to Asia, and the United States and Europe lose relevance, political affiliations between these powers and important industry stakeholders such as Russia and the Middle East also shift. Noreng explores these political affiliations and defines market indicators of political instability generated by the oil and gas industry which may affect its medium- to long-term sustainability.

The section continues with Chapter 3, "The Role of the Oil and Gas Industry in the Energy Transition", where **Soheil Saraji** and **Dayo Akindipe** explore the key role that the oil and gas industry could play in leading the energy transition and mitigating climate change. More specifically, the authors focus on three pillars of sustainable energy development, modernization and digitization, and underground energy storage. Saraji and Akindipe examine current efforts in sustainable energy development, as well as how a push for modernization and digitization could benefit these efforts, as well as novel ways to leverage the expertise of the industry into new fuel extraction methods.

In Chapter 4, "The Future of Fossil Fuels: Renewable Energy—Wind and Solar", **Binny Bagga** uses the case studies of Rystad Energy to explore the necessity of the transition to wind and solar energy sources if we are to achieve the COP26's established 1.5 °C goal, which aims to limit global warming to no more than 1.5 °C above pre-industrial levels. Bagga details the wind and solar demands that stem from the achievement of this goal, and the political and economic ramifications of this increased demand.

Finally, this section closes off with Chapter 5, "The next wave of natural gas in Brazil", **Jose Roberto Ferreira Savoia, André Castro Carvalho, Juliano Ribeiro de Almeida, and Luiz Eduardo Ganem Rubião,** uses a case study of the natural gas industry in Brazil to showcase the potential for producing renewable energy in the region, as well as the implications of government intervention in energy production activities.

**Section 2:** Sustainable frameworks and solutions for environmental challenges in the oil and gas industry

This section builds on the above with four chapters which highlight the imperative role the oil and gas industry must play in the energy transition. Using case studies, these chapters examine risk mitigation and offer solutions to ensure the energy transition involves a more sustainable oil and gas industry.

The section opens with Chapter 6, "The Social License to Operate Across the Energy Industry: Lessons for Low-Carbon Energy from Oil and Gas", in which **Siân Stephens** explores the concept of the Social Lisence to Operate, a popular concept which took form in the oil and gas industry. This chapter considers the similarities and differences between the local acceptance challenges faced by both the oil and gas industry, and renewable alternatives such as onshore wind. The chapter aims to extricate lessons learned from the social acceptance of oil and gas activities and apply these to the pushback reflected in other sustainable energy industries.

Chapter 7, "Carbon-negative Oil and Gas", by **Steven Bryant** examines energy supplies over the last century to show that replacing fossil fuels with renewables by 2050 will require very large growth rates, and that sustaining such rates for thirty years is uncommon. Bryant explores the timely idea of coupling established, already scaled technologies for injecting and producing fluids in subsurface hydrocarbon reservoirs, such as $CO_2$-enhanced oil recovery, with rapidly growing technologies to capture $CO_2$ from the atmosphere, such as direct air capture, examining how more carbon is removed from the atmosphere than is emitted during the production, processing, and combustion of oil. The author then discusses the advantages and drawbacks of carbon-negative oil relative to other forms of greenhouse gas removal.

Chapter 8 demonstrates the application of new technologies and how these can help increase the sustainability of oil and gas as it remains an important part of the energy demand. In "Two Technologies to Enable Environmental Sustainability of the Oil & Gas Industry", **Dandina Rao** and **Bikash Saikia** present a novel combustion technology, called HydroFlame (HF) (or Flame-in-Water) technology, to safely burn this hitherto-flared natural gas and to capture the flue gases of combustion and injecting into oil fields for enhancing oil recovery, proposing a dual technology scheme which provides the industry with a profitable means to considerably reduce (if not eliminate) GHG/$CO_2$ emissions from gas flares by enabling EOR in a sustainable manner.

The book concludes with Chapter 9, "The oil and gas sector and the UN SDGs: Geo-engineering as a solution to mitigate climate change", in which **Salim Ghettas** relates the risks associated with the oil and gas industry to the achievement of the UN's sustainable development goal. In detailing the risks entailed by many of the sector's activities and relating these to specific goals, Ghettas concludes that risk management can significantly improve the likelihood of achieving the UN SDGs and recommends specific actions which can be taken to this effect. Ghettas effectively demonstrates that the oil and gas industry, though it cannot be eliminated entirely, can be leveraged as a means to achieve a more sustainable future.

Ultimately, it is critical to evaluate the current implemented environmental programs and the advancement of sustainability in the oil and gas sector. Not only is the oil and gas industry an important part of the global economy through its trade potential and value generation, but it also represents an important source of employment and plays a large role in production processes globally. Nevertheless, the large volume of greenhouse gases emitted by its operations will cause significant environmental impacts regardless of government regulation levels or national policies. As national governments are pressured by these ongoing environmental concerns and the push toward a sustainable future, they must collaborate with corporations and market players to collectively address the role of the oil and gas industry in the energy transition. We hope that the chapters above can provide insightful directions toward this end.

## References

Anis, M. D., & Siddiqui, T. Z. (2015). Issues impacting sustainability in the oil and gas industry. *Journal of Management and Sustainability, 5*(4), 115–124. https://doi.org/10.5539/jms.v5n4p115

Charnois, G. K. (2021, October 21). Degrowth, steady state and circular economies: Alternative discourses to economic growth. *Society Register*, *5*(3), 75–94. https://doi.org/10.14746/sr.2021.5.3.05

Cherry, M. A., & Sneirson, J. F. (2011). Beyond profit: Rethinking corporate social responsibility and greenwashing after the BP oil disaster. *Tulane Law Review, 85*(4), 983. https://doi.org/10.2139/ssrn.1670149

Cox, E., Kelly, C., Murphy, B., & Rötttmer, N. (2022, May 16). *The ESG transformation—how to embrace it?* PwC. https://www.pwc.com/gx/en/issues/reinventing-the-future/take-on-tomorrow/esg-transformation.html

Dmitrieva, D., & Romasheva, N. (2020). Sustainable development of oil and gas potential of the arctic and its shelf zone: The role of innovations. *Journal of Marine Science and Engineering, 8*(12), 1003. https://doi.org/10.3390/jmse8121003

Gardas, B. B., Mangla, S. K., Raut, R. D., Narkhede, B., & Luthra, S. (2019). Green talent management to unlock sustainability in the oil and gas sector. *Journal of Cleaner Production, 229*, 850–862. https://doi.org/10.1016/j.jclepro.2019.05.018

Scanlan, S. J. (2017). Framing fracking: Scale-shifting and greenwashing risk in the oil and gas industry. *Local Environment, 22*(11), 1311–1337. https://doi.org/10.1080/13549839.2017.1345877

Slaper, T. F., & Hall, T. J. (2011). *The triple bottom line: What is it and how does it work?* Indiana Business Review. https://www.ibrc.indiana.edu/ibr/2011/spring/pdfs/article2.pdf

Stephenson, E., Doukas, A., & Shaw, K. (2012). Greenwashing gas: Might a 'transition fuel' label legitimize carbon-intensive natural gas development? *Energy Policy, 46*, 452–459. https://doi.org/10.1016/j.enpol.2012.04.010

United Nations Brundtland Commission. (1987). http://www.un-documents.net/our-common-future.pdf

Yuan, R., Behrens, P., Tukker, A., & Rodrigues, J. F. (2018). Carbon overhead: The impact of the expansion in low-carbon electricity in China 2015–2040. *Energy Policy, 119*, 97–104. https://doi.org/10.1016/j.enpol.2018.04.027

PART II

# Fundamentals of Sustainable Development in the Oil & Gas Industry

# CHAPTER 2

# Petroleum Industry Structural Transition

*Øystein Noreng*

## Introduction

This chapter discusses the changing patterns of the global petroleum industry and trade, focusing on China's rising importance, while also considering the potential effects of Russia's war on Ukraine. Historically, politics and international power relations have shaped the world's oil market together with conventional market forces through costs and prices. Investment patterns indicate that the world is not out of the coal age; it appears to be in the middle of the oil age and possibly at the beginning of a natural gas and renewables age. Investors, however, remain bullish on oil (Critchlow, 2019). Since alternatives to oil are neither cost competitive nor readily available, oil is likely, at least in this author's opinion, to remain in demand for a long time, even if within changing market structures.

A market structure can be understood as the arena of competition determined by a number of sellers meeting a number of buyers through a number of intermediaries. It can also be understood as the dispersal

Ø. Noreng (✉)
Professor Emeritus, Department of Leadership and Organizational Behavior, BI Norwegian Business School, Oslo, Norway
e-mail: onoreng@online.no



T. Walker et al. (eds.), *Sustainability in the Oil and Gas Sector*,
https://doi.org/10.1007/978-3-031-51586-6_2

of market power. Key concepts for understanding market structures are monopoly (a single seller), monopsony (a single buyer), oligopoly (few sellers), oligopsony (few buyers), and vertical integration (the inclusion of the value chain in one firm). Capital intensity and long lead times tend to limit access and dampen competition so that historically, the typical pattern of the oil industry has not corresponded to the image of a free market with open access, but rather one marked by barriers to entry that encourage collusion. Within this framework, shifting costs, prices, and profits have driven changes in company structures. External shocks, political conflicts, and wars impact the concentration of power and profits along the value chain.

Limited resource access and high capital requirements are inherent features of the oil and natural gas industry that give it a propensity for concentration of ownership and for imperfect competition. Volatile demand forces market stability to rely on spare supply capacity, the keeping of actual output below technical potential, and the setting of market prices above production costs. The modest impact of rising prices on oil demand implies that most consumers are more concerned about secure supplies than costs, providing incentives to seller cooperation, which in turn discourages competition. Consumers buy what they need for driving, heating, and other essential services while adjusting their budget if needed. The slow rate of replacement of capital assets and durable consumer goods enhances demand rigidity, impeding adaptation.

The oil industry has experienced long periods of remarkable stability, interrupted only by discontinuities which have yielded new company patterns. The First World War eliminated Germany from the competition over the Middle East's resources and left the international oil industry in the hands of British, French, and US interests until the 1973 Yom Kippur war. The key to the historical cartel was an oligopoly in control of trading as the strategic link in the value chain. The succeeding order has been based largely on producer power embodied by OPEC, the Organization of Petroleum Exporting Countries, and in recent years the OPEC+ (OPEC plus Russia). The 2022 Russia-Ukraine war appears to be triggering extensive changes, including the restructuring of the oil industry with China emerging as a powerful player. The concentration of oil demand in Asia could strengthen consumer power for a regional oligopsony.

The global oil market is not based on unlimited, open competition, rather, barriers to entering it make the market an oligopoly, where a few large sellers influence/control prices. Prices can stay well above production costs if consumers are willing to pay. For consumers, the most expensive oil barrel is the one that, in a pinch, is not available. Correspondingly, in a squeeze, consumers are willing to pay dearly for an additional barrel of oil. This underlines that for the public, oil is an input factor, that is, a necessity in the production and consumption processes. Trading makes oil a commodity, banking makes oil a financial object, and in both cases, it is a source of value to intermediaries.

These concerns give value to securing supplies at times in which prices are much higher than the cost of production (Dannreuther, 2017). Since the demand for oil is not highly price elastic, the risk is that increasing supply on the market will lead to lower prices rather than volume gains, which will result in revenue losses. In the oil market, it is sometimes more profitable not to produce, that is, to withhold oil from the market.

The petroleum industry has been the subject of successful coordination. The resulting economic rent and surplus profit are the object of strife between producing companies, traders, and governments of producer as well as consumer countries. The accumulation of economic rent provides equity capital, sheltering companies involved against fluctuations in prices and costs. The resulting robustness has helped many oil companies achieve strong market positions and long tenures. The counterpart to this robustness is a rigidity in company organization and management strategies. The oil industry is robust to variations in costs and prices, and so only major shocks can induce profound changes.

Market forces drove a transition away from coal in the twentieth century; oil was cheaper, more convenient, and cleaner. Although some governments at the time took measures to protect coal industries, *slowing* the shift, in the twenty-first century, governments have conversely pushed for a move away from oil, *accelerating* the shift. Energy availability and prices are as much the product of regulations, taxes, and subsidies, which relate political intentions, as they are of market forces, which mean relative costs.

The oil share of the world energy market is in decline, but the volumes extracted and consumed continue to rise, so too do the business figures and the industry turnover. Demand is moving to Africa and Asia and China has become the world's largest oil importer. The international oil industry is no longer dominated by the United States and European multinationals; Chinese, Russian, and Saudi companies are increasingly important. The US dollar is no longer the only petro-currency; the Chinese yuan holds a rising place in the oil trade.

These trends have been slowly changing the oil industry since the beginning of the twenty-first century. Russia's 2022 war in Ukraine revealed political trends with a potential impact on oil and natural gas trading patterns. Russia is highly affected as European customers have announced their intention to discontinue purchases of Russian oil and natural gas. Of equal importance is the refusal of certain countries, such as China and India, to follow suit in condemning Russia's war. Saudi Arabia's choice to continue the Organization of the Petroleum Exporting Countries' (OPEC+) supply policy, meaning pricing and production, in cooperation with Russia is also significant. The choice of currency for trading oil and natural gas may have significant implications on the global economy, where Russia and Saudi Arabia remain key players insofar as oil and natural gas remain vital to the world economy.

One view, however, is that "Peak Oil Demand," and not "Peak Oil," will occur worldwide in a few years' time, making the oil industry increasingly redundant, and giving governments and private investors reasons to divest (Muttit, 2020). From this perspective Russia and Saudi Arabia will lose economic weight and political clout as the world oil and natural gas markets shrink. The oil and gas industry would thus gradually become an energy industry.

An opposing view is that regardless of political inconvenience and climate risk, oil and natural gas will remain competitive and in demand for a long time (Yergin, 2020). In this case, worldwide oil consumption would continue to grow; oil and natural gas would therefore retain economic and strategic importance, but the oil industry would be increasingly anchored in Asia, including Russia and Siberia. The question is how these companies will score on efficiency and competitiveness, as well as on social and environmental accounts. Technical and managerial shortcomings would incite cooperation with international oil companies, if better managed (Seznec, 2015).

## The Issues

The prospect of man-made global warming raises stronger concerns in Europe and the United States than in the rest of the world. By 2020, countries outside the OECD accounted for sixty percent of the world's primary energy consumption and fifty-five percent of its oil demand.

Even with high annual growth rates in power generation from renewable sources such as solar, wind, and biomass, worldwide absolute progress is slow (Le Page, 2016).[1] The world's dependence on fossil fuels (natural gas, oil, and coal) has been constant since 1990, despite wide swings in energy prices. By the mid-1980s oil prices fell and the real price, measured in the purchasing power in US dollars, returned to the level it had reached in 1985 only by 2005.

The Middle East remains a key player in oil and natural gas due to its vast resources and low costs. The region is likely to remain financially important and attract the interest of China, Europe, India, Russia, and the United States. The United States, however, has a more vested interest in the financial surpluses and the arms markets of the region. Moreover, Russia has made a political comeback in the Middle East and is the key partner in OPEC+. China also has a wide range of economic and political interests in the region, while India is a rising economic and strategic actor. What results from these combined factors is a worldwide need for oil and natural gas. Until there is a breakthrough in electricity storage, oil and natural gas will remain competitive, at least in parts of the energy market. The best petroleum investment opportunities appear outside the OECD region, including Russia. International oil trade is increasingly a business between Middle Eastern and Russian suppliers and buyers in China and India.

Trends in the oil market have not followed the Peak Oil theory's forecasts. Demand has increased less than expected and supply has been more robust than anticipated. The price mechanism has worked, though sometimes in a brutal manner, with strong discontinuities and high social costs. Unfortunately for consumers and producers alike, oil prices are highly volatile and unstable at all levels.

Historically, the oil industry has tended toward increasingly efficient, clean, and ultimately cheaper energy technologies as consumers have become more educated and prosperous (Smil, 2017a, 2017b). Capital has been invested in machinery for energy to substitute the labor force (Beaudreau, 1998). Energy has also replaced manual labor and modern technology has allowed energy to replace mental labor, changing the modus operandi of the service sector (Smil, 2017a, 2017b). Since the early 1970s, energy market convulsions have reminded the world of

[1] Greg Muttit, "What for OPEC in the last generation of oil", in *Handbook of OPEC and the Global Energy Order*,London 2020, Routledge, pp. 338–355.

precarious balances. In 2020, the global COVID-19 pandemic caused a quasi-worldwide lockdown and incurred low energy prices. In 2021 and 2022, economic recovery and political conflict once again raised energy prices, diverting the world's attention from the potentially harmful effects of fossil fuels to the security and affordability of the energy they supply.

The new millennium has brought profound changes to the world economy and to the energy markets, with repercussions for international relations and political power. At the turn of the millennium, the United States was a global hegemon, an unchallenged leader having apparently won the Cold War against the Soviet Union. The diminished successor, Russia, was no match, nor was China; the European Union was a loyal ally, not a contender for power and influence. Twenty years later, the United States is being challenged by China, a new rival. Before its invasion of Ukraine, Russia appeared as a returning rival with solid finances and a robust oil and natural gas industry. Meanwhile, the European Union has shown signs of disagreement with the United States on several issues. Thus, global power dynamics may be shifting.

## The Oil Industry in Transition

The international oil industry has historically been dominated by American and European companies. However, Chinese, Russian, and Saudi oil companies are currently among the world's major oil corporations. China is the world's largest oil importer, with India steadily rising. As demand moves to Asia European and the American companies are losing relevance. For large Middle Eastern and Russian oil exporters, economic and political relations with China and India are becoming more important while those with Europe and the United States lose significance. A pertinent question to ask is to what extent the Shanghai Oil Futures Exchange, trading oil in yuan and gold, is a sign of change in financial markets.

By 2019, among the world's ten largest oil and gas companies, five were state-owned, of which two were Chinese (Sinopec and PetroChina), two were Russian (Rosneft and Gazprom), and the last was Saudi Arabia's Aramco, two were European and formerly state-owned (BP and Total), one was European, privately owned (Shell), and two were American and privately owned (Chevron and Exxon). The question remains to determine state-owned energy companies in China, Russia, and Saudi

Arabia will respond to challenges similar to those faced by their Western counterparts.

Trading in yuan allows the Chinese oil exchange to establish financial links which potentially short-circuit the US dollar and are outside US control. The US dollar's dominance in the international oil trade appears was established when the United States was the leading oil importer and American oil companies dominated Venezuela and the Middle East. In the "old oil days," i.e., before 2010, the oil market "axis" was between Washington and Riyadh; the balance between American imports and Saudi exports was often manageable and could stabilize the market. It made sense to have one currency, the US dollar, throughout the value chain. As rising demands shift towards Asia, the question of currency's effect on the market becomes increasingly important to consider.

## The Currency Weapon

When oil is billed and payable in a specific currency, its demand concurrently generates a demand for that currency. Seeing as the US dollar has been decoupled from gold since 1971, the international dollar demand has been crucial for the US economy. Its monopoly in the oil trade strengthened its dominance over world trade and the chosen reserve currency (Stokes, 2014). The latter has protected the United States from financial market sanctions, other than budget and payment balances. This logic prompted China to open a yuan oil exchange in 2018, and Russia is considering an initiative to invoice natural gas in rouble as of 2022.

The dollar's pre-eminence in the international economy dates to the post Second World War era, when the United States constituted almost half of the world's economy. As the gold reference imposed limits on the United States budgetary policies, it was suspended in 1971. Subsequently, the United States has since had large budget and trade deficits due to its confidence that the dollar would be widely accepted (Field, 2014). Simply put, the pre-eminence of the dollar allows the United States to print its own currency to pay anything to anyone and anywhere, fueling ambitions to lead the world's economy (Babones, 2015).

Primary sanctions imposed by the United States target exports and financial channels on countries such as Cuba, Iran, North Korea, and Venezuela to hinder their foreign trade, as well as on selected activities in countries such as China and Russia. Secondary sanctions apply to any company guilty of failing to comply with primary sanctions; they make the dollar a political weapon with the aim of controlling trade between third party countries. The risk is the emergence of a grand coalition of nations that do not accept US dominance (Hiro, 2018).

The threat of US sanctions encourages oil-exporting countries to look for alternatives to the dollar. Iran has chosen to invoice oil in euros, whereas Venezuela and Angola have chosen the yuan. In 2018, the United States imposed economic sanctions which impacted two billion people, nearly a third of the world's population, and one-fifth of the world economy. In return, the United States has found itself in economic conflict with many countries (Luft, 2018). Transactions now mostly intended to bypass US sanctions, avoid the United States, meaning the entire US banking system (Hosp, 2018). The risk for foreign companies and countries is to end up with frozen assets since sanctions also include US banks.

In addition, US sanctions prevent Iran from carrying out any trade in dollars. Consequently, it invoices oil exports in euros. A recent agreement between Iran and Turkey is to conduct bilateral trade in national currencies to avoid the US dollar. Russia sells oil to China in yuan. It is also a large seller of crude oil and refined products to Europe, invoiced in dollars, so far. Russian discontent at US sanctions provides further incentives to invoice in euros, though they face an issue with the EU's reluctance.

## The Great Financial Reshuffle

Since 2002, the United States, under presidents George W. Bush, Barack Obama, Donald Trump, and Joe Biden, has been running persistent budget deficits. In 2000, the Clinton administration left a budget surplus. In the following years, emergency spending after 9/11, the Iraq War, bank bailouts, and pandemic measures took their toll; from 2001 to 2020, the United States accumulated a current account deficit above US$10 trillion, at an annual deficit of 3.4 percent of the gross domestic product (GDP). Over this period, China has accumulated a current account surplus of US$3.6 trillion, at an annual average rate of 3.4 percent of its GDP. In Russia, the accumulated current account surplus is US$1.2 trillion, at an average annual rate of 5.4 percent of GDP.

Deficit financing stimulated domestic demand in the United States as well as imports from China, and over time, China responded by investing in export industries. The fact that US corporations outsource manufacturing from the United States to China has aided this process. Capital investment in US manufacturing and infrastructure has fallen. Consequently, the US trade balance has weakened. So far, the great economic reshuffle of the early twenty-first century has redistributed financial assets into north-west Europe, East Asia, the Gulf countries, and Russia; that is, away from the United States. Remarkably, the drivers of this redistribution of deficits and surpluses appear to be less related to oil than to policies. The United States has accumulated massive deficits and debts unrelated to falling oil imports. China is the mirror image, accumulating a large surplus while seeing oil imports rise.

When the United States went to war in Iraq, in March of 2003, the People's Republic of China had been a member of the World Trade Organization (WTO) for fifteen months. Until 1992, China was a net oil exporter. In 2022, however, oil imports exceed 10 million barrels a day (mbd), which makes China the leading oil importer, accounting for about one-fifth of the world oil market. China has a legitimate interest in entrenching its position in the world economy, as well as its weight in a largely oligopsonistic oil market, and to gain power and influence over oil prices (Meidan & Imsirovic, 2020).

In 2019, China accounted for twenty-three percent of world oil imports, balanced between the Middle East, Africa, South America, and Russia. China's oil imports are still growing, in absolute numbers as in share of world trade, which has strengthened its market power as one of a few large buyers. Declining self-sufficiency means an increasing exposure to oil market risk.

China's chief instruments are the national oil companies and oil trading. The Chinese government has majority ownership interests in several state-owned energy conglomerates with extensive international operations throughout the value chain (Carpenter, 2020).

## China and Middle East Oil

The weight of Chinese oil companies is indicative of a new oil order. For China, the Middle East (Iran and Iraq as well as the GCC countries) represents a source of increasing oil supplies, a market for consumer and investment goods, as well as an outlet for investments. Rising dependence on Middle Eastern oil has political consequences and raises security concerns as China sees a need to protect its energy interests in that region (Xuewen, 2014). Historically, China has wielded influence through "soft power," commercial and financial means, infrastructure projects, and humanitarian aid (Shambaugh, 2011). Recently, it has also opted for "hard power," highlighted by a military presence in the region, namely through its engagement in Syria (Eaddy, 2017). Middle Eastern turmoil has negative economic consequences for China, compromising oil supplies, trade, and investment. China has a vested interest in securing the oil supply lanes from the Gulf (Oosterveld, 2017), it also has a strong interest in securing positions for Chinese oil companies.

For China, Iran represents a complementary partner with the potential for long-term oil and gas deliveries, as well as a large home market as an outlet for investment and manufactured goods. However, there are important hurdles to a close relationship (Gardner, 2020). On the Iranian side, there is a preference for ties with Europe and a reluctance to be drawn into China's orbit. For China, one issue is that Iran physically cannot provide the oil volumes needed, so that it needs to balance relations and consider Saudi concerns about potential military and political threats from Iran.

Saudi Arabia represents an even more promising partner, with a large resource base more compatible with China's needs. The Saudi home market is, however, more limited. China has a minor participation in Saudi Aramco, as Saudi participates in the Chinese oil exchange by trading oil in yuan as well. Nevertheless, through military cooperation and arms trade, Saudi Arabia retains strong links with the United States; it has no Chinese or Russian weaponry. This fact may provide a clue to future economic links.

## The Shanghai Futures Oil Exchange

China is interested in trading in yuan, rather than in US dollars. As the major buyer of Saudi oil, China is significantly important to the Saudi economy. The Chinese envision a Sino–Arab cooperation based on complementary economic interests (Xuewen, 2014).[2] The International Energy Exchange (INE) is in the Shanghai Free Trade Zone, separated

[2] Qian Xuewen, "Sino-Arab Economic and Trade Cooperation: Situations, Tasks, Issues and Strategies".

from the internal Chinese economy. China grants oil sellers a discretionary currency regime, permitting the conversion of oil money into gold or any other currency. The Central Bank of Russia has opened a special Beijing office for this purpose.

The Shanghai Oil Futures Exchange serves a double purpose: first, through price formation in yuan it reduces the currency exchange rate risk in the domestic oil market, and second, it allows China to play a more important role in the world oil market. China's ambition, which is compatible with its long-term aim to promote the yuan as a leading international currency, is to establish a regional, and ultimately a global, marker of crude oil based in Shanghai (Prasad 2017).[3] A serious internal debt burden, insolvent companies, and a distorted financial sector would worsen by liberalizing reforms (Pettis, 2018).[4] The alternative to lifting currency controls in China would be a more widespread international use of the yuan. Any further growth, to become an international oil trading place and compete with London and New York, would be contingent on overcoming important hurdles. The Chinese yuan is not a freely convertible currency. As compensation, foreign oil sellers in Shanghai are permitted to exchange yuan for gold that can be repatriated

The Chinese project has often been dismissed by the West, especially by the oil community. Such a dismissive view overlooks the potential impact of US sanctions. The Chinese adopt a different point of view, in which the country's economy is exposed not only to an oil price risk, but also to a currency risk, insofar as oil is priced in another currency. Reasonably, the Chinese government is concerned about oil price volatility.

China's oil exchange project can be seen as an attempt to mitigate or eliminate exposure to currency risk in oil trading. Insofar as imported oil is priced in yuan, Chinese buyers run no currency risk. This may be a pragmatic, commercial consideration, which cuts costs. An ulterior economic motive may be to influence oil price formation—another reasonable concern for the world's largest oil importer. A final motive may be to assert power and political influence through the internationalization of the yuan, where oil trade would play an important role.

[3] Eswar S. Prasad. (2017). *Gaining currency*. Oxford: Oxford University Press.

[4] Michael Pettis. (2018). "Why beijing should dump its debt", *Foreign Policy*, January, pp. 27–28

The trading currency is not only a question of payment, but also of price formation. For China, oil price formation in yuan would help reduce volatility and risk, in addition to mitigating currency risk. These actions require an oil exchange and a benchmark crude, like Brent and the West Texas Intermediate (WTI), along with producers willing to take the risk of selling their crude in Chinese yuan.

In the longer run, a radical step for China might be to introduce a gold standard for the yuan, so that all holders of the Chinese currency would have the discretion to convert their yuan into gold or any other currency. Gold convertibility may be feasible for China, but it would require the lifting of capital controls and restrictions.

Trading in yuan allows the Chinese oil exchange to establish financial links which short-circuit the US dollar and outside US control. The dollar's dominance in international oil trade appears as a legacy from earlier times when the United States was the leading oil importer and US oil companies dominated in Venezuela and the Middle East.

The Chinese government faces the challenge balancing its global aspirations and its desire for control. Such aspirations intervene in its financial markets, which in recent years, has hindered foreign interest in trading in the yuan and in Chinese securities (Wildau & Mitchell, 2016). A serious internal debt burden, insolvent companies, and a distorted financial sector would be worsened by liberalizing reforms (Pettis, 2018). From experience, any liberal reforms which might threaten the Chinese Communist Party's control over the economy seem out of the question, in spite of inconveniences and losses. To sum up, despite representing a growing market for GCC oil as well as a leading supplier of manufactured goods, China is unlikely to appear as an attractive haven for GCC money.

## Russia—The Energy Market Master?

Russia, until 2021, was the world's leading natural gas and oil exporter and had been essential to the stability of the world's energy markets. In a few weeks, in the winter of 2022, the Russian government managed to discredit itself on several accounts: it no longer appears as a peaceful neighbor or as a trustworthy business partner. The Ukrainian crisis is obstructing Chinese plans for infrastructure connections in Eurasia, and consequently, the access of Chinese exporters to markets in Europe.

Russia's war in Ukraine has profoundly destabilized Europe's energy markets, compromising Russia's leading position in the European energy markets. In 2021, Russia exported 2.4 million barrels a day, mbd, of crude oil to Europe, in addition to approximately 1.4 mbd in refined products, including 0.8 mbd of diesel. In 2020, Russia exported 198 billion cubic meters of natural gas, of which 168 billion cubic meters, bcm, to Europe. One half of Russia's oil exports and eighty-five percent of gas pipeline exports went westward to Europe. The major outlets for Russian natural gas have been Germany, Italy, and Turkey.

Russia appears to have locked itself out of the European natural gas market to the benefit of competitors in the United States, Norway, North and West Africa, Qatar, Iran, Israel and Egypt, as well as buyers in China and India. Russia's exports of crude oil and refined products will have to find new outlets, likely in China and India. So far, Russia's war in Ukraine does not appear to be substantially impacting relations with fellow oil exporters in Iran, Iraq, and Saudi Arabia or with oil importers in China and India. It has, however, impacted relations with oil and natural gas importers in Europe.

With little foreign debt and a substantial reserve fund, Russia could weather several years of low oil prices as a result of its war in Ukraine, but at a high social cost. Russia runs the risk of a weakening currency and rising inflation harshly impacting the poorer parts of its population (Hedlund, 2015). Inflation could help lessen the pension burden; however, it carries a risk of social and political unrest.

With a resource base in tight oil and offshore prospects, Russia could maintain its current level of output, even in an environment of low prices. Government sanctions inhibit Western oil companies from new large-scale investment in Russia, and it appears that many companies may withdraw or scale down their presence. Russia has yet to see the wave of smaller, independent oil companies that have revitalized the petroleum industries in the United States and the North Sea. Opening up to newcomers would, however, challenge vested interests and the existing oligarchic structure of the Russian oil industry.

China would have to weigh the risks of closer entanglement with a weak Russian economy against a favorable bargaining position. Russia is wary of Chinese domination, but needs a strong partner and has energy to offer. China might choose to both lend resources and money to Russia against preferential access to Russian oil and gas, and peg the rouble to the yuan. China has the resources to buy into Russian oil companies. Such a deal might give Russian oil and gas preferential access to the Chinese market, with pricing in yuan, and a competitive advantage over Gulf oil, unless some Gulf exporters also would invoice oil for China in yuan.

In any case, the economic distress it is facing provides incentives for the Russian government to find a settlement of the Ukrainian crisis, preferably with France and Germany. With a military presence in the Middle East, Russia may aspire to influence GCC oil policies, especially as a potential partner of Iran and possibly Iraq. Any overt Russian pressure on the GCC countries has the potential to backfire, but a softer approach might facilitate the oil market's stabilization. The challenge for Russia's Middle Eastern policy is to maintain close relations with Iran and Iraq, while improving relations with Saudi Arabia and the other GCC countries. If successful, the payback could be considerable.

Rather than charge high oil prices, what Russia needs immediately is economic and political reform, as well as to overcome economic isolation and stagnation (Lo, 2015). The EU and US sanctions imposed in 2014 and 2017 have had a negative impact on the Russian oil industry, although not as much nor as quickly as anticipated and hoped for in Brussels and Washington (Mitrova et al., 2018). The objective has been to reduce export volumes of Russian oil and gas, not only to curb development.

Sanctions are not the only reason for stagnation and low productivity in large parts of Russia's oil and gas industries. From a petroleum geology perspective, much of Russia consists of mature petroleum provinces, i.e., areas that have been extensively explored, where the largest deposits have been found and developed, and much of the oil has been pumped out. Against this backdrop, the secular trend is rising costs and declining output, as the remaining resources are in old prospects in need of additional investment, or in new prospects with a remote location, technical obstacles, etc. These problems are not unique to Russia; they have for decades been evident in North America and the North Sea. The response of these regions to these challenges has been structural change in the oil industry.

## Conclusion: Imperfect Transition

At the time of writing, Germany has announced that it will discontinue purchases of Russian gas as of 2024. In response, Russia requested that EU customers with gas contracts in euros on immediate notice pay in rouble, otherwise supplies would halt. Russia's request was likely motivated by a desire to boost international demand for the rouble and will not likely be accepted. Historically, France has imported Russian gas through Germany; now Germany is likely to import overseas gas through France (Petrostrategies, 2022).

The financial repercussions of this could potentially be significant. Exclusion from Western banking and financial circuits will, by necessity, force Russia and the Russian oil and natural gas industries into the arms of China. Conditions appear ripe for a fragmentation of the oil market into distinctive circuits. One would be centered on the Shanghai Futures Oil Exchange, trading in yuan reference crudes for the Asian markets. It would first be supplied by Angola, Iran, Russia, and Venezuela, and subsequently with discretionary volumes by other producers targeting the Chinese market, such as Saudi Arabia. Japan might also have an interest in buying oil in Shanghai. The rest of the world might remain in the diminished traditional circuit based in London and New York, quoting oil prices in US dollars. Such an outcome would open possibilities for buying oil at a lower price and selling at a higher price, a situation beneficial to oil traders and brokers, but which would destabilize oil markets.

Historically, the international oil market has experienced several volatile periods which have been marked by wide price ranges for similar transactions, and often also political upheavals which affect market power strictures, and control of oil supplies. The 1973–1974 crisis is memorable fifty years later, compounded by the events of 1979–1980. In 2022, the stage may be set for another profound reshuffle, changing power relations, as well as supply and trading patterns.

The events of 2022 are a reminder of the salience of Russia in the world economy, not only in oil and gas matters. The war has halted food exports through the Black Sea from Ukraine and Russia, to the detriment of numerous African and Middle Eastern countries. It has disrupted supply chains for many commodities and products, including transit from China to Europe. From this perspective, Russia's war of attrition also targets Europe as a supporter of Ukraine. References to Russia as a medium-sized economy tend to overlook the strategic importance of a huge landmass and a bountiful resource base (Ferguson, 2022). Already in the late nineteenth century, Russian oil offered competition to US oil in the European market; in the twenty-first century, Russia and the United States compete in the European natural gas market.

Remarkably, after the chaos and mismanagement of the Yeltsin years, under Putin's governance, Russia has achieved financial stabilization, thanks in part to high oil and gas prices. According to the International Monetary Fund, IMF Data Base, from 2000 to 2021, Russia was running an average current account surplus corresponding to 5.9 percent of the gross national product, GDP. Twenty-one years of financial surplus amounted to US $1,400 trillion. Russia's accumulation of money has hardly been seen as a war chest. Indeed, if the intention had been war financing, the money would likely have been placed in greater safety, avoiding the risk that a large part would be frozen in Western institutions. Nevertheless, Russia's still considerable financial resources bolster oil and gas policy freedom; money in the bank relieves the need to sell oil and gas, neutralizing sanctions.

Since the dollar was decoupled from gold in 1971, the country's international position has largely been based in oil, the world's most important traded commodity. Most international oil transactions are made in dollars and since oil is paid for in dollars, oil demand creates a demand for dollars. Dominance in oil trading has bolstered the position of the dollar as the key currency in world trade and as the primary reserve currency. Until the winter of 2018, practically all international crude oil transactions were settled in US dollars, with the exception of countries under US sanctions, such as Iran and Venezuela. This facility has been essential to US power.

The willingness of foreigners to use their savings to purchase US debt is contingent on the international reserve currency status of the US dollar (Stokes, 2014). US sanctions compel several important countries to find alternatives to dollar trading. In 2022, alternatives to dollar payment for oil have emerged as an important issue for clients of the Russian oil companies, which points to a fragmentation of oil trading. In Asia, oil trading is likely to encourage the emergence of the yuan as a regional key currency (Hasegawa, 2018).

Before the dramatic events of 2022, strains to the incumbent oil order were evident, based on US dollar trading. The Shanghai Futures Oil Exchange is an important step in establishing an alternative to the United States dominated oil order. China can defend her oil market interests. For China, oil price formation in yuan would help reduce volatility and risk, in addition to eliminating the currency risk. Considering power relations in the world energy markets, accelerating change is not unlikely, affecting industrial structures as well as financial matters. China has a legitimate interest in entrenching its position in the world economy, as well as in a largely oligopsonistic market, i.e., dominated by a small number of large buyers, and to gain power and influence over oil prices (Meidan & Imsirovic, 2020). An important goal for China's petroleum strategy is to gain a foothold in countries on bad terms with the United States, among which Iran has been prominent for many years and has now been joined by Russia (Lorot, 2007).

China's chief instruments are the national oil companies and oil trading. The Chinese government has majority ownership interests in several state-owned energy conglomerates with extensive international operations throughout the value chain (Carpenter, 2020) The weight of Chinese oil companies signals a new oil order. The historical tandem of Saudi Arabia as the leading exporter and the United States the leading importer stabilizing the oil market, is no longer true. The United States is ceding to a new constellation of Asian buyers, with China in the forefront being supplied to a great extent by Middle Eastern producers. In terms of oil market structure, the Middle Eastern oligopoly (few sellers, facilitating coordination in OPEC) is encountering an Asian oligopsony (few buyers), putting the Middle Eastern suppliers and Russia in a strong bargaining position.

China is the major market for Gulf oil, with a preference for comprehensive bilateral economic ties and eventually to conduct trade in yuan. The new issues concern money as much as security, possibly with a petro-yuan challenging the petro-dollar. Oil is the world's most traded commodity; any large-scale move into yuan represents a risk for the US dollar and therefore the ability for the United States to project power around the world (Eichengreen, 2011). The issue is to what extent oil trading in yuan would enhance China's and even Russia's positions.

One possible outcome is that Russia will have to yield in Ukraine, and a domestic reshuffle would follow. Politically, the ground might become ready for large-scale joint ventures between Russian and US oil companies, possibly following the pattern of the earlier deals between Rosneft and ExxonMobil. A few major US oil companies would emerge sturdier, but the international industry would also in all likelihood include strong Russian oil and gas companies. Most likely, the US dollar would assert itself as the petroleum currency.

An opposite outcome would be a Russian victory. The Ukraine would be integrated into the Russian economy, and consequently Europe and the United States would likely terminate most of their economic transactions with Russia, for some time. Russia would be increasingly dependent on China, and the yuan would become a more important petroleum currency.

An intermediate outcome, perhaps most likely, would be a cease-fire, without a negotiated political settlement. Russian trade with Europa and the United States would resume slowly, but China would be a vital partner and Russia would be drawn into a yuan-zone. In this scenario, Russia's oil industry would become increasingly dependent on China's markets and good-will. Tighter links between Russia's energy potential and China's financial resources would challenge the position of the US dollar in world oil trade and enhance the bargaining power of Middle East oil exporters, not the least Saudi Arabia (Watkins, 2022).

**Acknowledgements** The author is thankful to Helen El Mallakh of ICEED, Boulder, Colorado, for editing the present paper.

## References

Babones, S. (2015, July–August). American hegemony is here to stay. *The National Interest*.

Beaudreau, B. C. (1998). *Energy and organization*. Greenwood Press.

Carpenter, J. W. (2020, June 16). *The 5 biggest Chinese oil companies*. Investopedia.

Critchlow, A. (2019, April 12). Saudi Aramco's success proves the oil age has a future. *The Telegraph*.

Dannreuther, R. (2017). *Energy security*. Polity Press.

Eaddy, A. (2017, October 25). *China's military shift in the middle east*. International Policy Digest. https://intpolicydigest.org/2017/10/25/china-s-military-shift-middle-east/

Eichengreen, B. (2011). *Exorbitant privilege*. Oxford University Press.

Ferguson, N. (2022, March 9). *The fates of Ukraine and Putin turn on 7 forces of history*. Bloomberg.

Field, D. (2014). Dollar hegemony. In L. P. Rochon et al. (Eds.), *Edward Elgar encyclopedia on central banking*. Edward Elgar.

Freeland, C. (2000). *Sale of the century*. Little, Brown and Company.

Gardner, D. (2020, July 29). Wary US watches for signs of Chinese-Iranian alliance. *Financial Times*.

Hasegawa, M. (2018). The geography and geopolitics of the renminbi: A regional key currency in Asia. *International Affairs, 94*(3), 535–554.

Hedlund, S. (2015, September 7). *False dawn for Russia's economy as cheap oil backs Kremlin into a corner*. Geopolitical Information Service (GIS).

Hiro, D. (2018, August 23). *Can Donald Trump unite the world (against himself)?* Tomgram. Retrieved from www.tomdispatch.com

Hosp, G. (2018, September 6). *Sind die US-Sanktionen ein Bumerang für die Leitwährung Dollar?* Neue Zürcher Zeitung.

Hudson, M. (2010, July 12). *Dollar Hegemony and the rise of China*. http://michael-hudson.com

Le Page, M. (2016, August 2). The renewables reality: Clean Energy Hasn't Risen for 25 Years. *New Scientist*.

Lo, B. (2015). *Russia and the new world disorder*. Royal Institute of International Affairs.

Lorot, P. (2007). *Le Siècle de la Chine*. Éditions Choiseul.

Luft, G. (2018, August 27). *The anti-dollar awakening could be ruder and sooner than most economists predict*. Yahoo Finance, CNBC News. https://ca.finance.yahoo.com

Meidan, M., & Imsirovic, A. (2020). *The shanghai oil futures contract and the oil demand shock*. OIES.

Mills, R. (2018, February). *Oil beyond 2018: What lies ahead for 'super OPEC'*. The Qamar Newsletter, 20.

Mitrova, T., Grushevenko, E., & Malov, A. (2018). *The future of oil production in Russia: Life under sanctions*. Skolkovo School of Management.

Muttit, G. (2020). What for OPEC in the last generation of oil. In *Handbook of OPEC and the global energy order* (pp. 338–355). Routledge.

Oosterveld, W. (2017, August 25). China in the Middle East: Testing the waters, linking the lands. *The Diplomat*. https://thediplomat.com/2017/08/china-in-the-middle-east-testing-the-waters-linking-the-lands/

Palley, T. I. (2006, June 20). *Why dollar hegemony is unhealthy*. Yale Global Online. https://yaleglobal.yale.edu/content/why-dollar-hegemony-unhealthy

Petrostrategies. (2022, September 25). *France will provide up to 350 GWh/d of gas to help Germany meet its needs this winter*.

Pettis, M. (2018, January). Why Beijing should dump its debt. *Foreign Policy*, pp. 27–28.

Seznec, J.-F. (2015). Politics of oil supply. In *Handbook of oil politics* (pp. 45–59). Routledge

Shambaugh, D. (2011). *China goes global*. Oxford University Press.

Smil, V. (2017a). *Energy and civilization* (p. 18). The MIT Press.

Smil, V. (2017b). *Energy transitions* (p. 23). Praeger.

Stanovaya, T. (2022, June 1). What the West (still) gets wrong about Putin. *Foreign Policy*.

Stokes, D. (2014). Achilles' deal: Dollar decline and US grand strategy after the crisis. *Review of International Political Economy, 21*(5), 1071–1094.

Watkins, S. (2022, September 13). *China and Russia move to disrupt the dollar's dominance in oil markets*. World Oil.
Wildau, G., & Mitchell, T. (2016, December 11). China: Renminbi stalls on road to being a global currency. *Financial Times*.
Xuewen, Q. (2014). Protecting China's energy interests in the Middle East. *Journal of Middle Eastern and Islamic Studies (in Asia)*, *8*(3), 48–59.
Yergin, D. (2020). *The new map* (p. 429). Allen Lane.

CHAPTER 3

# The Role of the Oil and Gas Industry in the Energy Transition

*Soheil Saraji and Dayo Akindipe*

## INTRODUCTION

The oil and gas industry (OGI) is among the world's largest, most complex, and crucial industries, involving upstream, midstream, and downstream sectors. The upstream sector is the first phase in the life cycle of oil and gas and consists of exploration and development operations, drilling and well completion, production and optimization, reservoir engineering, and reclamation. The midstream segment involves transporting, storing, and trading raw materials (oil and gas). Downstream operations include refining raw materials into more valuable products, product distribution, and transportation. The OGI played a significant role in the previous energy transition away from coal in the early twentieth century and has created much wealth over the past century (Murphy, 2019).

S. Saraji (✉)
University of Wyoming, Laramie, WY, USA
e-mail: ssaraji@uwyo.edu

D. Akindipe
National Renewable Energy Laboratory (NREL), Falls Church, VA, USA
e-mail: dayo.Akindipe@nrel.gov



T. Walker et al. (eds.), *Sustainability in the Oil and Gas Sector*,
https://doi.org/10.1007/978-3-031-51586-6_3

However, the use of fossil fuels has come with attendant issues that affect both the natural and human environments. Oil spills, gas flaring, post-combustion emissions, seismic tremors, and the Dutch disease are notable environmental and social issues that negatively connotate the OGI (Corden, 1984; McGarr et al., 2015; O'Rourke & Connolly, 2003). A significant contemporary challenge for the OGI is its lifecycle emissions, mostly greenhouse gases ($CO_2$, $CH_4$, and $N_2O$) and other toxic compounds (e.g., $SO_2$, NOx, and volatile organic compounds), that are respective precursors to the greenhouse effect and ground-level ozone (IPCC, 2014; US EPA, 2016). Climate scientists have unanimously opined that the exacerbating greenhouse effect, which leads to a rise in the global surface temperature, is the primary cause of imminent climate change (IPCC, 2014) and have recommended a 1.5 °C surface temperature rise limit over the pre-industrial baseline to mitigate its adverse effects (IPCC, 2018). The spotlight is now on the oil and gas industry and its response to climate challenges. Initial reluctance to accept the industry's contribution to the climate crisis has slowed progress in decarbonization efforts. However, as political and economic pressures intensify, and as ESG (environmental, social, and governance) become a global investment standard, industry players are now exploring ways to decarbonize existing operations and expand their energy portfolio to renewable and low-carbon sources (Beck et al., 2020; Oxford Institute for Energy Studies, 2020). The global drive for accelerated decarbonization in the energy industry has created the term *energy transition*. In its current use, energy transition connotes that the world's primary energy supply is shifting from carbon-intensive sources (fossil fuels) to renewable and low-carbon sources (e.g., wind, solar, hydrogen, and biogenic sources) (S&P Global, 2020). The future of fossil fuels lies in the ability of the industry to adapt to the market, the environment, and to social trends within the energy transition framework. Failure to do so could sidetrack net-zero carbon targets and sustainable development goals and render the industry obsolete.

This chapter explores the key role that the OGI could play in leading the energy transition and mitigating climate change. More specifically, we focus on three aspects: (a) sustainable energy development, (b) modernization and digitization, and (c) harnessing expertise in underground energy storage and offshore operations. First, we look at sustainable fossil fuel development, which mitigates carbon dioxide and methane emissions. Here, we discuss the current efforts and potential future developments in low-carbon fuels and Responsibly Sourced Gas (RSG) (DiChristopher, 2021; Russo, 2021). Second, we turn to the modernization of the industry via digital technologies such as Big Data Analytics (Choubey & Karmakar, 2021; Desai et al., 2021; Gai et al., 2020; Klein et al., 2018; Lu et al., 2019; Patel et al., 2020; Perrons & Jensen, 2015; Perrons & Nguyen et al., 2020; Tankimovich, 2018; Wanasinghe et al., 2020), Artificial Intelligence (Agwu et al., 2018; Bello et al., 2015; Bravo et al., 2013; Choubey & Karmakar, 2021; Gupta & Shah, 2021; Hanga & Kovalchuk, 2019; Li, Yu et al., 2021; Tariq et al., 2021; Tartakovsky et al., 2020), and Blockchain technology (Lu et al., 2019; Mehta et al., 2021; Perrons & Cosby, 2020; Saraji & Borowczak, 2021; Saraji & Khalaf, 2022; Wanasinghe et al., 2020). These modernizations aim to make the industry more efficient, reduce carbon emissions, and improve the safety and human welfare of its workers. Finally, we make a case for leveraging the expertise and infrastructure from the OGI in subsurface hydrocarbon extraction and offshore operations for developing underground energy storage (Bünger et al., 2016; Caglayan et al., 2020; Gai et al., 2020; Heinemann et al., 2021; Klein et al., 2018; Lysyy et al., 2021; Matos et al., 2019; Menéndez et al., 2019, 2020; Olsen et al., 2015; Tarkowski, 2019; Wanasinghe et al., 2020; Zivar et al., 2021), geologic sequestration of gigatons of $CO_2$ (Akindipe et al., 2021; Benson et al., 2005; Cuéllar-Franca & Azapagic, 2015; Hepburn et al., 2019; Li, Saraji et al., 2021; Meylan et al., 2015; Saraji et al., 2013, 2014), geothermal energy (Gong et al., 2020; Hamm et al., 2021; Li, Sun et al., 2021), and offshore solar and wind farms (Bigarelli et al., 2019; Solomin et al., 2019). In the following sections, we explore each of these pillars in more depth and provide examples of successful projects in each category.

## Pillar I: Low-Carbon Fuels

Based on California's Low Carbon Fuels Standard (LCFS), low-carbon fuels are those which inherently have minimal to net-zero carbon intensity over their lifecycle or have been engineered to significantly decrease their lifecycle carbon intensity compared to conventional fossil fuels (California Air Resources Board, 2020). Typical low-carbon fuels (LCF) are from biogenic sources (e.g., agricultural waste and wood biomass), while others are fossil-based sources such as responsibly sourced gas (RSG) and blue hydrogen. In the former class of LCF, the major energy source is from plants and trees, which, over their lifetime, have captured and stored significant amounts of atmospheric $CO_2$. Therefore, at the point of resource extraction, biogenic LCFs are carbon-negative. When these fuels are combusted for electricity and heat generation, the ensuing $CO_2$ emissions are counteracted by pre-stored $CO_2$, which makes the process almost carbon neutral. How close biogenic LCF can come to carbon neutrality depends upon other ancillary processes like transportation that contribute to the lifecycle emissions profile. In addition, the energy return on the energy invested (EROI) of most biofuels is currently very low, and the commercial potential of these resources as stand-alone fuels in the long term is uncertain (Murphy, 2019).

LCF from fossil sources include fuels derived from hydrocarbon extraction that have been strictly monitored for their emissions profile. Monitored emissions are mostly fugitive $CH_4$ which has 27–30 times the global warming potential (GWP) of $CO_2$ over a 100-year period (U.S. EPA, 2016). Other monitored emissions are $CO_2$ from gas flaring activities during source extraction. Although carbon neutrality is not achieved with emissions monitoring, these fuels are still categorized as LCF because of their lower lifecycle emissions compared to conventional fossil fuels (California Air Resources Board, 2020). In the following sections, we shall discuss different types of LCF in more detail and provide a suitable case study that the OGI can adopt.

### *Biomass, Bioethanol, and Renewable Natural Gas*

Biomass is composed primarily of solid fuels sourced from plants and animals (usually animal waste). They include renewable resources such as standing forests, waste (agricultural, human, municipal), and energy crops (Ram & Mondal, 2022; Saxena et al., 2009). The OGI is gradually increasing investments in biomass utilization for energy and producing non-fuel products. Between 2010 and 2018, BP and Shell spent 2.3% and 1.33% of their capital expenditures (CAPEX) on clean energy—biomass energy accounted for more than one-half of the CAPEX (Li et al., 2022). Within the same period, ExxonMobil derived all of its clean energy (0.22% of CAPEX) from biomass (Li et al., 2022). These percentages are meager compared to enormous amounts still being spent on fossil fuel production (IEA, 2020b). Therefore, the OGI needs to marry its annual pledges with active investments in bioenergy generation.

Bioethanol is a biofuel derived from the fermentation of crops and agricultural waste. It is mostly used as a renewable additive to gasoline or directly combusted as a biofuel (Mussatto et al., 2010). Feedstocks for bioethanol production are sugar-containing crops (e.g., sugarcane, sugar beet, and molasses), starch-containing grains (e.g., corn, barley, and wheat), and root crops (e.g., cassava and potato), and lignocellulosic biomass such as straw, agricultural waste, and crop and wood residues (Bušić et al., 2018; Mussatto et al., 2010). The downstream OGI is already using bioethanol in gasoline blends. In the United States, most of the gasoline sold contains at least 10% bioethanol (E10 blend) derived from corn starch, and up to 15% bioethanol in gasoline (E15 blend) has been allowed for medium-duty vehicles manufactured since 2001 (EIA, 2022). In other parts of the world, the bioethanol composition in gasoline is still very low or non-existent. For example, the European Union (EU) still limits ethanol content in gasoline to 10%—most EU countries use E5 (5%) gasoline (Gray, 2020). It is apparent that drastic policy changes, including consultations with both OGI stakeholders and automobile manufacturers, are required to enable higher bioethanol participation in the global low-carbon fuel mix.

Renewable natural gas (RNG) is another significant low-carbon biofuel that has gained traction. Also known as biomethane, this product is a high-purity gas derived from the anaerobic microbial degradation (or digestion) of food or agricultural and municipal solid waste. The low-quality biogas (containing 45–60% $CH_4$) derived from digestion is post-treated and upgraded to attain the acceptable purity levels (greater than 90% $CH_4$) required in methane-powered engines (U.S. EPA, 2020). The Clean Energy Fuels Corporation, based in California, is a major player being actively engaged by OGI companies. Since 2018, they have formed partnerships and joint ventures with BP, Chevron, and Total Energies. In December 2020, BP agreed to provide $50 million in investments to Clean Energy in developing and constructing RNG facilities (Clean Energy, 2020b). The joint venture was initiated in March 2021, specifically for carbon-negative RNG from dairy farms and other agricultural sites, to be used as a low-carbon fuel for road transportation (Clean Energy, 2021b). Total Energies recently signed a 100 million dollar-joint venture with Clean Energy to develop carbon-negative RNG production facilities in the United States and to expand Clean Energy's downstream RNG fueling infrastructure (Clean Energy, 2021a; Reuters, 2021a). Similarly, in July 2020, Chevron signed an $8 million agreement with Clean Energy to participate in their Adopt-a-Port program. Within this program, Chevron provides carbon-negative RNG to truck operators that haul goods from the Los Angeles and Long Beach ports and supplies RNG to stations near these ports. It also subsidizes the purchase of RNG-powered trucks and the cost of retrofitting existing trucks with RNG-capable engines (Clean Energy, 2020a). Thanks to its initial success, Chevron has invested an additional $20 million in expanding the Adopt-a-Port program (Clean Energy, 2021c). In September 2021, Shell launched its first American RNG plant in Junction City, Oregon. This facility uses cow manure and excess agricultural residues as feedstocks and is estimated to produce 736,000 MMBtu a year of RNG. Shell is also collaborating with RNG producers from dairy farms in Kansas and Idaho, which could potentially produce an additional 900,000 MMBtu of RNG annually (Shell, 2021).

### *Sustainable Aviation Fuels*

The aviation industry is one of the most carbon-intensive sectors worldwide. Despite the fact that the COVID-19 pandemic induced a slowing of emissions from air transport, the aviation industry still contributes between 2 and 3% of global $CO_2$ emissions (IEA, 2021c). The industry heavily relies on expensive and scarce carbon offsets, especially in developing markets. One major solution for low-carbon air transport is the use of sustainable aviation fuels (SAF). SAF is generally biogenic jet fuel derived from the conversion of biomass into a high-energy-density fuel. Conversion processes vary depending on the type of feedstock used. Common feedstocks include starch, sugar, animal fats, and vegetable oil (Michaga et al., 2021). These first-generation sources are gradually being replaced with second-generation oleo-chemical (e.g., used cooking oil) and lignocellulosic feedstocks (e.g., agricultural residues, nonedible biomass, and waste streams) that do not significantly affect food security (Michaga et al., 2021).

So far, SAF supply to aviation is still very low. In 2021, the proportion of SAF used in global air transport was a meager 0.05% of the 57 billion gallons of jet fuel consumed (IATA, 2021a, 2021b). Based on recent projections by the International Air Transport Association (IATA), about 119 billion gallons of SAF will be required to meet the 2050 net-zero goals of the international aviation industry (IATA, 2021a). One challenge limiting the use of SAF is the high cost of procuring and converting feedstocks to standard jet fuels. Another is interoperability issues, especially because the aviation industry is a global one (BP, 2021; Michaga et al., 2021). Therefore, SAF supply needs to be streamlined and accessible in multiple geographical locations worldwide. Currently, most of the supply is limited to North America and Europe; however, the Asian market is also coming on stream (Neste, 2022). Another issue is the challenge of compatibility with existing turbines and jet engines, which has restricted the SAF-to-conventional jet fuel blending ratio to 50% (Michaga et al., 2021).

The downstream OGI is the main supplier of fossil-derived jet fuels for the aviation industry. Major players include BP, Shell, and Total Energies. Among these legacy OGI companies, BP is the most active in the SAF market and, in collaboration with SkyNRG (a leading SAF producer), was the first to make SAF commercially available to the aviation industry at the Oslo Airport in Norway (BP, 2021). Other players in the SAF market are Neste, a Finnish downstream (mostly oil refining and product distribution) company that has now rebranded itself as a producer and supplier of renewable fuels. Neste is now a major global player in the SAF market, with a reach across North America, Europe, and Asia. It currently produces around 34 million gallons (100,000 tons) of SAF annually at its refinery in Porvoo, Finland (Neste, 2022). New production streams are expected to be operational in 2023 from refineries in Rotterdam (The Netherlands) and Singapore to increase annual capacity to 515 million gallons (1.5 million tons) (Neste, 2022). In addition, the company recently signed a joint venture agreement with the Marathon Petroleum Corporation (a leading OGI company in the United States) to convert Marathon's Martinez refinery in California to produce sustainable biofuels, including SAF (Reuters, 2022). This success story further exemplifies that the OGI needs to seriously consider converting conventional refineries to biorefineries for SAF to become mainstream.

### *Responsibly Sourced Gas*

As discussed previously, $CH_4$ as a greenhouse gas has eight times the global warming potential of $CO_2$, at least in the short and medium term. Therefore, $CH_4$ emissions across the value chain of natural gas production and supply are seriously concerning. If the OGI wants to continue supplying natural gas as a bridge fuel, there is a need for stricter regulation and regulation enforcement on $CH_4$ emissions. Responsibly sourced (natural) gas (RSG) is one product that offers a possible solution. RSG is natural gas that has been certified by third-party authorities to have minimal $CH_4$ pre-combustion emissions and meet global ESG best practices. Before fossil-based natural gas can be certified as RSG, a lifecycle (mostly Scope 1 and 2) emissions analysis and an ESG assessment are implemented across the upstream (e.g., fracking, production, and separation), transportation, and storage value chain (Russo, 2021).

Some OGI upstream and midstream companies in the United States and Canada are adopting this certification process due to investors' and stakeholders' (mainly gas utilities) need to more urgently decarbonize and adopt ESG standards (DiChristopher, 2021). Presently, RSG certifications are available through two leading independent companies—Equitable Origin and Project Canary. Equitable Origin uses its EO100™ certification standard to evaluate natural gas producers' compliance with RSG standards across five main criteria/principles: (i) corporate governance, transparency, and business ethics, (ii) human rights, social impacts, and community development (iii) indigenous peoples' rights, (iv) fair labor & working conditions, and (v) climate change, biodiversity and environment (Equitable Origin, 2017). In addition, participating producers are scored according to performance targets PT 1, PT 2, or PT 3 if they meet (PT 1), exceed (PT 2), or lead (PT 3) global best practices in ESG-based natural gas provision (Equitable Origin, 2017). Presently, the company has certified up to 10 Bcf of natural gas production from 18 producers in North America (DiChristopher, 2021). Similarly, Project Canary, through its TrustWell™ standard, monitors site-level $CH_4$ emissions at high resolutions and in real-time. They do so in conjunction with other ESG-relevant data, such as air quality, water usage, and land restoration (Project Canary, 2021).

RSG producers are exclusively medium-sized OGI companies aiming to differentiate their products from regular natural gas by demanding a premium over the market price. These companies include PureWest Energy, Southwestern Energy, Chesapeake Energy, Énergir, and Seven Generations Energy, all active in the North American gas market (DiChristopher, 2021; Russo, 2021). There is currently no indication of whether OGI majors will adopt RSG. This may be due to the fact that environmentalists could perceive RSG adoption as greenwashing fossil-based natural gas instead of focusing on renewables and other low-carbon ventures (Feinstein, 2022). Notwithstanding, the Norwegian-based major, Equinor ASA, has engaged both Equitable Origin and

Project Canary to certify natural gas produced from the Utica Shale basin through partnerships with Southwestern Energy and Chesapeake Energy (DiChristopher, 2021). The future of RSG will depend upon policy measures that make $CH_4$ monitoring and emissions mitigation mandatory (and not voluntary, as in the case of RSG certification) for natural gas producers. An example is the recent United States Environmental Protection Agency's (U.S. EPA's) proposed rule that aims to reduce $CH_4$ emissions from oil and gas activities by 41 million tons by 2035 (U.S. EPA, 2021).

## Pillar II: Modernization and Digitization

Facing challenges associated with the energy transition, the OGI will have to become technologically and commercially sophisticated in order to continue to be a part of the world's sustainable energy mix. OGI companies are looking for digital technology to drive efficiency and productivity, reduce carbon emissions, and transform their operations to meet these challenges. The industry generates huge amounts of data, which is often recorded manually across multiple, disconnected paper records or spreadsheets by siloed functional teams (*How Do You Reshape When Today's Future May Not Be Tomorrow's Reality? - Oil and Gas Digital Transformation and the Workforce Survey 2020*, n.d.). This data, if organized and processed in a timely manner, could be utilized toward achieving the digitization and modernization goals of the industry.

Some examples of utilizing advanced digital technologies to improve operations in the OGI are (Hanga & Kovalchuk, 2019): (a) utilizing real-time data streams generated by sensors to ensure better control and optimization of oil production, (b) robotics in offshore fields for drilling, inspection and damage control to enhance efficiency and personal safety, (c) wireless sensor networks to monitor and enhance production, as well as to detect and prevent issues with regard to health and safety, and (d) the radio-frequency identification (RFID) technology for asset management, oil rig site management, pipeline inspection, safety, and security, etc. In the following sections, we focus on three emerging digital technologies that have a massive potential to transform OGI, making it profitable in the energy transition era.

### *Internet of Things*

The Internet of Things (IoT) is a network of items embedded in smart devices (sensors and actuators) connected to the internet. The term "IoT" was coined by Kevin Ashton, executive director of the Auto-ID Center, in 1999, when he presented a radio-frequency identification (RFID)-based supply chain optimization system to Procter & Gamble (P&G) (Wanasinghe et al., 2020). The IoT enables machine-to-machine communication over a network without requiring human-to-computer interaction. The physical layer consists of the IoT nodes used for data acquisition and control of the OGI equipment and facilities (Elijah et al., 2021).

As discussed earlier, data is the core concept that drives the digital transformation of the OGI. IoT-based devices are at the heart of this transformation as they provide reliable data streams for various applications in upstream, midstream, and downstream operations. A recent literature review demonstrated that service companies are the main drivers of innovation in this space, far ahead of academic institutions and oil companies (Wanasinghe et al., 2020). In addition, the available literature was mainly focused on conceptual demonstrations rather than actual case studies (Wanasinghe et al., 2020). Nevertheless, several use cases are being tested in the industry in six critical areas (Wanasinghe et al., 2020): (i) remote monitoring, operation, and asset optimization (e.g., pressure relief valve, sucker-pump working condition, production and well monitoring/optimization, etc.), (ii) predictive maintenance, (iii) automation and control (e.g., automation of drilling systems, production systems, well completion systems, etc.), (iv) occupational safety and health compliances, situational awareness, and personnel tracking, (v) supply chain and fleet management, and (vi) security. For example, the use of wearable watches, smart helmets, and smart glasses by oil field engineers in offshore fields for real-time assistance, safety, and communication with the control room was highlighted by Hanga and Kovalchuk (Hanga & Kovalchuk, 2019) as a successful use case of IoTs in OGI.

However, there are serious challenges in deploying this technology at the larger scale. A comprehensive list of challenges provided by Wanasinghe et al. that include (Wanasinghe et al., 2020): (a) cybersecurity concerns, (b) lack of technological readiness, (c) lack of interoperability, adaptability, and standardization, (d) challenges in data storage and analytics, (e) maintenance cost, and obsolescence, and (f) mindset of employees. Among these challenges, cybersecurity concerns were the most cited constraints for the industry-wide adaptation of IoTs (Wanasinghe et al., 2020). Other concerns regarding a centralized IoT system are (Restuccia et al., 2019): (i) can help with illegitimate use of IoT data, for example, mass-surveillance programs. (ii) can expose the system to hacking through malicious activities, and (iii) challenges with authentication of IoT entities that will be primarily deployed in the wild with little supervision. IoTs are a relatively new technology, and further innovation is required for widespread adoption in the industry. Nevertheless, the IoTs, in combination with other digital technologies such as Artificial Intelligence, Big Data Analytics, Blockchain, provide a massive opportunity for the future of OGI.

### *Big Data Analytics and Artificial Intelligence*

As discussed in the previous section, the emergence of various IoT devices in the OGI accelerated the accumulation of massive data. Therefore, data processing and management have become a challenge for the industry and, at the same time, provided opportunities for the application of new data processing technologies such as Big Data analytics (BD), Artificial Intelligence (AI), and Machine Learning (ML). BD deals with the huge amount of data being collected from a variety of sources (volume), the speed at which the data is being collected in real-time (velocity), and the formats in which the data are collected (variety) (Elijah et al., 2021). BD analytics refers to the process of researching these massive amounts of data in order to uncover hidden patterns and correlations. BD has been used to help with exploration, drilling, oil recovery, and production (Elijah et al., 2021).

AI involves the use of computer algorithms in an attempt to mimic the operations of human brains or thoughts to understand and make decisions. AI can offer to handle the ever-increasing amount of data for prediction, prevention, and optimization (Hanga & Kovalchuk, 2019). ML is a subset of AI focusing on human-like learning with great potential in OGI applications, especially when it comes to analyzing and interpreting data. The main goals of ML are making predictions, performing clustering, extracting association rules, and making decisions from a piece of given information or data. It offers better ways of developing drilling plans, as well as diagnosing, monitoring, predicting, and performing real-time optimization at a minimal cost (Hanga & Kovalchuk, 2019). Evidence for the successful implementation of ML algorithms in the OGI are (Hanga & Kovalchuk, 2019): (i) maximizing the oil and gas production rate while minimizing the volume of produced water and sand in oil production, (ii) production pattern data recognition, (iii) minimizing the cost of lifting in the wellbore, (iv) enhancing reservoir modeling, and (v) applications in anomaly detection and preventive maintenance. ML can help identify patterns and predict failures based on relationships between valid readings.

These digital tools are also identified as building blocks of a futuristic vision of oilfields. i.e., intelligent oilfields (Elijah et al., 2021). Some of the characteristics of intelligent oilfields are self-diagnostics, control and monitoring systems, autonomous operations, the use of advanced mathematical models for control of equipment, and the real-time exchange of data for controlled objects. Overall, BD, AI, and ML have a massive potential for transforming the OGI into a safer and more efficient industry, thanks to the emergence and growth of many startup companies focused on bringing new technologies to various sectors in OGI.

### *Blockchain Technology*

Blockchain is a distributed ledger technology whose records are batched into timestamped blocks, and each block is identified by its cryptographic hash. Each block references the hash of the block that came before it, which establishes a link between the blocks, and thus creates a chain of blocks or a Blockchain. A blockchain network is a set of non-trusting writers sharing a digital database with no trusted intermediary. Properties of a Blockchain include: (i) a robust, truly distributed peer-to-peer system that is tolerant of node failures and (ii) transparency, verifiability, and auditability of the network's activity. Blockchain was started merely as a decentralized platform to secure cryptocurrencies by solving digital ownership or double-spending problems (Nakamoto, n.d.). It then evolved into a world computer enabling smart contracts, decentralized autonomous organizations, etc. (Buterin, n.d.). Currently, it is accepted as the potential future backbone of the internet (i.e., Web 3) (Wood, n.d.).

In OGI, Blockchain has emerged as a promising innovation that could play an essential role in delivering the technological and commercial capabilities that the sector will need to achieve its goals of modernization and digitization. It could offer operational cost reductions, increased efficiency, fast and automated processes, and transparency. Blockchain has much to offer in OGI, including blockchain-enabled transactional digital platforms for trading (Andoni et al., 2019), carbon accounting and the management of carbon emissions (Saraji & Borowczak, 2021), the design and construction of wells and facilities, the tracking of drilling equipment history and maintenance, the automation of drilling as well as the optimization of drilling operations, and supply chain management (Elijah et al., 2021). Current examples of employed applications include guaranteeing the authenticity of reservoir rock and fluid samples and creating a shared consensus about the progress of drilling campaigns (Perrons & Cosby, 2020). Another area of exploration is the integration of blockchain and IoT. This combination alleviates some of the challenges mentioned in the IoT section (e.g., centralization, non-repudiation, etc.). It also opens up new opportunities, such as enabling autonomous and self-organized machine-to-machine (M2M) communications, automatic and safe firmware updates, and data security.

A wide range of challenges has contributed to the slow adaptation of this technology in the industry, ranging from technical challenges, to unclear regulations and legal frameworks around this technology, and the lack of a technical workforce with the required skills to make use of it. Technical challenges include the lack of standardization and interoperability among technology platforms within the blockchain technology space and the inability of the blockchain (alone) to protect the integrity of the physical assets (Perrons & Cosby, 2020). The latter is known as the oracle problem and emerges when trying to build physical-digital bridges (Caldarelli, 2020). However, this is a fast-growing field, and the rate of innovation in the space is very promising. It is only a matter of time before commercial use cases emerge in the industry.

### *Challenges of Digitization and Modernization*

A recent online survey of oil and gas executives representing a cross-section of oil producers and service companies showed that there are many challenges to the adoption of technology within the industry, including organizational and cultural barriers, the ability to change in a timely manner, a lack of workers with the right skills and the challenge of training workers to use new technologies (*How Do You Reshape When Today's Future May Not Be Tomorrow's Reality?—Oil and Gas Digital Transformation and the Workforce Survey 2020*, n.d.). For example, one of the industry's promising areas for transformation and fast economic growth is the certification of low-emission fluids (e.g., Responsibly Sourced Gas (RSG)), which requires a standard process of monitoring, recording, and auditing the industry's carbon footprint. However, the absence of a globally accepted standard has hampered the success of early attempts to achieve this goal.

## Pillar III: Harnessing Subsurface and Offshore Expertise

Another way the OGI can thrive while undergoing an energy transition is by applying its expertise in subsurface resource exploration, extraction, production, and offshore operations to new fields. In the last century, the industry has recovered hydrocarbon resources from shallow and deep reservoirs (greater than 10,000 feet) with temperatures ranging from near-surface to very high temperatures (up to 250 °C) (DeBruijn et al., 2008). In addition, the complexities and challenges of offshore exploration and production have been successfully surmounted. These capabilities are useful in contemporary challenges encompassing energy security and sustainability, energy storage, and climate-change mitigation. In the following sections, we will discuss how the industry can actively lead the development and sustainable deployment of technologies that could provide solutions to these challenges.

### *Underground Hydrogen Generation and Storage*

Energy security is an important challenge in this technologically-driven modern age. Despite a contraction in the oil and gas industry in 2020 due to the COVID-19 pandemic, demand for energy continues to grow consistently (IEA, 2021a). In addition, climate-change issues, which have emanated from the combustion of fossil fuels since the industrial era, have been gaining global attention in recent years. Therefore, energy supply diversification and transition to renewable and low-carbon resources are proposed as the most sustainable pathway to energy security and climate-change mitigation. However, global utility-scale renewable energy (e.g., wind, solar, and geothermal) generation and supply pale in comparison to fossil-based (e.g., coal and natural gas) energy (IEA, 2021a). In addition, variable renewable energy sources such as wind and solar are insufficient to provide utility-scale baseload of electricity (Matek &

Gawell, 2015). Therefore, energy storage is paramount to consistently meet energy requirements, especially during periods of peak demand.

Hydrogen is attracting global attention as a key low-carbon energy carrier for decarbonizing hard-to-decarbonize sectors, such as aviation, shipping, trucking, cement production, and steelmaking (IEA, 2021d). In addition, hydrogen is expected to play a major role in mitigating the intermittency of wind and solar energy by balancing the energy supply from renewable energy plants and the energy demand of customers (i.e., peak shaving). Surface hydrogen storage requires cryogenic tanks where liquid hydrogen is stored below −253 °C (hydrogen's boiling point) (Langmi et al., 2022; Sundén, 2019). In cryogenic storage, about 35% of the energy stored is used to liquefy the gaseous hydrogen. Venting is occasionally required because the tanks can absorb heat from their surroundings, which causes the liquid they contain to boil (Sundén, 2019). Hydrogen can also be stored in metallic tanks as a compressed gas. However, in the long term, this storage method becomes unsafe because hydrogen can permeate the rigid structure of these metals due to its small atomic size and leak as well as cause extensive hydrogen embrittlement (i.e., making metals significantly less ductile) (Langmi et al., 2022; Murakami, 2019). Underground hydrogen storage (UHS) has been proposed to assuage these issues.

Hydrogen can be stored underground in aquifers, salt caverns, and depleted gas reservoirs (Bünger et al., 2016; Tarkowski, 2019; Zivar et al., 2021). These subsurface reservoirs have the suitable capacity, porosity, and permeability, among other reservoir properties, to allow for both the storage and production of hydrogen when needed. Although numerous underground gas storage sites worldwide are run by OGI producers, dedicated hydrogen storage sites are limited to four sites in operation. One is in Teesside in the United Kingdom, while the rest—Clemens Dome, Moss Bluff, and Spindletop—are located in Texas, United States (IEA, 2021d; Tarkowski, 2019; Zivar et al., 2021). Upscaling and commercializing this technology is necessary for hydrogen to become a mainstream carrier fuel. However, some existing challenges need to be addressed (Heinemann et al., 2021; IEA, 2021d; Lysyy et al., 2021; Matos et al., 2019). There are open areas for research and development that need to be implemented via industry-led collaborations with academic and research institutions. The OGI has extensive experience with such partnerships that have accelerated onshore and offshore exploration and production of hydrocarbons over the years. The direct transfer of research outcomes from lab-scale research to field pilots has been facilitated by professional organizations like the Society of Petroleum Engineers (SPE), the American Association of Petroleum Geologists (AAPG), and the Society of Exploration Geophysicists (SEG). As OGI majors become integrated energy companies with significant participation in the electric utility market, efficient, safe, and sustainable underground hydrogen generation and storage is increasingly necessary.

### *Geological Carbon Sequestration*

Atmospheric carbon dioxide has been described as the dominant greenhouse gas contributing to climate change. One major way to mitigate $CO_2$ emissions and their effects is through carbon capture, utilization, and storage (CCUS). CCUS is a four-step process that ultimately leads to geological $CO_2$ sequestration or the repurposing of $CO_2$ for other industrial uses (Benson et al., 2005; IEA, 2020a). Geological $CO_2$ sequestration is the only viable solution for large-scale carbon storage. The underground storage sites include deep saline aquifers, depleted hydrocarbon reservoirs, and non-mineable coal seams (Aminu et al., 2017; Benson et al., 2005). An extensive monitoring and verification program follows $CO_2$ injection to quantify and ensure storage integrity. Primary conditions for storage integrity in the aforementioned formations are a $CO_2$ impermeable caprock, good reservoir porosity and permeability, sealing faults (if faults exist), and extensive reservoir connectivity. Other factors affecting storage integrity include rock (geomechanical and geochemical) properties, brine salinity, well placement and completion, and well abandonment procedures (Aminu et al., 2017; Benson et al., 2005; Leung et al., 2014).

Since the 1950s, the OGI has been using $CO_2$ as a working fluid for oil recovery, first through the injection of carbonated water (i.e., $CO_2$-enriched brine) (Christensen, 1961; Hickok et al., 1960; Martin, 1951a, 1951b) and then via direct $CO_2$ injection for enhanced oil recovery—starting in the 1970s with the SACROC project (Han et al., 2010; Merchant, 2017). Through several pilot tests and injection optimization schemes, $CO_2$ utilization for enhanced oil recovery (EOR) has commercially produced several billion barrels of oil over the years. In both $CO_2$ injection approaches, significant amounts of the injected $CO_2$ are also stored as a distinct flowing phase or dissolved within the remaining oil and brine in the reservoir. $CO_2$-EOR projects are concentrated in North

America (mostly in the United States) (Global CCS Institute, 2021). This is due to a working infrastructure (e.g., $CO_2$ pipelines) and a market for $CO_2$-EOR in this area. For example, within the state of Wyoming, USA, ExxonMobil has been supplying $CO_2$ from its Shute Creek Treating Facility for EOR locally and around the Rocky Mountain region through existing pipeline networks since the 1990s (Parker et al., 2011).

Direct injection of $CO_2$ for storage is still emerging but rapidly accelerating. The first field-scale injection of $CO_2$ for dedicated storage was accomplished by Statoil (now Equinor) in their Sleipner Field, offshore Norway. This saline aquifer $CO_2$ storage project started in 1996, and is still operational, storing about 1 Mt of $CO_2$ annually. As of May 2022, there are six dedicated (non-$CO_2$ EOR) commercial $CO_2$ storage projects worldwide—in the United States (Illinois-Decatur), Canada (Quest), Norway (Sleipner and Snøhvit), Australia (Gorgon), and just recently Iceland (Orca) (Global CCS Institute, 2021). The Orca project is the first commercial DAC (Direct Air Capture) project with an annual capture capacity of 4,000 tons. $CO_2$ is stored in a mafic formation where it is mineralized—another industry first (Carbfix, 2021; Climeworks, 2021; Reuters, 2021b). Other carbon-intensive countries like China and Brazil are intensifying their CCUS efforts through dedicated storage and $CO_2$-EOR projects at different stages of development (Global CCS Institute, 2021).

Although the technology behind geological carbon storage has been applied for many years, the number of commercial projects and the total annual $CO_2$ storage considerably lag behind storage requirements for 2050 net-zero carbon goals. Specifically, 40 Mt of $CO_2$ (2020 data) is being stored annually, whereas a storage rate of 5,000 Mt per year is needed to meet the 2050 goal of 220 Gt of total $CO_2$ stored prescribed by the International Energy Agency (IEA, 2021b). However, based on current storage potential estimates, existing underground storage sites have the capacity to store up to 55,000 Gt of $CO_2$ (IEA, 2021b). OGI's existing infrastructure and subsurface expertise could help accelerate the rate of adaptation of CCUS as a critical mid-term solution in the energy transition.

### *Geothermal Energy*

In geothermal energy systems, the natural heat energy from the earth's crust/core is harnessed for electricity generation and heating. Geothermal energy is one of the oldest forms of energy manifested in surface systems like geysers, warm springs, and fumaroles in regions of the world with a high level of volcanic activity. The heat energy within hot water and wet/dry steam has been a primary energy source for millennia. These surface systems are directly linked to hydrothermal reservoirs in the subsurface. Analogous to hydrocarbon reservoirs, hydrothermal reservoirs are formed when hot water and steam migrate upward from deeper hotter rocks near the earth's core through faults and fissures toward the earth's surface. However, before reaching the surface, the migrating fluids could become trapped when they reach a region of an impermeable layer of rock (serving as a caprock), thereby forming a hydrothermal reservoir.

Conventional hydrothermal systems are found in places like California in the United States, Indonesia, Japan, and Iceland (i.e., regions with high volcanic activity). In such plants, wells are drilled to produce hot water and steam, which in turn are used to generate electricity. The cold water is then re-injected to maintain reservoir pressure and increase heat recovery (also known as flashing). Recently, enhanced geothermal systems (EGS) have been developed. These are man-made reservoirs formed by injecting water and other fracking fluids to induce fractures in hot low-permeability rocks. EGS is usually first implemented on existing hydrothermal wells (in-field EGS) and can be gradually extended to other adjacent reservoirs (near-field EGS). However, EGS is still an evolving technology, with most projects still at the pilot testing stage.

Most EGS wells do not go beyond 5,000 miles deep, where temperatures of up to 250 °C have been recorded. However, plans are underway to drill deeper wells that are more than 6,000 miles deep. At this depth, in situ water is in a supercritical state (critical pressure and temperature of the water are 330 °C and 220 bar, respectively). When water becomes supercritical, its specific enthalpy (i.e., the energy it can hold per unit mass) almost doubles at the same temperature. Therefore, a substantially higher thermal energy is derived from such systems. This scheme, which is still being researched, is called hot-rock EGS. Recent research has shown that it is more cost-effective than ordinary EGS.

From the preceding discussion, it is obvious that, in the future, geothermal systems will not just increase in number and scale but also in depth. This development will pose a major challenge to the global energy industry because of the very high temperatures that have rarely been encountered in other subsurface exploration and production ventures like oil and gas production. Drill bits, string, tubing, casings, cements, and sensors would need to be redesigned and fabricated with materials enabled to withstand such super-elevated temperature and pressure conditions. Well planning and design have to be optimized to avoid issues around overpressurization and blowouts. Extensive rock and fluid characterizations at such conditions would need to be carried out. Since EGS is fracking-intensive, the geomechanical properties of these reservoir systems need to be determined. EGS is heavily reliant on fracking, which is banned in some states in the U.S. (e.g., New York, Massachusetts) and other countries.

The OGI is well primed for geothermal energy production due to its vast experience with directional drilling of vertical and lateral wells and hydraulic fracturing (fracking). However, geothermal energy production creates bigger challenges, which can spur similar industrial innovation as was seen with deep water offshore hydrocarbon production. Presently, the budding geothermal energy market is becoming attractive to investors, and many startup companies founded by former OGI experts (such as Fenovo, Geothermix) are springing up. Oil majors are not particularly active in this market. However, it is very probable that they will join in as the cost barriers lessen, just as they have in the broader renewables markets (wind, solar, and hydro).

### *Offshore Technology for Renewable Energy: Wind and Solar*

Wind and solar energy together comprise the majority of the renewable energy portfolio today. Overall costs of electricity generation from these sources have substantially decreased in the past two decades—with solar even becoming cheaper than non-renewable electricity from natural gas in some regions. One major challenge brought about by these resources is the space required to harness the energy they supply, especially with regard to utility-scale electricity generation with photo-voltaic (PV) panels and wind turbines. Most of the world's solar and wind energy come from land-based installations on the rooftops of residential and commercial buildings and wind turbine installations on land. The ongoing trend of wind and solar energy installations and the rising demand for low-carbon and renewable energy could significantly impact the amount of land available for other uses.

One way to increase wind and solar energy generation without necessarily changing the amount of land being used is by accelerating the development of offshore renewable energy. Some countries in Western

Europe that do not have sufficient land area for onshore installations (e.g., Denmark and Sweden) are spearheading this technology. The OGI has decades of experience developing offshore drilling and production platforms suitable for shallow and deep water operations (Bigarelli et al., 2019; Solomin et al., 2019).

## Conclusion

The OGI has been transforming in order to find its place in a world undergoing a global energy transition. There are several internal and external forces that are fuelling this transformation. First, with much of the world's "easy oil" already produced, OGI companies will have to use increasingly sophisticated technologies to find and deliver these energy sources to the market (Perrons & Cosby, 2020). Second, the expectations placed upon the sector by many of its stakeholders have grown considerably with regard to environmental stewardship, safety, and human welfare (Perrons & Cosby, 2020). Third, the market volatility in the O&G sector, the dwindling demand for oil due to the impact of COVID-19, predictions of a long-term decline in demand, and the significant reduction in capital investment in the industry (Elijah et al., 2021) have all significantly affected the OGI.

To face these challenges and continue to be a part of the world's source of sustainable energy, the industry will require an increased degree of technological and commercial sophistication. The OGI offers opportunities to employ digital technology to drive efficiency and productivity into operations, help develop standards and technologies for low-carbon fuels, and provide its subsurface and offshore expertise in various areas related to energy/carbon storage, geothermal energy extraction, and offshore wind and solar industry.

## References

Agwu, O. E., Akpabio, J. U., Alabi, S. B., & Dosunmu, A. (2018). Artificial intelligence techniques and their applications in drilling fluid engineering: A review. *Journal of Petroleum Science and Engineering, 167*, 300–315. https://doi.org/10.1016/j.petrol.2018.04.019

Akindipe, D., Saraji, S., & Piri, M. (2021). Salt precipitation during geological sequestration of supercritical $CO_2$ in saline aquifers: A pore-scale experimental investigation. *Advances in Water Resources, 155*, 104011. https://doi.org/10.1016/j.advwatres.2021.104011

Aminu, M. D., Nabavi, S. A., Rochelle, C. A., & Manovic, V. (2017). A review of developments in carbon dioxide storage. *Applied Energy, 208*, 1389–1419. https://doi.org/10.1016/j.apenergy.2017.09.015

Andoni, M., Robu, V., Flynn, D., Abram, S., Geach, D., Jenkins, D., McCallum, P., & Peacock, A. (2019). Blockchain technology in the energy sector: A systematic review of challenges and opportunities. *Renewable and Sustainable Energy Reviews, 100*, 143–174. https://doi.org/10.1016/j.rser.2018.10.014

Beck, C., Rashidbeigi, S., Roelofsen, O., & Speelman, E. (2020). *The future is now: How oil and gas companies can decarbonize* (Energy Transition and Decarbonization). McKinsey & Company. https://www.mckinsey.com/industries/oil-and-gas/our-insights/the-future-is-now-how-oil-and-gas-companies-can-decarbonize

Bello, O., Holzmann, J., Yaqoob, T., & Teodoriu, C. (2015). Application of artificial intelligence methods in drilling system design and operations: A review of the state of the art. *Journal of Artificial Intelligence and Soft Computing Research, 5*(2), 121–139. https://doi.org/10.1515/jaiscr-2015-0024

Benson, S., Anderson, J., Bradshaw, J., Deguchi, G., Gale, J., Heidug, W., Holloway, S., Keith, D., Lloyd, P., Thomson, J., Zarlenga, F., Zhou, D., Celia, M., Lombardi, S., Oldenburg, C., Stevens, S., Borm, G., & Hawkins, D. (2005). Underground geological storage. In B. Metz, O. Davidson, H. de Coninck, M. Loos, & L. Meyer (Eds.), *IPCC Special report on carbon dioxide capture and storage* (pp. 195–276). Cambridge University Press. https://www.ipcc.ch/site/assets/uploads/2018/03/srccs_chapter5-1.pdf

Bigarelli, L., Lidozzi, A., di Benedetto, M., Solero, L., & Bifaretti, S. (2019). Model predictive energy management for sustainable offshore oil and gas platforms. *2019 21st European Conference on Power Electronics and Applications (EPE '19 ECCE Europe)*, 1–10. https://doi.org/10.23919/EPE.2019.8914962

BP. (2021, July). *What is sustainable aviation fuel (SAF) and why is it important? | News and views*. Air BP. https://www.bp.com/en/global/air-bp/news-and-views/views/what-is-sustainable-aviation-fuel-saf-and-why-is-it-important.html

Bravo, C., Saputelli, L., Rivas, F., Pérez, A. G., Nikolaou, M., Zangl, G., de Guzmán, N., Mohaghegh, S., & Nunez, G. (2013). State of the art of artificial intelligence and predictive analytics in the E&P industry: A technology survey. *SPE Journal, 19*(04), 547–563. https://doi.org/10.2118/150314-PA

Bünger, U., Michalski, J., Crotogino, F., & Kruck, O. (2016). 7—Large-scale underground storage of hydrogen for the grid integration of renewable energy and other applications. In M. Ball, A. Basile, & T. N. Veziroğlu (Eds.),

*Compendium of hydrogen energy* (pp. 133–163). Woodhead Publishing. https://doi.org/10.1016/B978-1-78242-364-5.00007-5

Bušić, A., Marđetko, N., Kundas, S., Morzak, G., Belskaya, H., Ivančić Šantek, M., Komes, D., Novak, S., & Šantek, B. (2018). Bioethanol production from renewable raw materials and its separation and purification: A review. *Food Technology and Biotechnology, 56*(3), 289–311. https://doi.org/10.17113/ftb.56.03.18.5546

Buterin, V. (n.d.). *Ethereum: A next-generation smart contract and decentralized application platform*. 36.

Caglayan, D. G., Weber, N., Heinrichs, H. U., Linßen, J., Robinius, M., Kukla, P. A., & Stolten, D. (2020). Technical potential of salt caverns for hydrogen storage in Europe. *International Journal of Hydrogen Energy, 45*(11), 6793–6805. https://doi.org/10.1016/j.ijhydene.2019.12.161

Caldarelli, G. (2020). Understanding the blockchain oracle problem: A call for action. *Information, 11*(11), 509. https://doi.org/10.3390/info11110509

California Air Resources Board. (2020). *Low carbon fuel standard*. California Air Resources Board. https://ww2.arb.ca.gov/sites/default/files/2020-09/basics-notes.pdf

Carbfix. (2021, September 7). *The world's largest direct air capture and $CO_2$ storage plant is ON*. Carbfix Website. http://carbfix.com/the-worlds-largest-direct-air-capture-and-co2- storage-plant-is-on

Choubey, S., & Karmakar, G. P. (2021). Artificial intelligence techniques and their application in oil and gas industry. *Artificial Intelligence Review, 54*(5), 3665–3683. https://doi.org/10.1007/s10462-020-09935-1

Christensen, R. J. (1961, May 26). *Carbonated waterflood results—Texas and Oklahoma*. https://doi.org/10.2118/66-MS

Clean Energy. (2020a, July 7). *Chevron partners with clean energy on adopt-a-port initiative to reduce emissions*. Clean Energy Fuels. https://www.cleanenergyfuels.com/press-room/chevron-partners-with-clean-energy-on-adopt-a-port-initiative-to-reduce-emissions

Clean Energy. (2020b, December 21). *Clean energy to make more carbon-negative fuel available for transportation with BP*. Clean Energy Fuels. https://www.cleanenergyfuels.com/press-room/clean-energy-to-make-more-carbon-negative-fuel-available-for-transportation-with-bp

Clean Energy. (2021a, March 4). *Clean energy and total sign joint venture to develop carbon-negative fuel and infrastructure*. Clean Energy Fuels. https://www.cleanenergyfuels.com/press-room/clean-energy-and-total-sign-joint-venture-to-develop-carbon-negative-fuel-and-infrastructure

Clean Energy. (2021b, March 10). *Clean energy and BP create JV to invest in RNG fuel production*. Clean Energy Fuels. https://www.cleanenergyfuels.com/press-room/clean-energy-and-bp-create-jv-to-invest-in-rng-fuel-production

Clean Energy. (2021c, May 11). *Chevron, clean energy fuels extend adopt-a-port initiative to reduce emissions*. Clean Energy Fuels. https://www.cleanenergyfuels.com/press-room/chevron-clean-energy-fuels-extend-adopt-a-port-initiative-to-reduce-emissions

Climeworks. (2021). *Orca is Climeworks' new large-scale carbon dioxide removal plant*. Climeworks Website. https://climeworks.com/roadmap/orca

Corden, W. M. (1984). Booming sector and Dutch disease economics: Survey and consolidation. *Oxford Economic Papers, 36*(3), 359–380. https://www.jstor.org/stable/2662669

Cuéllar-Franca, R. M., & Azapagic, A. (2015). Carbon capture, storage and utilisation technologies: A critical analysis and comparison of their life cycle environmental impacts. *Journal of $CO_2$ Utilization, 9*, 82–102. https://doi.org/10.1016/j.jcou.2014.12.001

DeBruijn, G., Skeates, C., Greenaway, R., Harrison, D., Parris, M., James, S., Mueller, F., Ray, S., Riding, M., Temple, L., & Wutherich, K. (2008). High-pressure, high- temperature technologies. *Oilfield Review*, 46–60. https://www.slb.com/-/media/files/oilfield-review/high-pressure-high-temperature

Department for Transport. (2021, February 25). *Introducing E10 petrol: Outcome and summary of responses*. GOV.UK. https://www.gov.uk/government/consultations/introducing-e10-petrol/outcome/introducing-e10-petrol-outcome-and-summary-of-responses

Desai, J. N., Pandian, S., & Vij, R. K. (2021). Big data analytics in upstream oil and gas industries for sustainable exploration and development: A review. *Environmental Technology & Innovation, 21*, 101186. https://doi.org/10.1016/j.eti.2020.101186

DiChristopher, T. (2021, September 14). *Market for responsibly sourced gas begins to take root, stakeholders say*. S&P Global—Market Intelligence. https://www.spglobal.com/marketintelligence/en/news-insights/latest-news-headlines/market-for-responsibly-sourced-gas-begins-to-take-root-stakeholders-say-66578408

EIA. (2022, April 7). *Biofuels explained: Ethanol*. U.S. Energy Information Administration (EIA). https://www.eia.gov/energyexplained/biofuels/ethanol.php

Elijah, O., Ling, P. A., Abdul Rahim, S. K., Geok, T. K., Arsad, A., Kadir, E. A., Abdurrahman, M., Junin, R., Agi, A., & Abdulfatah, M. Y. (2021). A survey on industry 4.0 for the oil and gas industry: Upstream sector. *IEEE Access, 9*, 144438–144468. https://doi.org/10.1109/ACCESS.2021.3121302

Equitable Origin. (2017). *EO100™ standard for responsible energy development*. Equitable Origin. https://energystandards.org/wp-content/uploads/2020/10/EO100-Standard-for-Responsible-Energy-Development_2017_PT.pdf

Feinstein, L. (2022, February 10). *Responsibly sourced gas: Boon or boondoggle?* Sightline Institute. https://www.sightline.org/2022/02/10/responsibly-sourced-gas-boon-or-boondoggle/

Gai, H., Beath, J., Fang, J., & Lou, H. H. (2020). Alternative emission monitoring technologies and industrial internet of things–based process monitoring technologies for achieving operational excellence. *Current Opinion in Green and Sustainable Chemistry, 23*, 31–37. https://doi.org/10.1016/j.cogsc.2020.04.009

Global CCS Institute. (2021). *The global status of CCS: 2021.* https://www.globalccsinstitute.com/wp-content/uploads/2021/11/Global-Status-of-CCS-2021-Global-CCS-Institute-1121.pdf

Gong, F., Guo, T., Sun, W., Li, Z., Yang, B., Chen, Y., & Qu, Z. (2020). Evaluation of geothermal energy extraction in Enhanced Geothermal System (EGS) with multiple fracturing horizontal wells (MFHW). *Renewable Energy, 151*, 1339–1351. https://doi.org/10.1016/j.renene.2019.11.134

Gray, R. (2020, March 9). *Why raising the alcohol content of Europe's fuels could reduce carbon emissions.* Horizon: The EU Research and Innovation Magazine. https://ec.europa.eu/research-and-innovation/en/horizon-magazine/why-raising-alcohol-content-europes-fuels-could-reduce-carbon-emissions

Gupta, D., & Shah, M. (2021). A comprehensive study on artificial intelligence in oil and gas sector. *Environmental Science and Pollution Research.* https://doi.org/10.1007/s11356-021-15379-z

Hamm, S. G., Anderson, A., Blankenship, D., Boyd, L. W., Brown, E. A., Frone, Z., Hamos, I., Hughes, H. J., Kalmuk, M., Marble, A., McKittrick, A. M. W., Metcalfe, E., Morse, L. J., Nieto, A., Payne, J., Porse, S. L., Prisjatschew, A., Stutz, G. R., Tasca, C., ... Winick, J. (2021). Geothermal Energy R&D: An Overview of the U.S. Department of energy's geothermal technologies office. *Journal of Energy Resources Technology, 143*(10). https://doi.org/10.1115/1.4049581

Han, W. S., McPherson, B. J., Lichtner, P. C., & Wang, F. P. (2010). Evaluation of trapping mechanisms in geologic $CO_2$ sequestration: Case study of SACROC northern platform, a 35-year $CO_2$ injection site. *American Journal of Science, 310*(4), 282–324. https://doi.org/10.2475/04.2010.03

Hanga, K. M., & Kovalchuk, Y. (2019). Machine learning and multi-agent systems in oil and gas industry applications: A survey. *Computer Science Review, 34*, 100191. https://doi.org/10.1016/j.cosrev.2019.08.002

Heinemann, N., Alcalde, J., Miocic, J. M., Hangx, S. J. T., Kallmeyer, J., Ostertag-Henning, C., Hassanpouryouzband, A., Thaysen, E. M., Strobel, G. J., Schmidt-Hattenberger, C., Edlmann, K., Wilkinson, M., Bentham, M., Haszeldine, R. S., Carbonell, R., & Rudloff, A. (2021). Enabling large-scale hydrogen storage in porous media—The scientific challenges. *Energy &*

*Environmental Science, 14*(2), 853–864. https://doi.org/10.1039/D0EE03536J

Hepburn, C., Adlen, E., Beddington, J., Carter, E. A., Fuss, S., Mac Dowell, N., Minx, J. C., Smith, P., & Williams, C. K. (2019). The technological and economic prospects for $CO_2$ utilization and removal. *Nature, 575*(7781), 87–97. https://doi.org/10.1038/s41586-019-1681-6

Hickok, C. W., Christensen, R. J., & Ramsay, H. J. J. (1960). Progress review of the K&S carbonated waterflood project. *Journal of Petroleum Technology, 12*(12), 20–24. https://doi.org/10.2118/1474-G

*How do you reshape when today's future may not be tomorrow's reality? - Oil and Gas Digital Transformation and the Workforce Survey 2020*. (n.d.). TRUE Global Intelligence. ey.com/oilandgas/digitalskills

IATA. (2021a). *Net zero 2050: Sustainable aviation fuels*. IATA. https://www.iata.org/contentassets/b3783d24c5834634af59148c718472bb/factsheet_saf-.pdf

IATA. (2021b). *Industry Statistics: Fact Sheet*. IATA. https://www.iata.org/en/iata-repository/publications/economic-reports/airline-industry-economic-performance---october-2021---data-tables/

IEA. (2020a). *CCUS in clean energy transitions*. IEA. https://www.iea.org/reports/ccus-in- clean-energy-transitions

IEA. (2020b). *The oil and gas industry in energy transitions*. International Energy Agency. https://iea.blob.core.windows.net/assets/4315f4ed-5cb2-4264-b0ee-2054fd34c118/The_Oil_and_Gas_Industry_in_Energy_Transitions.pdf

IEA. (2021a). *Global energy review 2021*. International Energy Agency. https://iea.blob.core.windows.net/assets/d0031107-401d-4a2f-a48b-9eed19457335/GlobalEnergyReview2021.pdf

IEA. (2021b, April). *The world has vast capacity to store $CO_2$: Net zero means we'll need it – Analysis*. IEA. https://www.iea.org/commentaries/the-world-has-vast-capacity-to-store-co2-net-zero-means-we-ll-need-it

IEA. (2021c, November). *Aviation—Fuels & technologies*. IEA. https://www.iea.org/fuels-and- technologies/aviation

IEA. (2021d). *Global Hydrogen Review 2021*. IEA. https://iea.blob.core.windows.net/assets/5bd46d7b-906a-4429-abda-e9c507a62341/GlobalHydrogenReview2021.pdf

IPCC. (2014). *AR5 climate change 2014: Mitigation of climate change—IPCC*. https://www.ipcc.ch/report/ar5/wg3/

IPCC. (2018). *Summary for policymakers—Global warming of 1.5 °C*. https://www.ipcc.ch/sr15/chapter/spm/

Klein, L., Ramachandran, M., van Kessel, T., Nair, D., Hinds, N., Hamann, H., & Sosa, N. (2018). Wireless sensor networks for fugitive methane emissions monitoring in oil and gas industry. *IEEE International Congress on*

*Internet of Things (ICIOT), 2018*, 41–48. https://doi.org/10.1109/ICIOT.2018.00013

Langmi, H. W., Engelbrecht, N., Modisha, P. M., & Bessarabov, D. (2022). Hydrogen storage. In T. Smolinka & J. Garche (Eds.), *Electrochemical power sources: Fundamentals, systems, and applications* (Chapter 13, pp. 455–486). Elsevier. https://doi.org/10.1016/B978-0-12-819424-9.00006-9

Leung, D. Y. C., Caramanna, G., & Maroto-Valer, M. M. (2014). An overview of current status of carbon dioxide capture and storage technologies. *Renewable and Sustainable Energy Reviews, 39*, 426–443. https://doi.org/10.1016/j.rser.2014.07.093

Li, D., Saraji, S., Jiao, Z., & Zhang, Y. (2021a). $CO_2$ injection strategies for enhanced oil recovery and geological sequestration in a tight reservoir: An experimental study. *Fuel, 284*, 119013. https://doi.org/10.1016/j.fuel.2020.119013

Li, H., Yu, H., Cao, N., Tian, H., & Cheng, S. (2021b). Applications of artificial intelligence in oil and gas development. *Archives of Computational Methods in Engineering, 28*(3), 937–949. https://doi.org/10.1007/s11831-020-09402-8

Li, M., Trencher, G., & Asuka, J. (2022). The clean energy claims of BP, Chevron, ExxonMobil and Shell: A mismatch between discourse, actions and investments. *PLoS ONE, 17*(2), e0263596. https://doi.org/10.1371/journal.pone.0263596

Li, Y., Sun, R., Li, Y., Hu, B., & Dong, J. (2021c). An enhanced role understanding of geothermal energy on compressed air energy storage in aquifers considering the underground processes. *Journal of Energy Storage, 44*, 103483. https://doi.org/10.1016/j.est.2021.103483

Lu, H., Guo, L., Azimi, M., & Huang, K. (2019). Oil and gas 4.0 era: A systematic review and outlook. *Computers in Industry, 111*, 68–90. https://doi.org/10.1016/j.compind.2019.06.007

Lysyy, M., Fernø, M., & Ersland, G. (2021). Seasonal hydrogen storage in a depleted oil and gas field. *International Journal of Hydrogen Energy, 46*(49), 25160–25174. https://doi.org/10.1016/j.ijhydene.2021.05.030

Martin, J. W. (1951a). The use of carbon dioxide for increasing the recovery of oil. *Quarterly Bulletin, the Interstate Oil Compact, 10*(1), 50.

Martin, J. W. (1951b). Additional oil production through flooding with carbonated water. *Producers Monthly, 15*(9), 18.

Matek, B., & Gawell, K. (2015). The benefits of baseload renewables: A misunderstood energy technology. *The Electricity Journal, 28*(2), 101–112. https://doi.org/10.1016/j.tej.2015.02.001

Matos, C. R., Carneiro, J. F., & Silva, P. P. (2019). Overview of large-scale underground energy storage technologies for integration of renewable energies and criteria for reservoir identification. *Journal of Energy Storage, 21*, 241–258. https://doi.org/10.1016/j.est.2018.11.023

McGarr, A., Bekins, B., Burkardt, N., Dewey, J., Earle, P., Ellsworth, W., Ge, S., Hickman, S., Holland, A., Majer, E., Rubinstein, J., & Sheehan, A. (2015). Coping with earthquakes induced by fluid injection. *Science, 347*(6224), 830–831. https://doi.org/10.1126/science.aaa0494

Mehta, D., Tanwar, S., Bodkhe, U., Shukla, A., & Kumar, N. (2021). Blockchain-based royalty contract transactions scheme for Industry 4.0 supply-chain management. *Information Processing & Management, 58*(4), 102586. https://doi.org/10.1016/j.ipm.2021.102586

Menéndez, J., Fernández-Oro, J. M., Galdo, M., & Loredo, J. (2020). Efficiency analysis of underground pumped storage hydropower plants. *Journal of Energy Storage, 28*, 101234. https://doi.org/10.1016/j.est.2020.101234

Menéndez, J., Ordóñez, A., Álvarez, R., & Loredo, J. (2019). Energy from closed mines: Underground energy storage and geothermal applications. *Renewable and Sustainable Energy Reviews, 108*, 498–512. https://doi.org/10.1016/j.rser.2019.04.007

Merchant, D. (2017, July 17). *Enhanced oil recovery—The history of $CO_2$ conventional wag injection techniques developed from lab in the 1950's to 2017*. https://doi.org/10.7122/502866-MS

Meylan, F. D., Moreau, V., & Erkman, S. (2015). $CO_2$ utilization in the perspective of industrial ecology, an overview. *Journal of $CO_2$ Utilization, 12*, 101–108. https://doi.org/10.1016/j.jcou.2015.05.003

Michaga, M. F. R., Michailos, S., Hughes, K. J., Ingham, D., & Pourkashanian, M. (2021). 10— Techno-economic and life cycle assessment review of sustainable aviation fuel produced via biomass gasification. In R. C. Ray (Ed.), *Sustainable biofuels* (pp. 269–303). Academic Press. https://doi.org/10.1016/B978-0-12-820297-5.00012-8

Murakami, Y. (2019). 21—Hydrogen embrittlement. In Y. Murakami (Ed.), *Metal fatigue* (2nd ed., pp. 567–607). Academic Press. https://doi.org/10.1016/B978-0-12-813876-2.00021-2

Murphy, D. (2019). *Renewable energy in the 21st century*. Trubooks.

Mussatto, S. I., Dragone, G., Guimarães, P. M. R., Silva, J. P. A., Carneiro, L. M., Roberto, I. C., Vicente, A., Domingues, L., & Teixeira, J. A. (2010). Technological trends, global market, and challenges of bio-ethanol production. *Biotechnology Advances, 28*(6), 817–830. https://doi.org/10.1016/j.biotechadv.2010.07.001

Nakamoto, S. (n.d.). *Bitcoin: A Peer-to-peer electronic cash system*. 9.

Neste. (2022). *Neste annual report 2021.* https://www.neste.com/sites/neste.com/files/attachments/corporate/investors/corporate_governance/neste_annual_report_2021.pdf

Nguyen, T., Gosine, R. G., & Warrian, P. (2020). A systematic review of big data analytics for oil and gas industry 4.0. *IEEE Access, 8*, 61183–61201. https://doi.org/10.1109/ACCESS.2020.2979678

NOAA. (2021). *State of the climate: Global climate report for annual 2020* [Online Report]. NOAA National Centers for Environmental Information. https://www.ncdc.noaa.gov/sotc/global/202013

Olsen, J., Paasch, K., Lassen, B., & Veje, C. T. (2015). A new principle for underground pumped hydroelectric storage. *Journal of Energy Storage, 2*, 54–63. https://doi.org/10.1016/j.est.2015.06.003

O'Rourke, D., & Connolly, S. (2003). Just oil? The distribution of environmental and social impacts of oil production and consumption. *Annual Review of Environment and Resources, 28*(1), 587–617. https://doi.org/10.1146/annurev.energy.28.050302.105617

Oxford Institute for Energy Studies. (2020). Decarbonization pathways for oil and gas. *Oxford Energy Forum, 121*, 1–40. https://www.oxfordenergy.org/wpcms/wp-content/uploads/2020/03/OEF121.pdf

Parker, M. E., Northrop, S., Valencia, J. A., Foglesong, R. E., & Duncan, W. T. (2011). $CO_2$ management at ExxonMobil's LaBarge field, Wyoming, USA. *Energy Procedia, 4*, 5455–5470. https://doi.org/10.1016/j.egypro.2011.02.531

Patel, H., Prajapati, D., Mahida, D., & Shah, M. (2020). Transforming petroleum downstream sector through big data: A holistic review. *Journal of Petroleum Exploration and Production Technology, 10*(6), 2601–2611. https://doi.org/10.1007/s13202-020-00889-2

Perrons, R. K., & Cosby, T. (2020). Applying blockchain in the geoenergy domain: The road to interoperability and standards. *Applied Energy, 262*, 114545. https://doi.org/10.1016/j.apenergy.2020.114545

Perrons, R. K., & Jensen, J. W. (2015). Data as an asset: What the oil and gas sector can learn from other industries about "Big Data." *Energy Policy, 81*, 117–121. https://doi.org/10.1016/j.enpol.2015.02.020

Project Canary. (2021, September 10). *How to tap certified responsibly sourced gas as a quick win in the transition to a clean energy future.* Project Canary. https://www.projectcanary.com/white-paper/how-to-tap-certified-responsibly-sourced-gas-as-a-quick-win-in-the-transition-to-a-clean-energy-future/

Ram, M., & Mondal, M. K. (2022). Biomass gasification: A step toward cleaner fuel and chemicals. In B. Gurunathan, R. Sahadevan, & Z. A. Zakaria (Eds.), *Biofuels and bioenergy* (Chapter 13, pp. 253–276). Elsevier. https://doi.org/10.1016/B978-0-323-85269-2.00008-3

Restuccia, F., Kanhere, S. D. andSalil S., Melodia, T., & Das, S. K. (2019). *Blockchain for the Internet of things: Present and future*. http://arxiv.org/abs/1903.07448

Reuters. (2021a, March 4). *Clean energy, total sign JV for renewable natural gas production*. Reuters. https://www.reuters.com/article/us-clean-energy-fuels-total-rng-idUSKBN2AW1AB

Reuters. (2021b, September 13). *World's largest plant capturing carbon from air starts in Iceland*. Reuters. https://www.reuters.com/business/environment/worlds-largest-plant-capturing-carbon-air-starts-iceland-2021-09-08/

Reuters. (2022, March 2). *Neste says to become first global renewable fuels producer*. Reuters. https://www.reuters.com/business/energy/neste-team-up-with-us-oil-company-marathon-produce-renewable-fuels-2022-03-02/

Russo, T. N. (2021). Responsibly sourced gas: Time to change the natural gas industry's narrative. *Climate and Energy, 37*(7), 22–27. https://doi.org/10.1002/gas.22215

Saraji, S., & Borowczak, M. (2021). *A blockchain-based carbon credit ecosystem* [White Paper]. http://arxiv.org/abs/2107.00185

Saraji, S., Goual, L., Piri, M., & Plancher, H. (2013). Wettability of supercritical carbon dioxide/water/quartz systems: Simultaneous measurement of contact angle and interfacial tension at reservoir conditions. *Langmuir, 29*(23), 6856–6866. https://doi.org/10.1021/la3050863

Saraji, S., & Khalaf, C. (2022). Blockchain applications in the energy industry. In P. M. Tehrani (Ed.), *Regulatory aspects of artificial intelligence on blockchain* (pp. 159–180). IGI Global. https://doi.org/10.4018/978-1-7998-7927-5.ch008

Saraji, S., Piri, M., & Goual, L. (2014). The effects of $SO_2$ contamination, brine salinity, pressure, and temperature on dynamic contact angles and interfacial tension of supercritical $CO_2$/brine/quartz systems. *International Journal of Greenhouse Gas Control, 28*, 147–155. https://doi.org/10.1016/j.ijggc.2014.06.024

Saxena, R. C., Adhikari, D. K., & Goyal, H. B. (2009). Biomass-based energy fuel through biochemical routes: A review. *Renewable and Sustainable Energy Reviews, 13*(1), 167–178. https://doi.org/10.1016/j.rser.2007.07.011

Shell. (2021, September 28). *Shell starts production at Shell New Energies Junction City, its first US renewable natural gas facility*. Shell: 2021 Media Releases. https://www.shell.us/media/2021-media-releases/shell-starts-production-at-shell-new-energies-junction-city-its-first-us-renewable-natural-gas-facility.html

Solomin, E., Kaixuan, G., Yanming, J., & Minghan, D. (2019). Offshore PV and Wind Based Energy Generation. *2019 International Conference on Industrial Engineering, Applications and Manufacturing (ICIEAM)*, 1–6. https://doi.org/10.1109/ICIEAM.2019.8742965

S&P Global. (2020, February 24). *What is Energy Transition?* S&P Global - Articles. https://www.spglobal.com/en/research-insights/articles/what-is-energy-transition

Sundén, B. (2019). Hydrogen. In B. Sundén (Ed.), *Hydrogen, batteries and fuel cells* (Chapter 3, pp. 37–55). Academic Press. https://doi.org/10.1016/B978-0-12-816950-6.00003-8

Tankimovich, M. R. (2018). *Big data in the oil and gas industry: A promising courtship* [Thesis]. https://doi.org/10.15781/T2804Z300

Tariq, Z., Aljawad, M. S., Hasan, A., Murtaza, M., Mohammed, E., El-Husseiny, A., Alarifi, S. A., Mahmoud, M., & Abdulraheem, A. (2021). A systematic review of data science and machine learning applications to the oil and gas industry. *Journal of Petroleum Exploration and Production Technology, 11*(12), 4339–4374. https://doi.org/10.1007/s13202-021-01302-2

Tarkowski, R. (2019). Underground hydrogen storage: Characteristics and prospects. *Renewable and Sustainable Energy Reviews, 105*, 86–94. https://doi.org/10.1016/j.rser.2019.01.051

Tartakovsky, A. M., Marrero, C. O., Perdikaris, P., Tartakovsky, G. D., & Barajas-Solano, D. (2020). Physics-informed deep neural networks for learning parameters and constitutive relationships in subsurface flow problems. *Water Resources Research, 56*(5), e2019WR026731. https://doi.org/10.1029/2019WR026731

US EPA. (2016, January 12). *Global greenhouse gas emissions data* [Overviews and factsheets]. https://www.epa.gov/ghgemissions/global-greenhouse-gas-emissions-data

U.S. EPA. (2016, January 12). *Understanding global warming potentials* [Overviews and factsheets]. https://www.epa.gov/ghgemissions/understanding-global-warming- potentials

U.S. EPA. (2020). *An overview of renewable natural gas from biogas* (EPA 456-R-20-001). United States Environmental Protection Agency. https://www.epa.gov/sites/default/files/2020-07/documents/lmop_rng_document.pdf

U.S. EPA. (2021). *Reducing methane from the oil and natural gas source category*. United States Environmental Protection Agency. https://www.epa.gov/system/files/documents/2021-11/epas-proposed-oil-and-gas-rules.presentation-11.2.2021.pdf

Wanasinghe, T. R., Gosine, R. G., James, L. A., Mann, G. K. I., de Silva, O., & Warrian, P. J. (2020). The Internet of things in the oil and gas industry: A systematic review. *IEEE Internet of Things Journal, 7*(9), 8654–8673. https://doi.org/10.1109/JIOT.2020.2995617

Wood, D. G. (n.d.). *Polkadot: Vision for a heterogeneous multi-chain framework*, 21.

Zivar, D., Kumar, S., & Foroozesh, J. (2021). Underground hydrogen storage: A comprehensive review. *International Journal of Hydrogen Energy, 46*(45), 23436–23462. https://doi.org/10.1016/j.ijhydene.2020.08.138

CHAPTER 4

# The Future of Fossil Fuels: Renewable Energy—Wind and Solar

*Binny Bagga*

## INTRODUCTION

In May 2021, the International Energy Agency (IEA) released a bold statement which affirmed that extraction and development of new oil and gas fields must stop immediately and no new coal-fired power stations (barring projects already sanctioned for the year) are to be built if the world is to stay within the safe limits of global heating and meet the goal of net zero emissions by 2050. This proposal is part of a scenario outlined in the IEA's report on ways to achieve net zero carbon dioxide emissions by 2050, a prerequisite to meet the Paris climate accord goal of limiting global warming to 1.5 °C above pre-industrial levels (Bonckaert et al., 2021).

The UN's Intergovernmental Panel on Climate Change (IPCC), in February 2022, also emphasized the fears of the impact of climate change and the urgency to deal with its effects in order to limit the global temperature increase. The authors of the sixth assessment report highlight that

B. Bagga (✉)
Rystad Energy, Oslo, Norway
e-mail: bagga.binny@gmail.com



T. Walker et al. (eds.), *Sustainability in the Oil and Gas Sector*,
https://doi.org/10.1007/978-3-031-51586-6_4

the world will face unavoidable climate hazards in the next two decades with global heating of 1.5 °C above pre-industrial levels—the warming level ascribed as the aspirational target in the landmark 2015 Paris Agreement. They further underscore the reality that coal and other fossil fuels are choking humanity, and a continued reliance on fossil fuels makes the global economy and energy security vulnerable to geopolitical shocks and crises (Pörtner et al., 2022).

To tackle climate change, some countries have already taken initiative by banning the exploration of fossil fuels. In 2017, France's parliament passed a law to ban the production of oil and gas in all its territories by 2040. No new permits for extracting fossil fuels can be issued and no existing licenses are able to be extended past the deadline. In 2020, Denmark agreed to ban new exploration and end oil and gas production in the North Sea by 2050. It became the second country in Europe to set a date for the complete phase-out of oil and gas production after France. Ireland followed suit, introducing a legislation in February 2021 to ban licenses on new oil and gas exploration. Then in May 2021, Spain approved a climate law that will put an end to the production of fossil fuels across all its territories by 2042. The ruling bans all new coal, gas, and oil exploration effective immediately, as well as enshrining in law the prohibition of fossil fuel vehicles by 2040, and a goal to generate 74% of the country's electricity from renewable energy by 2030. In July 2021, Greenland also banned all new oil and gas exploration citing climate concerns (Frost, 2022).

There is no doubt that the world has already entered an era which gradually phases out the fossil fuel industry. At the same time, there is no denying the fact that modern society relies on oil, and if oil were to disappear tomorrow, numerous areas and commodities including air travel, cosmetics, contact lenses, shoes, key medicines, and hypodermic syringes, among others, would be affected.

The demand for oil must be reduced in the coming years. However, as we still remain dependent on oil and gas as we increasingly deploy more renewable energy sources, investments in this field are also required to meet the residual demand of oil throughout this transition. A planned and controlled transition from a society dependent on fossil fuels to a more sustainable one is very important. This will entail securing economic growth and development along with the reduction of carbon emissions.

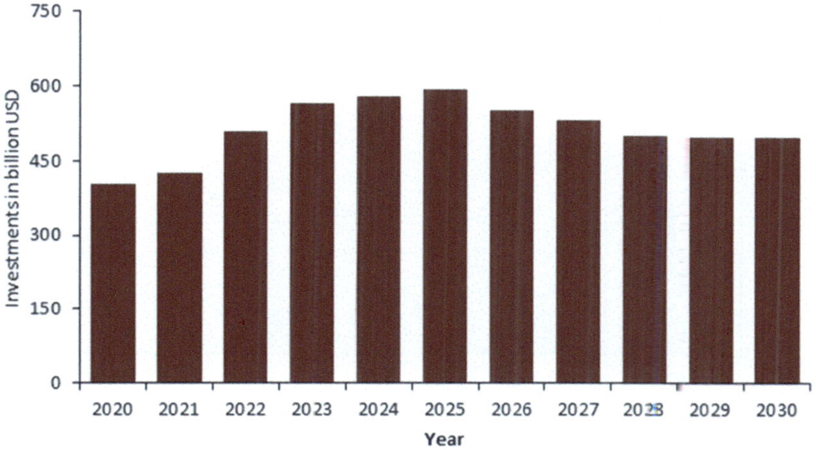


**Fig. 4.1** Upstream oil and gas investments by year (*Note* Copyright 2022 by Rystad Energy. Reprinted with permission)

According to the estimates of Rystad Energy—an independent energy research and business intelligence company—the global upstream investments within the oil and gas industry are expected to grow by a mere 2% over the period 2020 to 2030 (as shown in Fig. 4.1). This stands in stark contrast to the expected growth of the renewables industry—which is expected to exhibit a higher growth across all energy sectors (i.e., offshore wind, onshore wind & solar among others). Figure 4.1 indicates upstream oil and gas investments will grow by a compound annual growth rate of 2% during the period 2020 to 2030.

## Current State of Renewables Industry

Renewables are the backbone of the energy transition and imperative if we are to achieve net zero emissions. Understanding the current state of the renewable energy industry along with its future growth potential in light of regulatory and policy frameworks, funding availability, and the state of supply chains will, to a great extent, determine the future of the fossil fuel industry.

Figure 4.2 indicates that the combined annual installed capacity of both solar and wind energy reached close to 176 Gigawatts (GW) in

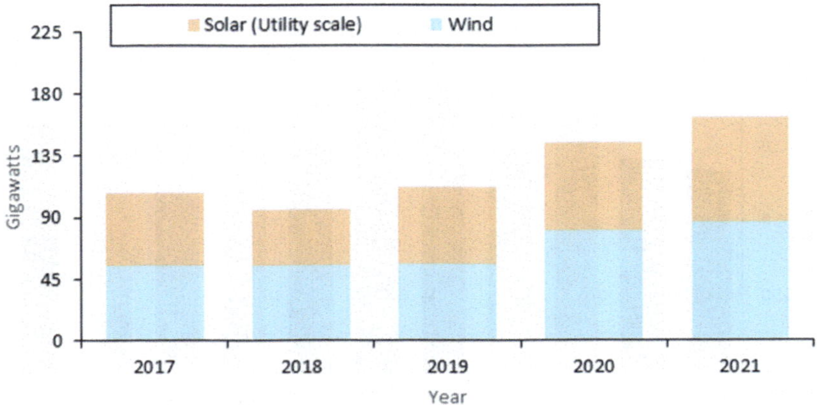


**Fig. 4.2** Renewables, annual installed capacity by energy source (*Note* Copyright 2022 by Rystad Energy. Reprinted with permission)

2021. This represents a 55% increase in annual installed capacity relative to 2017 figures i.e., 114 GW. These two sources of renewable energy (wind and solar) have been deployed in full force across the world in the past few years. The expansion is led by continuous policy support in many countries, ambitious net zero goals announced by nations and improving cost competitiveness of wind and solar photovoltaic (PV) energy. Figure 4.2 indicates the annual renewables installed capacity during the period 2017 to 2021.

### *Wind Energy*

Figure 4.3 shows the annual installed capacity of wind energy increased at compound annual growth rate of 12% from 2017 to 2021. The onshore wind installed capacity contributed almost 90% of the additions in the wind energy over the period.

#### *Onshore Wind Energy*

The annual onshore wind installed capacity additions stood at 69.7 GW in 2021 in comparison with 52.2 GW in 2017. Additionally, the installation of onshore wind increased by 48% in 2020 to 74.9 GW in comparison

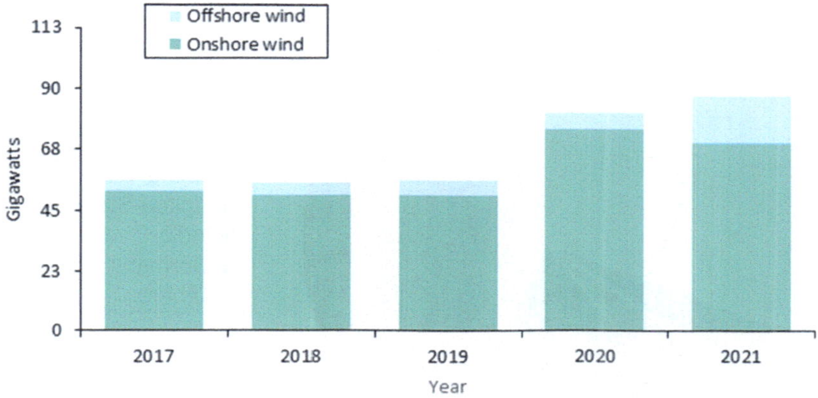


**Fig. 4.3** Wind energy, annual installed capacity by year (*Note* Copyright 2022 by Rystad Energy. Reprinted with permission)

with 2019 levels (as shown in Fig. 4.3). A large part of the installation in 2020 was driven by developers in China that rushed to complete projects before their subsidies expired. Figure 4.4 shows that China has led the world in the onshore wind capacity additions for the period 2017 to 2021. This was followed by the United States (US) and Germany (Fig. 4.4).

Taylor (2020) shows that China circulated $15.6 billion of renewable subsidies in 2017, accounting for 9% of the world's total subsidies. In fact, "in China, India and the rest of the world, onshore wind received large shares of the total renewable power generation subsidy. Some 43% of China's renewable power generation subsidies went to onshore wind in 2017" (p. 32). The developments of onshore wind have long been subsidized in the country, allowing the industry to thrive while the levelized cost of energy has been higher than grid-parity power prices. Despite the phase-out of the onshore wind subsidies in 2020, China continued to announce large-scale renewable energy projects in 2021.

In the United States, Bowers states that:

> The timing and magnitude of wind turbine installations are often driven by tax incentives. The US production tax credit (PTC), a per-kilowatt hour credit for electricity generated by eligible renewable sources, was first

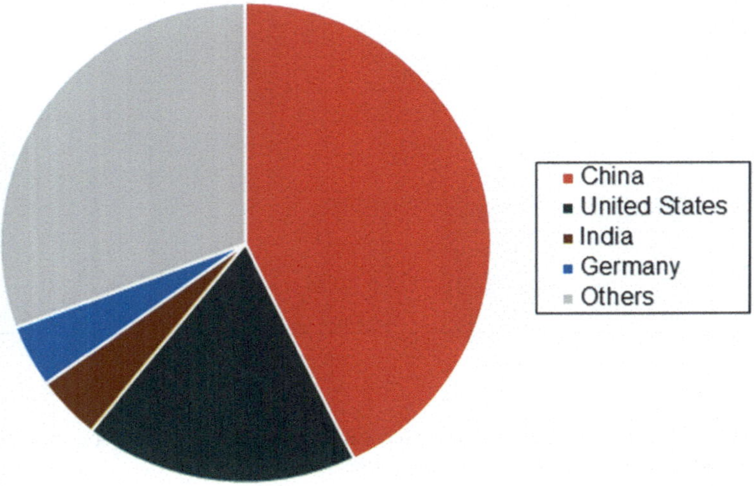


**Fig. 4.4** Annual onshore wind, installed capacity by country, 2017 to 2021 (*Note* Copyright 2022 by Rystad Energy. Reprinted with permission)

enacted in 1992 and has been extended and modified in the years since. (Bowers, 2021)

The US onshore wind installation reported its highest-ever year of new installations in 2020. This was driven by the planned phase-out of the PTC, project developers now had to chase the 2020 deadline to qualify for the PTC's full value. This record in installations happened despite the fact that that the Internal Revenues Service (IRS) extended the commissioning deadline for projects that started construction in 2016 and 2017 from four years to five to ease pressure on developers, as it recognized the disruption of COVID-19 on supply chain and project construction execution (Internal Revenue Bulletin, 2021). At the end of December 2020, the Senate extended the PTC for another year at 60% of its original rate (Bowers, 2021). In August 2022, the US government passed the Inflation Reduction Act, the single largest clean energy, health, and tax spending bill in history. Solar PV, wind, storage, nuclear, hydrogen, carbon capture, utilization and storage, and geothermal will benefit from investment and production tax credits, which will reassure developers. The Inflation Reduction Act has reassured developers over vital lifelines for project economics for the coming years. The bill will continue the current production tax credit (PTC) at $0.15/kWh and the investment tax credit (ITC) at 30% until 2024. In 2025, all tax credits will roll into a singular, technology-agnostic clean energy ITC or PTC. The bill will start with base rates of $0.003/kWh and 6% for the PTC and ITC, respectively.

Germany has led Europe with its onshore wind installations for years. The country saw steep growth in 2016 to 2017 largely due to its national carbon emissions reduction target (Bundesverband Wind Energie, 2018). Furthermore, the industry was supported with radical changes to its renewable energy support regime (from predetermined feed-in-tariffs to auctions). However, the industry struggled in years since, with onshore wind installations in 2019 emerging as some of the lowest in the decade. The downfall was caused by several factors, including severe regulatory bottlenecks. These bottlenecks led to fewer permits being awarded, and thus, declining installations (Amelang & Wehrmann, 2022). To address these issues, Germany revised its Renewable Energy Act in December 2020. The new act came into force on January 1, 2021, and aims to see renewables account for 65% of the country's energy mix by 2030. In addition to speeding up the approval and construction process of onshore wind farms, the law proposed removing limitations on grid expansions, especially for capacity additions in northern German states—a move designed to encourage developers to actively participate in future auctions (Green Dealflow, 2021).

*Offshore Wind Energy*

The global offshore wind annual capacity additions grew to 17.7 GW in 2021 relative to a mere 3.8 GW in 2017. Specifically, in 2021, this is a near tripling of 2020's record value of 6.3 GW (refer Fig 4.3). China was the main driver for the surge in commissioning levels in 2021 as the country's full feed-in-tariffs were set to be phased out from 2022 onward. As such, developers raced to reach the 2021 deadline to receive full feed-in-tariffs support. Figure 4.5 indicates the annual offshore wind energy installed capacity during the period 2017 to 2021.

China also overtook the United Kingdom (UK) as the world's largest offshore wind nation, a position held by the UK since 2009 (Fig. 4.5). As of the end of 2021, Germany, the Netherlands, Denmark, and Belgium had the highest installed base of capacity apart from the two leading nations, China and the UK. Figure 4.6 indicates the offshore wind energy installed capacity of China and UK.

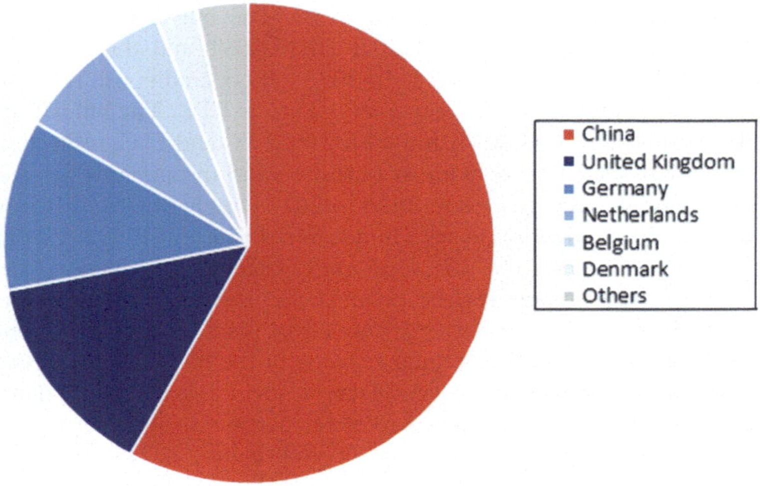


**Fig. 4.5** Annual offshore wind, installed capacity by country, 2017 to 2021 (*Note* Copyright 2022 by Rystad Energy. Reprinted with permission)

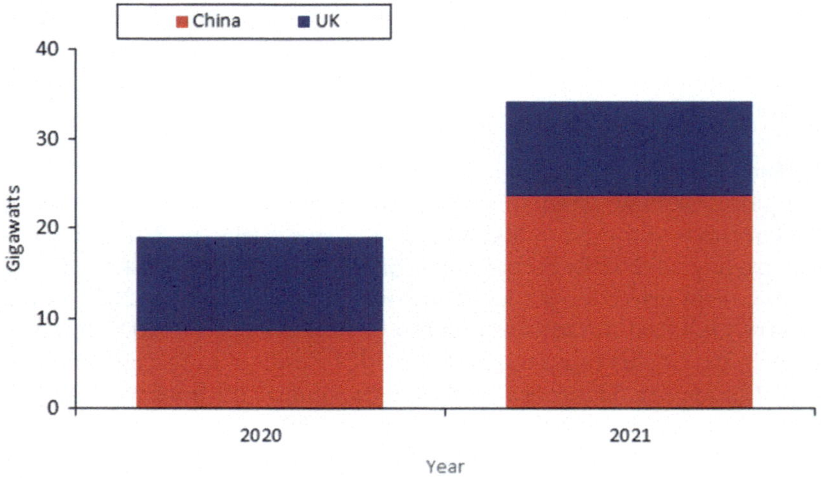


**Fig. 4.6** Offshore wind, installed capacity of China and the UK, by year (*Note* Copyright 2022 by Rystad Energy. Reprinted with permission)

### *Solar Energy*

Around the world, countries and companies are investing in solar generation capacity on an unprecedented scale, and consequently, costs continue to fall and technologies improve. While solar energy is abundant, it represents a tiny fraction of the world's current energy mix, though this is changing rapidly.

China, followed by the United States and India, have had the highest capacity additions in utility-scale solar PV from 2017 to 2021 (refer to Fig. 4.7). In 2021, over 160 GW of solar power was installed, among which 76.4 GW is utility-scale. Asia and North America installed most of the utility-scale solar capacity in 2021, amounting to roughly 70% of total utility-scale installations worldwide. In a significant majority of countries worldwide, utility-scale solar PV is the least costly option for adding new electricity capacity, especially amid rising natural gas and coal prices. As of the beginning of 2022, China ranked first in the world in terms of installed PV capacity, onshore wind, as well as offshore wind capacity.

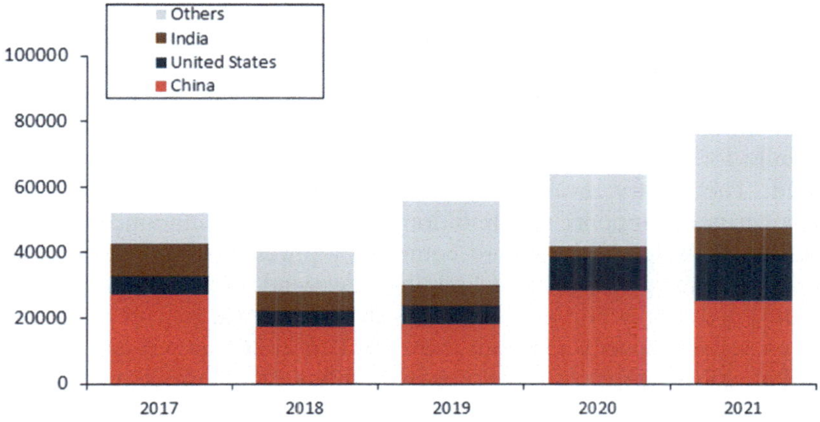


**Fig. 4.7** Annual solar, installed capacity by country, 2017 to 2021 (*Note* Copyright 2022 by Rystad Energy. Reprinted with permission)

## The Changing Global Energy Mix

The world currently gets the majority of its primary energy supply from fossil fuels. This needs to change if the international community is to limit global warming to 1.5 °C above pre-industrial levels. To meet this target, the current global energy mix must undergo a significant transformation to replace a large part of the energy that is currently supplied by fossil fuels. This would require that the two major renewable sources of energy, i.e., wind and solar, to meet a greater proportion of power generation needs through 2050.

Instead of fossil fuels, the energy sector would be based largely on renewable energy. Two-thirds of total energy supply in 2050 is from wind, solar, bioenergy, geothermal, and hydro energy. Solar becomes the largest source, accounting for one-fifth of energy supplies. Solar PV capacity increases 20-fold between now and 2050, and wind power 11-fold. Net zero means a huge decline in the use of fossil fuels. They fall from almost four-fifths of total energy supply today to slightly over one-fifth by 2050. Fossil fuels that remain in 2050 are used in goods where the carbon is embodied in the product such as plastics, in facilities fitted with CCUS, and in sectors where low-emissions technology options are scarce (Bouckaert et al., 2021).

As per the IEA, the renewables capacity additions are expected to grow faster than ever in the period between 2021 and 2026 and will account for almost 95% of the increase in global power capacity through 2026. The agency revised its forecast in 2021 from a year earlier, as stronger policy support and ambitious climate targets announced during COP26 outweighed the record commodity prices increases observed in 2021, impacting the costs of building new wind and solar PV installations. Further, the IEA's report notes that China will remain the leader in renewables capacity additions from 2021 to 2026 and will account for 43% of global renewable capacity growth, followed by Europe, the United States, and India. These four markets combined will account for around 80% of renewable capacity expansion worldwide (Abdelilah et al., 2021). The targets and policies introduced by these four markets has positively impacted the future growth outlook.

On July 14, 2021, the European Union's (EU) unveiled its 'Fit for 55' package with a binding target of achieving carbon neutrality by 2050. In its package, the EU raised its 2030 climate ambition, by committing to cut emissions by at least 55% by 2030, compared to 1990 levels

(European Commission, 2021). Rapid deployment in the region is now being driven by member countries implementing larger auction volumes, corporations contracting for more renewable electricity, and consumers continuing to install large residential solar.

As for China, the country has committed to reach carbon neutrality before 2060 and has formulated nearer-term targets, such as 1,200 GW of total wind and solar PV capacity by 2030 (Abdelilah et al., 2021). In November 2021, India pledged to achieve net zero carbon emissions by 2070 (British Broadcasting Corporation, 2021). The country further announced that it would expand its installed capacity of renewables to 500 GW by 2030, and that half of the nation's power-generating capacity would be based on renewable energy by 2030 (Vishnoi, 2021). According to the Government of India, the total installed capacity for renewable energy in the country stood at 151.4 GW as of 31 December 2021 (Manohar, 2022). The United States also laid out its plan to reach net zero greenhouse gas emissions by 2050 in November 2021 (The White House, 2021).

## Wind Energy Outlook

The IEA estimates the onshore wind additions through 2026 to be almost 25% higher on average than in the period between 2015 and 2020. China, Europe, and the United States together account will account for 80% of global onshore wind expansion between 2021 and 2025. The offshore wind market is also set to grow at a rapid rate in the coming years as countries look to reduce emissions and combat climate change, and "total offshore wind capacity is forecast to more than triple by 2026. By then, offshore wind additions are expected to account for one-fifth of the global wind market, a major milestone" (Abdelilah, et al., 2021, pp. 15, 28).

Many countries have set ambitious offshore wind targets for 2030, which is expected to lead this industry to reach a new height between 2020 and 2030. In the coming years, offshore wind developments are expected to expand in new markets beyond the UK, Germany, Belgium, Denmark, and the Netherlands. This includes large-scale projects that are expected to be commissioned in the United States, Chinese Taipei, South Korea, Vietnam, and Japan.

In China's case, rapid cost declines and strong provincial level policies could drive up offshore wind installations. Additionally, the country has already set for itself wind energy targets to be achieved by 2030. While in the United States, the early commissioning of large-scale pipelines could push growth. The country aims to achieve 30 GW of offshore wind installations by 2030 (The White House, 2021, ). South Korea, as part of policy targets set in 2018, is aiming to install 12 GW of offshore wind by 2030 (Tachev, 2021). While Japan, in 2020, set an offshore wind target of 10 GW to reach by 2030 (*The Japan Times*, 2020).

Vietnam too has ambitious wind power development plans in the Association of Southeast Asian Nations. The country's target is to reach 11.8 GW of wind power capacity by 2025. The country's offshore wind potential generated from the wind at sea is much larger than onshore wind (Nguyen, 2022). According to the World Bank's Offshore Wind Roadmap for Vietnam, offshore wind could play a significant role in sustainability and has the potential to supply 12% of Vietnam's electricity by 2035 (World Bank Group, 2021).

With the current pace of development in offshore wind developments, the spending in the offshore wind sector is increasingly closing the gap against offshore oil and gas investments, per Rystad Energy. Further, spending on offshore wind is forecasted to surpass that of offshore oil and gas in several key markets by 2030. The energy research firm states that while the global crossing point is further out in time, countries and regions that prioritize offshore wind are expected to see a gradual decline in offshore oil and gas investment and the inevitable crossover (Fløtre, 2021). China and the UK—the two largest offshore wind nations by operational capacity—already reached this crossing point in 2017 and 2020, respectively. Europe is expected to be the world's largest offshore wind region by 2030. Europe and Asia (excluding China) are expected to see clear and opposite trends between the two industries. For Europe, investment levels in offshore wind have been high for some time, making it the most mature offshore wind region in the world. With the decline in offshore oil and gas investment and capex budget cuts by E&P companies during the pandemic, offshore wind and offshore oil and gas capex levels nearly intersected in 2022. The offshore wind industry in Asia (excluding China) is still in its infancy, but capacity is expected to see rapid growth during the decade. In the short-to-medium term, intertidal wind farms in Vietnam and conventional offshore wind in Taiwan are expected to drive capital investment toward 2025 (Fløtre, 2021). Figure 4.8 shows the development trends of annual global offshore oil and gas capex vs. global offshore wind capex.

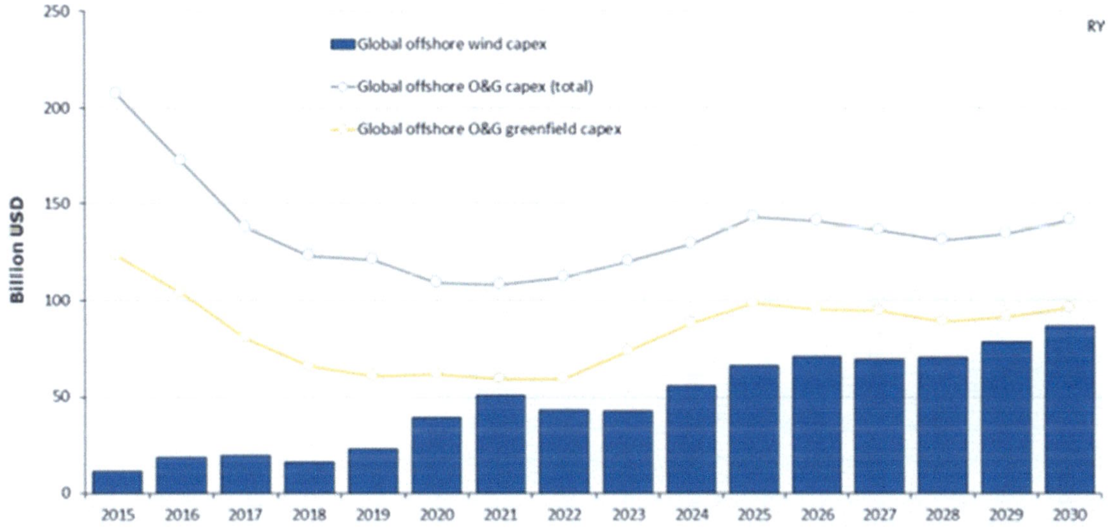


**Fig. 4.8** Annual global offshore oil and gas capex vs. global offshore wind capex (*Note* Copyright 2022 by Rystad Energy. Reprinted with permission)

## Solar Energy Outlook

The expansion of solar PV capacity between 2022 and 2026 is expected to be almost double that of the previous five years. Currently, utility-scale projects continue to provide over 60% of all solar PV additions worldwide. The rise in solar energy is expected to be most in key markets such as China, Europe, the United States, and India. At the same time, considerable growth potential remains in nascent markets such as sub-Saharan Africa and the Middle East. The policy initiatives in China, the EU and India are boosting the deployment of commercial and residential PV projects (Abdelilah et al., 2021).

## E&P Companies Energy Transition

By 2050, the upstream oil and gas landscape will be unrecognizable as the majority of energy needs will be met by the renewable energy. From its current contribution of 80% to the global energy mix, fossil fuel's contribution is estimated to reach only 20% if we are able to limit global warming to 1.5 °C above pre-industrial levels (Bouckaert et al., 2021). 2050 may seem a lifetime away in years, but change is just around the corner for oil and gas companies. For these companies, going "beyond the barrel" will really mean maximizing returns from the barrel and applying some appreciable portion of those gains to developing low-carbon and negative-carbon energy and energy-related opportunities. For the exploration and production (E&P) companies' evolution is necessary, and there will be opportunities to create value along the way.

During the past five years, more upstream E&P companies have increased investments in clean energy across the electricity value chain, but specific investments vary with company types and core markets. These companies have undertaken numerous approaches to energy transition with all of them moving at different paces, in different directions, and with different guiding philosophies. Companies such as Exxon, Shell, BP, Oxy, Suncor, TotalEnergies, Saudi Aramco, and many others have rolled out their low-carbon or net zero initiatives.

ExxonMobil is planning to invest more than $15 billion on initiatives to lower greenhouse gas emissions over the next six years, with a significant share earmarked for scaling up carbon capture and storage, hydrogen, and biofuels (Woods W. D.). Chevron aims to spend $10 billion on total capital investment by 2028, including $2 billion to lower the carbon intensity of Chevron's operations. Chevron has a more focused carbon-mitigation strategy with low-carbon fuels, hydrogen and carbon capture, and storage at its core (Chevron, 2021).

In April 2021, Shell presented its Energy Transition Strategy publication to shareholders for an advisory vote. The publication sets out the company's target to achieve net zero emissions by 2050, with Shell's short- and medium-term climate targets, customer-focused decarbonization strategy, capital allocation, and approach to climate-related policy and advocacy. A key pillar of the strategy states that by 2030, Shell aims to double the electricity it sells, delivering the equivalent of more than 50 million households with renewable electricity (Shell, 2021a, 2021b). Italian major contributor Eni aims to install 60 GW of renewable energy projects by 2050, with an interim target of 15 GW of capacity by 2030. BP has an ambitious target of 50 GW renewables installed capacity by 2030. As of the end of 2021, with its renewables pipeline and 4.4 GW developed to final investment decision, the company is on its track for having developed 20 GW renewables power capacity by 2025 (BP, 2022). While the French-headquartered TotalEnergies wants to be "no more an oil and gas company but an energy company," it aims to have 100 GW of gross wind and solar energy generation capacity by 2030, building on the company's short-term pledge of having developed 35GW by 2025 (TotalEnergies, 2022a, 2022b). Companies such as BP and Shell have ambitious targets for renewable energy growth and could match or even surpass the current market leaders NextEra and Orsted, the major renewable energy developers. Shell, TotalEnergies, BP, Repsol, Equinor, Eni, Galp Energia, and Petronas have set themselves renewable energy targets to be reached between 2026 and 2030, and used 2021 to bulk up pipelines.

Clearly, European E&P companies are taking the lead here with ambitious plans for renewable energy, as their path to energy transition lies with investments in the low-carbon energy systems of the future. This transition also means that companies will gradually redirect some of their oil and gas investments to their renewable's portfolio. The US companies have started to join their European counterparts in making low-carbon investment plans. However, in comparison with their European counterparts they have a more focused carbon-mitigation strategy with low-carbon fuels, hydrogen and carbon capture and storage at its core. Figure 4.9 shows the TotalEnergies energy transition roadmap.

To achieve their medium and long-term low-carbon and renewables investment targets, the many E&P companies undertook significant

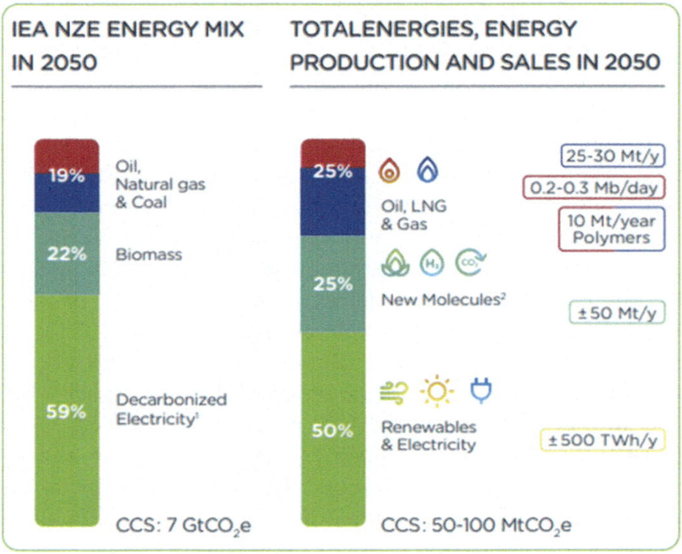


**Fig. 4.9** TotalEnergies roadmap to 2050 (*Note* TotalEnergies Sustainability & Climate 2022 Progress Report)

mergers, acquisitions, and joint ventures in 2021. Shell announced the acquisition of solar and energy storage developer Savion in December 2021 (Shell, 2021a, 2021b), while Eni and Shell entered a joint venture with partners RedRock and Iberdrola, respectively, to bid in the 10 GW Scotwind tender (Eni, 2021) (Iberdrola, 2021). To date, solar PV retains its position as the favorite renewable energy source of E&P players, followed by offshore wind. Shell, TotalEnergies, BP and Repsol's renewable energy portfolios are dominated by solar PV, while Equinor's is dominated by offshore wind.

Despite all of these efforts, the investment by E&P companies outside their core business areas is less than 5% of their total capital expenditures. As per an IEA report published in January 2020, the investment to date by oil and gas companies outside their core business areas has been less than 1% of their total capital spent. Further, McGlade et al. determine that a significant change in overall capital allocation is required to accelerate energy transitions (McGlade et al., 2020).

## Current State of Renewables Supply Chain

To achieve the net zero target and to ensure an easy transition to renewables, a robust supply chain is required. Any pressure on the renewables supply chain could easily derail the global energy transition targets and can have strong implications for the environment. Mainly, supply chain challenges could stifle renewables adoption rates.

### *Solar Supply Chain*

The solar PV manufacturing chain consists of five main components: polysilicon, ingots, wafers, cells, and modules. Figure 4.10 shows the five major components of solar PV manufacturing chain.

Polysilicon is the key feedstock for the production of solar cells. After the polysilicon arrives at the ingot factory as a sack of chunks, it is shaped into either multicrystalline or monocrystalline ingots by melting it and allowing it to cool slowly into solids. Ingots are then sliced into wafers. The doped wafers are electrically connected and sealed into cells, then finally strung and assembled into the modules that are installed onto roofs or into open spaces. The module is the core component of a solar PV system. The majority of global PV module shipments use crystalline silicon technology. Each of the five steps of the value chain uses a variety of specialized materials and equipment. Furthermore, the production of each of these components requires very different processes and competencies. There are additional components that are added to manage the flow of electricity. This includes inverters, which convert direct current

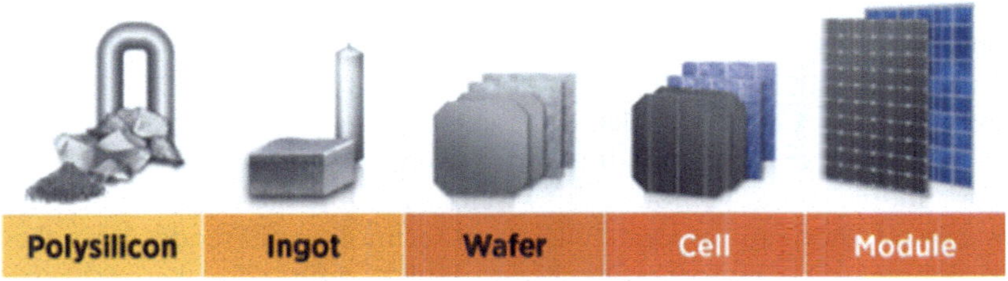


**Fig. 4.10** Solar PV manufacturing chain (*Source* Solar Photovoltaics—Supply Chain Deep Dive Assessment, US Department of Energy, p. 13, 2022)

electricity from the modules into alternating current for connection to the grid.

Manufacturing of components across the upstream value chain—including ingots, wafers, cells, and modules—is largely dominated by Chinese players, with only a handful of US and South Korean companies. Basore and Feldman note the following:

> A significant portion of PV-component supply, varying by the stage of the supply chain, comes from China. While a considerable (but minority) portion of cells, modules, and polysilicon can be sourced outside of China, the global PV supply chain is almost entirely dependent on ingot and wafers from China. Additionally, many of the other pieces of the module supply chain, such as the manufacturing of production-facility equipment and balance-of-module components (e.g., glass, aluminum frames), are predominantly located in China. China also manufactures a significant share of balance-of-PV-system components, including inverters (which convert the dc output from PV modules to ac power used by the electrical grid) as well as aluminum and steel used for mounting PV modules. By 2035, a high decarbonization scenario would require significant expansion of several parts of the supply chain. (Basore & Feldman, 2022, p. 7)

The polysilicon market is the most consolidated within the solar supply chain. This is due to high capital expenditure required to establish a polysilicon facility and in turn discourages competition and lowers overall market growth. Basore and Feldman emphasize that "the ingot production process alone requires greater than 70% of the total energy to produce a wafer. Therefore, it is advantageous to site ingot production near large, inexpensive sources of energy, and global ingot capacity reflects these trends" (Basore and Feldman, 2022, p. 31). As for the wafer market, it is also consolidated owing to high capex and vertical integration across the supply chain, dominated by Chinese players and a few western companies like Canadian Solar.

The market consolidation is comparatively less within the solar cell and solar module industry. Both cell as well as module factories can be built faster, and they can respond quicker to technological trends and policy developments like import tariffs. Most of the leading cell makers are vertically integrated companies that own wafer and/or module manufacturing as well.

Module makers are also heavily reliant on the supply of external components such as PV glass and aluminum frames. As a result, securing reliable supply of high-quality product is essential for module manufacturers. Here, China is also home to the largest manufacturers of key materials such as PV glass and aluminum frames. However, it is easier for the module manufacturers to expand their operations in other countries in response to tariffs or other policies as they face low technical and financial barriers.

### *Wind Supply Chain*

The main components contained in a typical utility-scale wind turbine are foundations, towers, blades, hubs, and drivetrains. The drivetrain sits within the nacelle and converts the rotational energy from the blades into electricity. Figure 4.11 shows the major components of wind supply chain.

Concrete is the predominant material used in onshore wind farms (by mass), while steel takes the lion's share for offshore wind

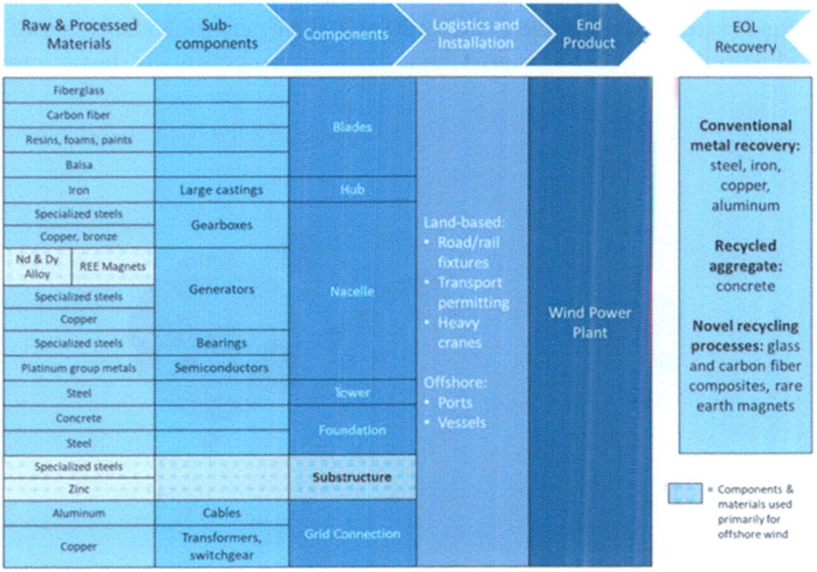


**Fig. 4.11** Schematic diagram that details the relationships of these supply chain elements, for both land based and offshore wind (*Note* US Department of Energy, Wind Energy—Supply Chain Deep Dive Assessment, p. 16)

projects. Concrete, land-based foundations and steel sub-sea foundations contribute the majority to this, but the nacelle and tower also require steel (Refer to Fig. 4.10). Mostly, the concrete tends to be locally sourced, whereas China remains a key steel producer (Refer to Figs. 4.12 and 4.13). Figure 4.12 shows the major steel producing regions in the world based on total production of crude steel.

Figure 4.13 shows the major steel producing regions in the world based on total production of crude steel.

Glass fiber reinforced plastic material is primarily used in wind turbine blades. Most production comes from China.

Polymer materials are used in various wind turbine subcomponents, including as resin in composites, coatings on blades and towers, cable exteriors, in foam core for some blades, and in auxiliary equipment. The primary source of polymer materials is petrochemical feedstocks, although production of polymers from bio-based feedstocks has been demonstrated.

Another raw material 'rare earth magnets' makes electrical motors and generators more efficient and enhances their performance. Its global production is concentrated in China, with all processing of heavy rare

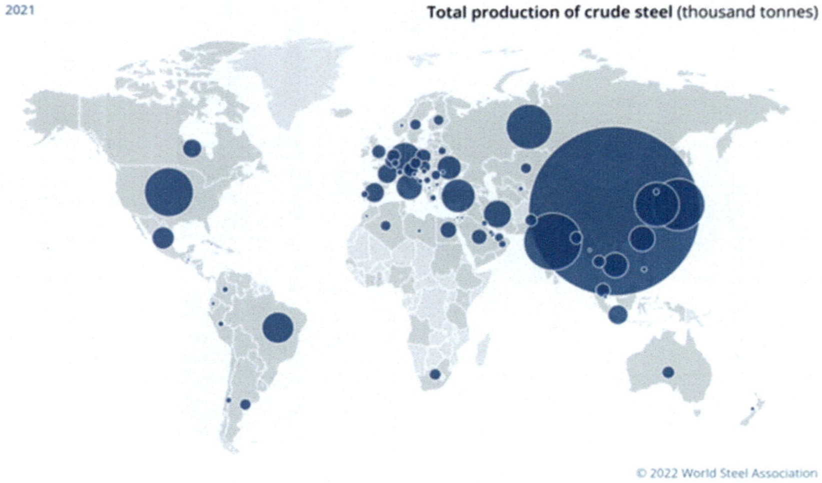


**Fig. 4.12** Top steel producing regions in 2021 (*Note* World Steel Organization, Steel Data Viewer)

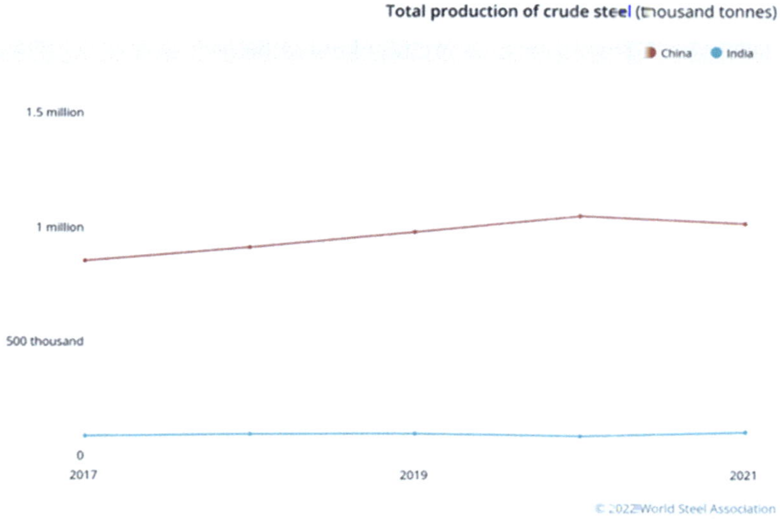


**Fig. 4.13** Top steel producing countries in 2021 (*Note* World Steel Organization, Steel Data Viewer)

earth elements—including dysprosium and terbium—taking place there (U.S. Department of Energy, 2020).

Europe, China, India, and the United States are major wind manufacturing hubs but each of the country imports certain materials and components. However, more than 50% of the world's wind turbine manufacturing or assembly plants are situated in China. Overall, the wind supply chain has both local as well as global characteristics.

## Challenges in Achieving a Clean Energy Transition

More than 100 countries are promising to cut emissions of methane by 30% by 2030. All of these countries are increasingly capitalizing on renewable energy sources to mitigate their climate induced vulnerabilities. Additionally, by early 2021, 160 countries had active targets for renewable power at the national level, as included in national laws, official strategies and plans (Hawila et al., 2022). All of this means that renewables need to grow at a fast rate. However, renewables adoption can face a myriad of challenges. A few major ones are highlighted below.

### *Climate Finance*

Achieving a rapid clean energy transition depends on the ability of the global community to direct global financial capital toward sustainable assets. The International Renewable Energy Agency (IRENA) has estimated that the deployment of energy transition-related technologies required to put the world on the 1.5 °C pathway will necessitate $131 trillion of aggregate investment between 2021 and 2050. This represents an average annual funding requirement for the energy sector of about $4.4 trillion between 2021 and 2050. When it comes to renewable power, which is identified as one of the major avenues for the energy transition, the required annual investment amounts to nearly $1 trillion for the 2021 to 2050 period, more than triple the renewable energy power investment of about $300 billion estimated for 2020 (Hawila et al., 2022).

Figure 4.14 shows the total investment by technology as per planned energy scenario, i.e., where current plans will lead to and IRENA's 1.5 °C scenario.

A rapid clean energy transition requires enhancing access to low-cost finance for clean energy projects. This requires large energy companies to channel their retained earnings from the balance sheets. Plus, there needs to be an open funding from a range of companies and external sources—notably banks and the enormous pools of capital in financial markets. There is also a need to make drastic cuts and/or a repurposing of current investments in fossil fuels over the coming years and decades to clean energy.

Public commitments have already been made by some for financing. At the United Nation's (UN) climate change conference 26, a total of 39 signatories, including several countries and multi-lateral development banks, signed a statement on aligning international public finance with the clean energy transition and committed to "ending direct public support for the international unabated fossil fuel energy sector by the end of 2022, except in limited and clearly defined circumstances that are consistent with a 1.5 °C warming limit and the goals of the Paris Agreement" (COP26, 2021).

Private financiers are also increasingly joining coalitions aiming to scale up capital required for the transition to a climate safe economy, as can

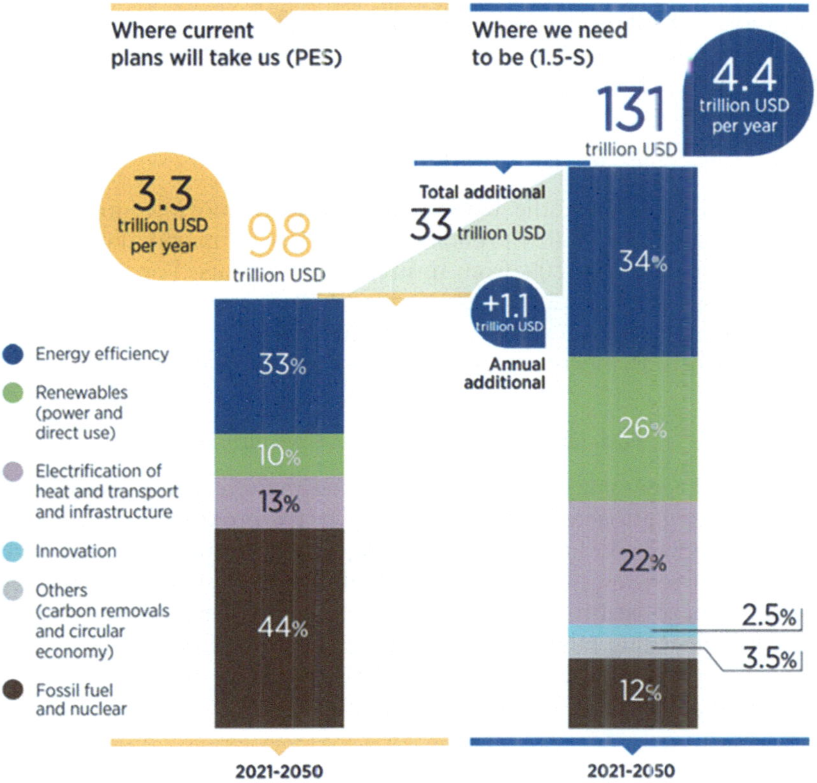


**Fig. 4.14** Total investment by technology in the Planned Energy Scenario (PES) and IRENA's 1.5 °C Scenario (2021–2050) (*Note* NDCs and renewable energy targets in 2021, Are we on the right path to climate-safe future? International Renewables Energy Agency)

be seen in the launch of the Glasgow Financial Alliance for Net Zero with a rapidly growing membership that includes over 450 firms from 45 countries (Hawila et al., 2022).

The global climate finance architecture, however, extends well beyond the Paris agreement entities and occurs through multilateral, bilateral, regional, and national climate change channels. Owing to its large and decentralized scope, climate finance flows are difficult to estimate and monitor. IRENA analysis indicates that while public financing to for the renewables energy in developing countries has grown in the recent past, it is still too little, not flowing sufficiently to the country's most in need (Hawila et al., 2022).

### *Re-directing Big Oil Investments*

For big oil companies, the biggest hinderance to moving into renewable energy is the so-called profitability gap. The oil majors traditionally expect returns of 15%-20% from upstream investments. For renewables, the return is on average 5% to 10%, at most 15% with clever financial engineering. Companies often reference lower returns as a barrier to investing more heavily in the increasingly competitive world of renewables.

### *Policies and Support by the Government*

In advanced economies, there are various challenges related to permitting and grid integration for the wind and solar PV projects. This leads to lower-than-planned capacity being awarded in government auctions. The stop-and-go policies, the lack of grid availability, and risks concerning off-takers' financial health are all hurting investor confidence and negatively impacting financing rates in case of emerging and developing economies. Lack of remuneration and targeted policy support for flexibility are also an issue in all countries (Abdelilah et al., 2021).

### *Renewables Power Generation Costs and Supply Chain Challenges*

The cost of developing renewable energy is becoming more and more competitive in the energy landscape. For the period from 2010 to 2020, there was a dramatic improvement in the cost competitiveness of solar and wind power technologies. As per IRENA, between 2010 and 2020, the cost of electricity for utility-scale solar PV fell by 85%, followed by concentrating solar power by 68%, onshore wind by 56%, and offshore wind by 48% (International Renewable Energy Agency, 2021). These all lead to increased adoption of renewable energy i.e., solar PV, onshore solar, and offshore solar across the globe.

However, since the beginning of 2020, the prices of key raw materials required in solar and wind supply chain have increased dramatically. There are multiple reasons for price hike including supply chain shortages driven by increase in demand, COVID-19-related logistics challenges and so on. The price of solar-grade polysilicon increased to RMB 249/kg ($39.3/kg) as on February 15, 2022, its highest since 2011 as per Jinko Solar, a major solar manufacturer. Further, the manufacturer stated that the price is up more than 400% since the start of June 2020 and there has been a 280% year-on-year growth (Bellini, 2022). The price of steel, a major component needed by wind suppliers, has also shot up by 50% since the beginning of 2020. Other raw material where prices have increased include copper by 60% and aluminum by 80% during the same period. On the top of that, the freight cost has been on an increasing trajectory since the first quarter of 2021 (European Commission, 2022). Strong demand for these renewables sources of energy and the effect of inflation is jointly creating a destructive mix on the industry. In sum, the rising prices are now leading to reversal of cost reduction trend that was observed during the last decade. If the commodity prices remain high in 2022, additional investments will be needed to deploy the same level of installed capacity as planned and could lead to delay in financing of projects already in pipeline. Some support to renewables is provided by high oil and natural gas prices (2022) which has improved the cost competitiveness of wind and solar PV.

A large dependence on China in case of both wind and solar raw materials/manufacturing capacity poses another threat in smooth energy transition. Local supply chains/smooth trade-flow is prerequisite for the transition to take place.

## Conclusion

The push to limit global warming has slowed down investments in upstream oil and gas, while wind and solar energy continue to exhibit high growth signs driven by policy support and improved cost competitiveness. The energy transition continues to encounter a number of obstacles, including the need for a robust renewables supply chain, a lack of grid availability, and insufficient funding for renewables projects, particularly in emerging and developing nations. While stakeholders from the oil and gas industry have revised their strategic priorities, set clear intentions and tangible goals to decarbonize, and expanded into the renewable energy sectors, the pace of adoption of renewables could be stifled by the challenges faced by the industry. In order to change the current course of global warming, we must work toward replacing the majority of the world's primary energy supply sourced from fossil fuels by renewable sources. The future of fossil fuels is heavily reliant on how quickly we can overcome the numerous hurdles confronting the renewables industry.

This chapter highlights the need for policies that explicitly support the clean energy transition. Governments and stakeholders cannot lose sight of the progress made in the renewable energy sector and must take steps to mitigate increasing costs in the supply chain and to support investments in renewable energy projects. This responsibility is shared not only by government officials, but major stakeholders such as banks and corporations. To achieve a successful sustainable energy transition, access to low-cost finance for clean energy projects, building new infrastructure, ensuring the development of policies and regulatory framework, development of a robust and resilient supply chain are crucial.

## General Annex

### *Abbreviations and Acronyms*

| | |
|---|---|
| GW | Gigawatts |
| E&P | Exploration and Production |
| EU | European Union |
| IEA | International Energy Agency |
| IPCC | Intergovernmental Panel on Climate Change |
| PV | Photovoltaic |
| UK | United Kingdom |
| US | United States |

## References

Abdelilah, Y., Baha, R H., Criswell, T., Bojek, P., Briens, F., Moorhouse, G., & Jiménez, G. R. (2021, December 1). *Renewables 2021: Analysis and forecast to 2026*. International Energy Agency, pp. 14, 22. https://iea.blob.core.windows.net/assets/5ae32253-7409-4f9a-a91d-1493ffb9777a/Renewables2021-Analysisandforecastto2026.pdf

Amelang, S. & Wehrmann, B. (2022, January 21), *German onshore wind power—Output, business and perspectives*. Clean Energy Wire. https://www.cleanenergywire.org/factsheets/german-onshore-wind-power-output-business-and-perspectives

Baranowski, R., Cooperman, A., Gilman, P., Office of Energy Efficiency and Renewable Energy, & Lantz, E. (2022, February 2022).

*Wind energy—Supply chain deep dive assessment*. U.S. Department of Energy. https://www.energy.gov/sites/default/files/2022-02/Wind%20Supply%20Chain%20Report%20-%20Final%202.25.22.pdf

Basore P., & Feldman D. (2022, February 2022). *Solar photovoltaics—Supply chain deep dive assessment*. U.S. Department of Energy. https://www.energy.gov/sites/default/files/2022-02/Solar%20Energy%20Supply%20Chain%20Report%20-%20Final.pdf

Bellini E. (2022, February 2022). Polysilicon price reaches $39.3/kg—The highest since 2011. *PV Magazine*. https://www.pv-magazine.com/2022/02/22/polysilicon-price-reaches-39-3-kg-the-highest-since-2011/#:~:text=%E2%80%9CThe%20latest%20announced%20price%20of,2020%2C and%20280%25%20YoY%20growth

Bouckaert S., Pales A. F., McGlade C., Remme U., Wanner B., Varro L., Abergel T., Arsalane Y., Bains P., Menendez J. M. B., Connelly E., Crow D., Dasgupta A., Delmastro C., Goodson T., Gouy A., Hugues P., Lee L... Wetzel D. (2021). *Net zero by 2050—A roadmap for global energy sector*, *International Energy Agency*, p. 21. https://iea.blob.core.windows.net/assets/deebef5d-0c34-4539-9d0c-10b13d840027/NetZeroby2050-ARoadmapfortheGlobalEnergySector_CORR.pdf, https://www.iea.org/reports/net-zero-by-2050

Bowers, R., (2021, January 28). *U.S. wind energy production tax credit extended through 2021*. U.S. Energy Information Administration. https://www.eia.gov/todayinenergy/detail.php?id=46576

BP. (2022, February 8). *BP update on strategic progress*. https://www.bp.com/en/global/corporate/news-and-insights/press-releases/bp-update-on-strategic-progress.html

British Broadcasting Corporation. (2021, November 2). *COP26: India PM Narendra Modi pledges net zero by 2070*. https://www.bbc.com/news/world-asia-india-59125143

Bundesverband Wind Energie, (2018, January 25). *Ausbauzahlen für das Gesamtjahr 2017 in Deutschland Windenergie an Land: Starker Zubaupfad im Übergangsjahr, EEG reparieren und Klimaschutz stärken*. https://www.wind-energie.de/presse/pressemitteilungen/detail/ausbauzahlen-fuer-das-gesamtjahr-2017-in-deutschland-windenergie-an-land-starker-zubaupfad-im-uebergа/

Chevron. (2021, September 14). *Chevron accelerates lower carbon ambitions*. https://www.chevron.com/stories/chevron-accelerates-lower-carbon-ambitions

COP26. (2021, December 4). *Statement on international public support for the clean energy transition. UN Climate Change Conference (COP26) at the SEC—Glasgow 2021*. https://ukcop26.org/statement-on-international-public-support-for-the-clean-energy-transition/

Eni. (2021, July 12). *Red rock power and Eni partner up for Scotwind*. https://www.eni.com/en-IT/media/press-release/2021/07/red-rock-power-eni-partner-scotwind.html

Eni. (2022). *Renewables at the centre of our strategy*. https://www.eni.com/en-IT/operations/energy-evolution/renewable-energy.html

European Commission. (2021, July 14). *European green deal: Commission proposes transformation of EU economy and society to meet climate ambitions*. https://ec.europa.eu/commission/presscorner/detail/en/IP_21_3541

European Commission. (2022, March 9). *What is the impact of increasing commodity and energy prices on solar PV, wind and biofuels?* https://clean-energy-islands.ec.europa.eu/news/what-impact-increasing-commodity-and-energy-prices-solar-pv-wind-and-biofuels

Fløtre, A. (2021, November 1). *Offshore wind spending is closing the gap against O&G, will exceed it in more regions by 2030*. Rystad Energy. https://www.rystadenergy.com/newsevents/news/press-releases/offshore-wind-spending-is-closing-the-gap-against-OG-will-exceed-it-in-more-regions-by-2030/

Frost, R. (2022, January 14). *The end of fossil fuels: Which countries have banned exploration and extraction?* Euronews. https://www.euronews.com/green/2021/08/12/the-end-of-fossil-fuels-which-countries-have-banned-exploration-and-extraction

Green Dealflow. (2021, January 21). *Germany and the new Renewable Energy Act 2021*. https://greendealflow.com/germany-new-renewable-energy-act-2021

Hawila, D., Rana, F., Strinat, C., & Lozo S. (2022, January). *NDCs and renewable energy targets in 2021, Are we on the right path to climate-safe future?* International Renewables Energy Agency. https://www.irena.org/-/media/Files/IRENA/Agency/Publication/2022/Jan/IRENA_NDCs_RE_Targets_2022.pdf

Iberdrola. (2021, July 16). *Iberdrola and Shell work together to bid on the first floating offshore wind projects in the United Kingdom*. https://www.iberdrola.com/press-room/news/detail/iberdrola-shell-together-bid-first-floating-offshore-wind-projects-united-kingdom

*Internal Revenue Bulletin: 2021–29*. (2021, July 19). Internal Revenue Service. https://www.irs.gov/irb/2021-29_IRB#NOT-2021-41

International Renewable Energy Agency. (2021, June). *Renewables Power Generation Costs in 2020*, p. 3. https://www.irena.org/-/media/Files/IRENA/Agency/Publication/2021/Jun/IRENA_Power_Generation_Costs_2020.pdf

Manohar, A. (2022, March). *India has the largest renewable energy expansion plan globally*. Invest India. https://www.investindia.gov.in/sector/renewable-energy

McGlade, C., Waldron, M. & Gould T. (2020, January). *The oil and gas industry in energy transitions*. International Energy Agency,

p. 7. https://iea.blob.core.windows.net/assets/4315f4ed-5cb2-4264-b0ee-2054fd34c118/The_Oil_and_Gas_Industry_in_Energy_Transitions.pdf

Nguyen, C. (2022, January 10). *How can investors seize Vietnam's wind power potential*. Vietnam Briefing. https://www.vietnam-briefing.com/news/how-can-investors-seize-vietnams-wind-power-potential.html/#:~:text=Vietnam%20has%20the%20most%20ambitious,MW)%20by%202030%2C%20respectively

Pörtner, H., Roberts. D. C., Adams, H., Adelekan, I., Adler, C., Adrian, R., Aldunce, P., Ali, E., Begum, R. A., Friedl, B. B., Kerr, R. B., Biesbroek, R., Birkmann, J., Bowen, K., Caretta, M. A., Carnicer, J., Castellanos, E., Cheong, T. S., Chow, W... & Thomas, A., (2022, February 28). *Intergovernmental panel on climate change—Sixth assessment report on climate change*, pp. 9–11. https://www.ipcc.ch/report/ar6/wg2/downloads/report/IPCC_AR6_WGII_FinalDraft_TechnicalSummary.pdf

Shell. (2021, April 15). *Shell presents energy transition strategy publication to shareholders for advisory vote*. https://www.shell.com/media/news-and-media-releases/2021/shell-presents-energy-transition-strategy-publication-to-shareholders-for-advisory-vote.html

Shell. (2021, December 14). *Shell acquires solar and energy storage developer Savion, further expanding its global renewable power business*. https://www.shell.com/media/news-and-media-releases/2021/shell-acquires-savion.html

Taylor, M. (2020, April). *Energy subsidies: Evolution in the global energy transformation to 2050*. International Renewable Energy Agency, p. 31. https://www.irena.org/-/media/Files/IRENA/Agency/Publication/2020/Apr/IRENA_Energy_subsidies_2020.pdf

Tachev, V. (2021, October 14). *Wind energy in South Korea—Opportunities and challenges*. Energy Tracker Asia. https://energytracker.asia/wind-energy-in-south-korea-opportunities-and-challenges/#:~:text=As%20a%20part%20of%20its,MW%20the%20country%20has%20today

The White House. (2021, March 29). *Fact Sheet: Biden administration jump-starts Offshore Wind Energy Projects to Create Jobs*. https://www.whitehouse.gov/briefing-room/statements-releases/2021/03/29/fact-sheet-biden-administration-jumpstarts-offshore-wind-energy-projects-to-create-jobs/

The Japan Times. (2020, December 16). *Japan aims to be world's No. 3 offshore wind power producer in 2040*. https://www.japantimes.co.jp/news/2020/12/16/business/japan-offshore-wind-power

TotalEnergies. (2022, February 15). *Solar and wind: Our ambition in renewable energies*. https://totalenergies.com/energy-expertise/exploration-production/renewable-energies/solar-energy-and-wind-energy

TotalEnergies. (2022, March 24). Sustainability & climate 2022 progress report. https://totalenergies.com/system/files?file=documents/2022-03/Sustainability_Climate_2022_Progress_Report_EN.pdf

U.S. Department of Energy. (April, 2020). Critical materials rare earths supply chain: A Situational white paper. *Office of energy efficiency & Renewables energy*. https://www.energy.gov/sites/prod/files/2020/04/f73/Critical%20Materials%20Supply%20Chain%20White%20Paper%20April%202020.pdf

Vishnoi, A. (2021, December 14). 2030 renewable energy target: Panel to be set up soon for 'Mission 500GW'. *The Economics Times*. https://economictimes.indiatimes.com/industry/renewables/2030-renewable-energy-target-panel-to-be-set-up-soon-for-mission-500gw/articleshow/88267104.cms

World Bank Group. (2021, June). *Offshore wind roadmap for Vietnam*, p. xvii. https://documents1.worldbank.org/curated/en/261981623120856300/pdf/Offshore-Wind-Development-Program-Offshore-Wind-Roadmap-for-Vietnam.pdf

World Steel Organization. (2022). *Crude steel production: Street data viewer*. https://worldsteel.org/steel-by-topic/statistics/annual-production-steel-data/P1_crude_steel_total_pub/CHN/IND

Woods, W. D. (2021, November 9). *Why we're investing $15 billion in a lower-carbon future*. ExxonMobil. https://corporate.exxonmobil.com/News/Newsroom/News-releases/2021/1109_Why-we-are-investing-15-billion-in-a-lower-carbon-future

CHAPTER 5

# The Next Wave of Natural Gas in Brazil

*José Roberto Ferreira Savoia, André Castro Carvalho, Juliano Ribeiro de Almeida, and Luiz Eduardo Ganem Rubião*

## Introduction

Brazil is currently seeing a third wave in the demand for natural gas production and distribution in the country. The first came in the 1980s, when offshore production was popularized, the second came in 2010, when Brazil negotiated production rights with Bolivia and secured the expansion of its Natural Gas (NG) sector by connecting Bolivia to Porto

J. R. Ferreira Savoia (✉) · A. C. Carvalho · J. R. de Almeida · L. E. G. Rubião
Fundação Instituto de Administração, University of Sao Paulo, Sao Paulo, Brazil
e-mail: jrsavoia@usp.br

A. C. Carvalho
e-mail: andcastrocar1@gmail.com

J. R. de Almeida
e-mail: julianoalmeida@usp.br

L. E. G. Rubião
e-mail: luiz.rubiao@biosafelab.com.br



T. Walker et al. (eds.), *Sustainability in the Oil and Gas Sector*,
https://doi.org/10.1007/978-3-031-51586-6_5

Alegre, introducing the industry to five Brazilian states. In addition, in the State of São Paulo, there is significant potential for producing renewable natural gas from the tailings of sugar and alcohol plants, landfills, effluent treatment stations, and farms that adopt intensive farming models. This volume of gas can strategically guarantee energy security. In contrast, the transition of the energy matrix accelerates in response to the water crisis and boosts the supply of energy generated by wind and solar power plants. Production vouchers for solar and wind sources can be supported by natural gas, which can be the primary source for generating units directly connected to production in reservoir-to-wire generation system. It can also be transported and distributed through gas pipelines or cryogenic trucks as liquefied natural gas (LNG) to consumption points.

The Brazilian Constitution enshrines the distribution of gas via pipelines to three concessionaires that serve the State of São Paulo and are regulated and inspected by the Agência Reguladora de Serviços Públicos do Estado de São Paulo (ARSESP). In 2021, the agency held a public hearing to discuss the early renewal of the concession of the primary gas distribution concessionaire in the state, Companhia de Gas de São Paulo—COMGÁS. This process allowed for a broad discussion of the intricacies of natural gas distribution which we summarize and discuss in this chapter. This chapter explores the third wave of natural gas consumption in Brazil. It begins by conceptualizing the sustainability of the industry and exploring the potential for the expansion of the production of natural gas in the country. It then looks at the increased demand for natural gas and the means of supply that characterize this third wave. The following section details the current management of the natural gas industry with the example of the Companhia de Gas de São Paulo (COMGÁS), the primary gas distribution concessionaire in the state. The chapter concludes with policy suggestions for the federalization of the natural gas industry in Brazil.

## The Path to Sustainability

*The fossil fuel economy has reached its limits. We want to leave a healthy planet for the next generation and good jobs and growth that does not harm our* nature. **Ursula von der Leyen. "European Green Deal: Commission proposes transformation of economy and society to meet climate ambitions." (2021)**

The most recent evaluation of the International Energy Agency (IEA), conducted in 2020, reports that the global energy demand dropped by 5% in 2020, while $CO_2$ emissions related to energy decreased by 7%, and energy investments fell by 18%. The impacts of these events vary according to the fuel source. For natural gas, the demand fell by 3%. This relative resilience can be partially explained by the fuel exchange in the generation of electricity (IEA, 2021). The most significant change occurred in the United States, where the demand for gas for electricity generation increased by approximately 2%, despite the decline in the overall electricity demand. The level of energy consumption rose significantly in India, China, and other emerging economies throughout 2021 as a result of the global economic recovery. Despite concerns raised by the ongoing Russia-Ukraine conflict, the "global electricity demand is expected to grow at a much faster pace of 3% per year over the 2023–2025 period compared with the 2022 growth rate" (IEA, 2023).

Governments and organizations worldwide have announced preventative strategies to achieve zero net emissions (an energy transition) in three to four decades. The European Commission has taken the global lead in climate change, revealing an ambitious plan to reduce the European Union's (EU) carbon emissions by 55% from 1990 to 2030 and achieve carbon neutrality by 2050. Its European Ecological Pact will have 600 million investments from the Recovery Plan of the Next Generation EU and the EU budget for the next seven years. In addition, the EU foresees a total review of the bloc's economy, including the elimination of the sale of new cars with combustion engines by 2035 and the introduction of import taxes to penalize products from countries less committed to the low-carbon strategy (Patric, 2021). In response, US President Joe Biden announced the United States' commitment to adhere to the Paris Accords and the country's transition to zero emissions by 2050. Democratic congressmen recently announced a proposal for "carbon taxation" measures on imported goods from countries that do not respect sustainability protocols. Further, according to the Ministry of Economy, Trade, and Industry in Japan, the country's energy transition strategy aims to double the share of renewable energy to 36%-38% of the matrix by 2030, compared to the less than 20% observed today (Segal, 2021). As a result, the share of fossil fuels should drop from more than 75% to approximately 40% in the matrix. Furthermore, in April 2021, at the Climate Leaders' summit held in the United States, Japanese Prime Minister Yoshihide Suga presented a new intermediate climate goal for the country, aiming at a 46% reduction in greenhouse gas emissions by 2030 and the achievement of carbon neutrality by 2050. China also launched another critical initiative by announcing its 14$^{th}$ Five-Year Strategic Plan (IEDI, 2021). It recognized natural gas as a clean fuel and reaffirmed its importance for optimizing the country's energy structure. Among the measures listed in the Plan to reinforce "energy security," the following are cited:

1. The exploitation of natural gas on the high seas;
2. The expansion of the capacity of the gas distribution network;
3. The search for interconnectivity;
4. Supply diversification; and
5. An increased production capacity of gas turbines and large liquefied natural gas (LNG) transport vessels, aiming to ensure the country's self-sufficiency in energy supply.

These examples demonstrate that although fossil fuels still play an essential role among energy sources, a significant change in the energy matrix is projected for the future. There are numerous examples in which the energy industry has already initiated the transition to (a) low-carbon fossil fuels, (b) large-scale use of renewable energy, and (c) more intelligent energy systems with greater technological content. In this process of structural transformation, energy sources are changing from solid (firewood and coal) and liquid (petroleum) to natural gas (Caineng et al., 2018), which will be the dominant fossil fuel after 2030 (Caineng et al., 2018; IEA, 2020).

Over the last few years, the percentage of use of natural gas in the global energy matrix has grown to approximately 25%. The expansion of the shale gas supply in the United States, the expansion of LNG exports in various parts of the world, and the increase in production in Asia contributed to this increase. Natural gas also has advantages over other fossil energy sources. The first derives from its energy capacity: the calorific value of natural gas is much higher than that of mineral coal and close to that of oil. The second is that natural gas produces cleaner burning when it occurs under appropriate conditions, resulting in neutrality regarding the emission of pollutants such as sulfur oxides, solid particles, and other toxic derivatives. This aspect of natural gas makes its use more efficient and allows an improvement in air quality. Table 5.1 shows that natural gas emits approximately 27% less $CO_2$ than oil and

**Table 5.1** Comparison of natural gas—$CO_2$ emissions

| *NG compared to:* | *Reduction in $CO_2$ emission (%)* |
|---|---|
| Coal | 44 |
| Oil | 27 |
| Fuel oil | 33 |
| Gasoline | 26 |
| *Diesel* oil | 27 |
| GLP | 17 |

*Source* Teixeira et al. (2021)

44% less than coal. It is important to note that natural gas contributes to the reduction of $CO_2$ and the drastic, almost integral, reduction of other toxic pollutants and particles harmful to health present in burning these fuels.

Natural gas also presents itself as the more sustainable option in terms of risk management. The IEA (2020) states that reducing methane leakage is the most crucial factor, in terms of cost-effectiveness, to reduce emissions from the oil and gas industry and to maintain the relevance of natural gas while transiting toward reducing a zero-carbon economy. Another potential for the future growth of natural gas stems from developing new technologies for transforming methane into hydrogen. This more revolutionary approach allows multiple uses for gas (DNV GL, 2020). Gains in both the economy and the environment may be achieved using natural gas in the short and medium term. However, this is not always the case, particularly with regard to expensive alternative energy sources. Therefore, industrialized countries have chosen to lead the transition toward a low-carbon economy, since renewable energies have yet to reach sufficient maturity to meet all the countries' needs.

## Brazil: Potential for Expanding the Use of Natural Gas and Biogas

In Brazil, natural gas and biogas represent 18% of the total energy matrix. The country is the fourth-largest global producer, generating a significant amount of renewable energy. However, the country's largest source of carbon emissions, responsible for more than 40% of emissions, is forest management, where fires substantially increase the amount of $CO_2$ in the atmosphere.

Similar to other developed countries, Brazil is increasingly implementing renewable energies in combination with energy generated from gas in order to reduce its dependence on fossil fuels which emit carbon more intensively (such as coal and petroleum derivatives). As a result, we anticipate that the New Gas Law's provisions will cause the generation of coal and oil to decline by almost 70% by 2029. The recent discoveries of large natural gas reserves in the pre-salt production fields, which totaled 2.55 billion barrels of oil equivalent (BOE), will also contribute to this projected decarbonization. Thus, by 2030, the consumer market will have approximately 140 million $m^3$/d of natural gas available, doubling the current supply (ANP, 2020) and reaching 14% of the Brazilian energy matrix (Compass, 2021a).

Petrobras is the leading producer and distributor of natural gas in the country, operating at all stages of the production and distribution process. The company is responsible for the natural gas production pipeline flow in the Campos and Santos Basins (Routes 1, 2, and in the future 3). In addition, it controls three LNG import terminals in Brazil, with a capacity of 41 million $m^3$/day. This monopoly situation led to the establishment of changes in the scope of its action by the New Gas Law. The sector will increase its efficiency by aiming to increase competition through selling assets and transport activities.

The Companhia de Gas de São Paulo (COMGÁS), a primary natural gas distributor in the region, actively participates in gas distribution by expanding the pipeline network and interconnecting its regions. The arrival of gas from the pre-salt can increase efficiency, leverage operations, and deliver energy at a competitive cost for the resumption of industrialization in the country. At the same time, the dependence on other sources of fuel and energy will be mitigated, jobs will be generated, and tax collection in the commercialization of fuels will be introduced in the State of São Paulo (Fig. 5.1).

According to Teixeira et al. (2021):

> in Brazil, on the one hand, there is an enormous untapped potential for natural gas on the country's coast, especially in the pre-salt layer. On the other hand, there is great potential for biogas in the interior, which can be produced from agricultural and forest waste. Therefore, why not start developing a network of gas pipelines from the coast toward the interior to enable not only the production of biogas in rural areas but also its distribution in small and medium-sized cities, even though it is necessary to

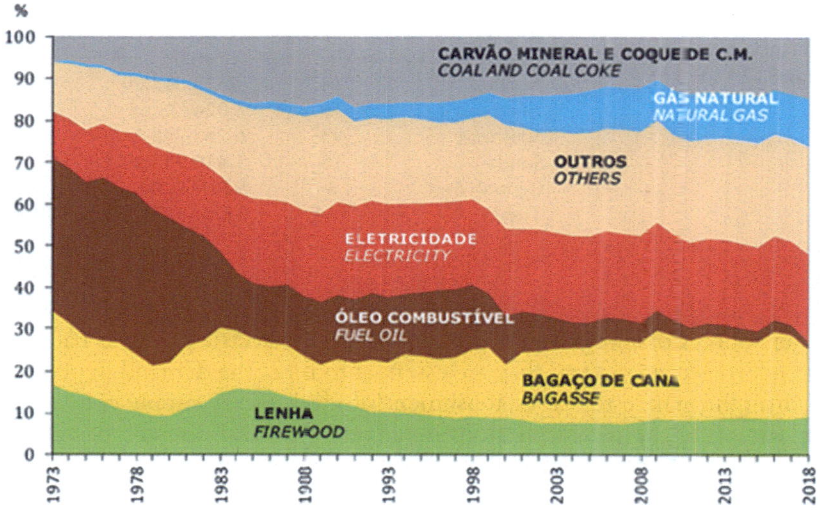


**Fig. 5.1** Brazilian energy matrix–1973 to 2018 (in %) (*Source* Metronlab [2021])

rely on virtual pipelines to make the bridge between the consumer market and the pulverized production of biogas? Countries with dense gas pipeline networks will be able to better plan and ensure gas supply. They may even consider distributing hydrogen production from gas or have the possibility, in the future, of having the natural gas infrastructure to transport and distribute hydrogen.

The growing importance of natural gas in energy markets worldwide amplifies the need for adequate infrastructure and planning for its distribution to use the input proactively and provide energy security (Feijoo et al., 2019). In other words, natural gas is an element of transition and energy security.

### *The Generation of Electricity from the Supply of Natural Gas to Thermoelectric Plants*

Thermoelectric plants have become a guaranteed element to stabilize the Brazilian electrical system. Therefore, their crucial role in the Brazilian electricity generation matrix cannot be ignored. Due to the seasonality of

**Table 5.2** Natural gas thermoelectric plants in Brazil (2020)

| *Region* | *No. of Plants* | *Power (kW)* | *%kW* |
|---|---|---|---|
| North | 14 | 1.528.843,00 | 9,8 |
| Northeast | 35 | 5.026728,65 | 32,1 |
| Southeast | 95 | 6.768.998,54 | 43,2 |
| South | 15 | 1.410.953,20 | 9,0 |
| Central-West | 5 | 920.974,00 | 5,9 |
| **Total** | **164** | **15.656.497,39** | **100,00** |

*Source* ANEEL (2020)

other sources of energy and the ability of thermoelectric plants to back up the hydroelectric system, they are essential to meet the demand in periods of drought, where the re-establishment of ideal energy supply conditions can extend for up to several months per year. Thermal dispatch to natural gas reduces the dependence on rainfall occurrence, attenuating the effects of seasonality and ensuring less dependence on reservoirs.

Once this process is established, natural gas producers can anchor their investments in critical players such as thermal power plants. Concurrently, investors in this segment can count on the diversification of energy sources and cost-effective alternatives.

In addition, with the potential to significantly reduce emissions and toxic pollutants, it is clear that there is an opportunity to replace existing oil and coal thermoelectric generation parks with natural gas plants. Furthermore, future expansions will involve the use of natural gas; therefore, thermal generation is favored by the Brazilian system instead of options for oil or coal thermal power plants. Natural gas has been the primary fuel used in the generation of energy in the country's thermoelectric plants due to its advantages and energy power, responsible for approximately 35.2% of the generation capacity (Leal et al., 2021). In 2020, 164 thermoelectric plants in Brazil used natural gas as fuel, with a power of 15,656 MW (Table 5.2).

### *Cleaner Transport*

Gas can also provide savings and environmental advantages when used in transportation by replacing gasoline or diesel oil. For instance, in Brazil, mainly due to differences in pricing policies and taxes between fuels, natural gas showed a significant increase in consumption for automotive purposes.

Within the scope of its Annual Program for Research and Technological Development and Conservation and Rationalization of the Use of Natural Gas in the State of São Paulo, 2016/2017, COMGÁS contracted the Health and Sustainability Institute to conduct a study to assess the impacts on public health and its economic valuation due to the diffusion of compressed natural gas (CNG) in collective public transport and light vehicles in six metropolitan regions. The report concluded that the substitution of diesel for CNG in public transport plays an essential role in air quality and public health, and it should be considered a target of public policies because:

1. The bus fleet is responsible for approximately 25% of the emissions of particulate matter (PM2.5); that is, it accounts for a quarter of the emissions that result in mortality and public hospitalizations;
2. The replacement of 50% of the diesel fleet for CNG in passenger transport would reduce the mortality caused by pollution by PM2.5 by 41% in large centers;
3. The estimated economic cost avoided with the reduction of early deaths and, consequently, the increase in production in these two metropolitan regions would reach R$4.5 billion in the period in question.

Table 5.3 summarizes a feasible strategy to improve the Brazilian energy matrix considering operational measures in all sectors for the next ten years.

## The New Gas Market and the Increase in Demand and Supply

### *Brazil's New Gas Market*

The creation of the New Natural Gas Market in Brazil opened the possibility of concomitant development of suppliers and consumers of natural gas. From the suppliers' side, gas distributors in São Paulo, for example, now seek diversification, a decrease in the dependence on gas from Bolivia, and an increase in the share of gas produced in the Santos Basin.

**Table 5.3** A strategic approach to reaching higher sustainability in the energy sector

| *1—Industry* | *Replace more polluting sources such as fuel oil at a feasible operational cost* |
|---|---|
| 2—Electrical Sector: | Replace more polluting sources such as coal, diesel, and fuel oil and favor using renewable energy sources. The thermoelectric plants became an indispensable element of excellent stability for the Brazilian electrical system. Therefore, its key role in the Brazilian electricity generation matrix cannot be dispensed. Replacing the oil and coal-fired thermoelectric generation parks with natural gas, as well as having the essential use of natural gas in future thermal generation expansions, will help in avoiding blackouts and supply failures |
| 3—Transportation | Natural gas can replace diesel in public transportation and improve air quality in cities and cargo transportation. It also increases metropolises' quality of life |
| 4—Infrastructure and Intercommunication Sharing | The pipelines built by the natural gas segment can be advantageous for biogas production projects, enabling its production and commercialization in the field and small and medium-sized cities |
| 5—Expansion of Investments: | Stricter environmental, social, and governance sustainability requirements have been embraced by investors, creditors, risk agencies, and governments to support companies. As a result, at the beginning of 2020, global sustainable investment in the five leading financial markets reached US$ 35.3 trillion, an increase of 15% from 2018 to 2020. In addition, industrialized countries have also been increasing their use of natural gas for decades. These all serve as the link in the shift to a low-carbon economy |

(continued)

**Table 5.3** (continued)

| | |
|---|---|
| *1—Industry* | *Replace more polluting sources such as fuel oil at a feasible operational cost* |
| 6—Evolution of the Energy Matrix: | In many countries, the use of natural gas is already at maturity. In Brazil, however, there are several opportunities to expand supply, thanks to the potential of the pre-salt layer, such as its consumption by families, industries, and trade |
| 7—Economic, Social, and Environmental Results: | Natural gas provides short- and medium-term possible results. Other alternative sources demand high-cost technological changes. Extracting and using gas represents income, employment and tax collection, environmental quality, and energy security for the country |

They also wish to expand the distribution network and significantly increase the number of customers to increase demand and stimulate gas producers in the Santos Basin to direct more offshore gas to the consumer market. Figure 5.2 shows that a considerable portion of the gas produced today still needs to be made available for the Santos Basin market. The availability to the market in December 2021 was only 32% of the total produced. As a result, a higher percentage was destined for reinjection in the fields, and a non-negligible portion (approximately 2% of the total produced) was burned on the platforms.

According to a 2020 study on the use of pre-salt natural gas (Oliveira da Silva et al., 2020), an operator can send offshore natural gas to one of several locations. The gas can be:

1. Compressed and reinjected, to allow advanced oil recovery;
2. Compressed, flowed to the continent, and processed on land;
3. Processed and compressed still in the open sea (Floating Compressed Natural Gas—FCNG);
4. Processed and liquefacted still in the open sea (floating liquefied natural gas—FLNG); or
5. Converted into liquid products (LPG, naphtha, diesel, and kerosene) still in the open sea (floating gas to liquid—FGTL).

| Basin | Internal Consumption | Gas Flare | Available | Injection | Production |
|---|---|---|---|---|---|
| Santos | 7.299 | 1.881 | 29.856 | 53.741 | 92.778 |
| Campos | 5.442 | 1.065 | 8.599 | 22 | 15.127 |
| Solimões | 445 | 197 | 6.623 | 6.546 | 13.811 |
| Parnaíba | 23 | 7 | 3.403 | 0 | 3.432 |
| Camamu | 58 | 3 | 2.442 | 0 | 2.504 |
| Recôncavo | 98 | 59 | 1.612 | 387 | 2.156 |
| Espírito Santo | 288 | 33 | 593 | 0 | 914 |
| Potiguar | 63 | 46 | 667 | 0 | 776 |
| Alagoas | 2 | 16 | 480 | 0 | 497 |
| Amazonas | 1 | 6 | 99 | 0 | 107 |
| Tucano Sul | 4 | 0 | 90 | 0 | 94 |
| Sergipe | 24 | 17 | 0 | 2 | 43 |
| Barreirinhas | 0 | 0 | 0 | 0 | 0 |
| Total Geral | 13.747 | 3.329 | 54.465 | 60.698 | 132.239 |

**Fig. 5.2** Distribution of natural gas movement by production basin (in Mm3/d) (*Source* ANP [2021])

In addition to these options, the use of gas to produce electric energy on the high seas with transmission to the continent is currently being evaluated. This option will be implemented through a floating power generation plant (FPGP). It would be an offshore version of the RTW (Reservoir to Wire) strategy in onshore gas fields directly connected to TPPs (Thermoelectric Plants).

The main factors identified in the study above as barriers to increasing the commercial use of pre-salt gas are associated with the investment in natural gas flow and processing infrastructure and the development of a healthy relationship between the supply and consumption of natural gas. Consequently, it becomes simpler for FPSO operators to enable other offshore gas monetization alternatives with these two elements. Thus, the New Natural Gas Market will cause an increase in the demand and supply of natural gas **consistently** to stimulate both consumers and gas producers, making it feasible to justify the necessary investments in infrastructure.

### *Consequences of an Increased Supply and Demand of Natural Gas*

Industrial energy consumption is mainly aimed at the generation of thermal and mechanical energy (28.8 MM $m^3$/day in 2018) and the self-production of electricity (1.5 MM $m^3$/day). The consumption of natural gas (essential methane) as a raw material in 2018 was only 1.8 MM $m^3$/day. The largest total natural gas consumers are the chemical, ceramic, pig iron, steel, paper, and cellulose industries. These industries consumed approximately 66% of the total verified in 2018.

Due to their high levels of consumption, the industrial and thermal generating sectors are essential for supporting the consistent growth of desired demand. In Brazil, the industrial sector is the primary consumer of natural gas, with high and continuous daily consumption levels. According to data from the National Energy Balance (EPE, 2018), in the base year of 2018, the industry was responsible for 35% of the annual demand for natural gas from 2006 to 2018. In Brazil, natural gas is used in industrial settings as an energy input and raw material, mainly for producing nitrogen fertilizers (urea, ammonium sulfate, and ammonium nitrate).

Nitrogen fertilizers are produced from ammonia, which can be produced by the Haber–Bosch process, which involves the reaction between the $N_2$ of atmospheric air and the $H_2$ obtained from the steam reforming of methane from natural gas. Today, Brazil has an insufficient production of these fertilizers and is therefore strongly dependent on imports. The strategic issue of greater independence concerning imports was highlighted by the sanctions resulting from the war in Ukraine. The expectation is that, at least in the medium term, Brazil will resume maximum production in all existing units in the country, complete the works of units not yet finished, and make investments in new units that will further increase the demand for natural gas.

Another industry that can benefit greatly from increased natural gas usage is the thermoelectric industry, particularly if it adopts a more prominent role, rather than as a backup plan in case of the depletion of hydroelectric reservoirs. Instead, continuously operating thermoelectric plants would be ideal for enabling this consumption increase, especially if installed in regions not yet served by a transport and distribution network but with good potential for gas consumption. The concept would be to fund the initial investment with the demand for a thermoelectric plant, for which a transport network with some capacity slack would be installed.

The capacity slack could then be used to service additional industrial, commercial, residential, and automotive clients. In principle, the theory is that large-volume industrial consumers of methane (either for energy production or as raw material in chemical processes) and permanent thermoelectric plants can, through the signing of contracts in the free market of natural gas, contribute significantly to the growth in demand and encourage the increase in supply of natural gas. The projected growth in the industrial natural gas demand has led to several projections from Brazil's leading natural gas producers and suppliers, and we discuss these below.

### *The Expansion of Natural Gas Infrastructures in Brazil*

Figure 5.3 shows the natural gas distribution profile of COMGÁS, the largest distributor in São Paulo (Brazil), by type of customer/application over 19 years. Figure 5.4 shows the relative evolution of the number of customers per type of application in the same period.

With consistent growth in the gas consumer base and volume consumed, greater availability of offshore gas in the market is needed.

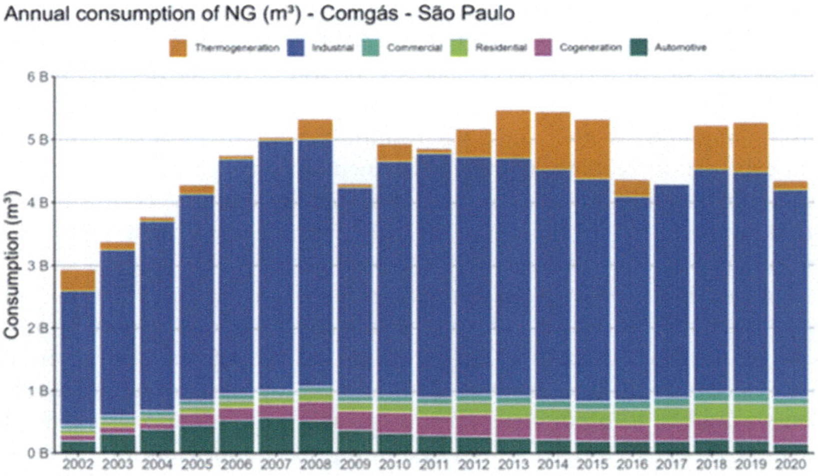


**Fig. 5.3** Natural gas distribution profile of COMGÁS, by type of customer/application over 19 years

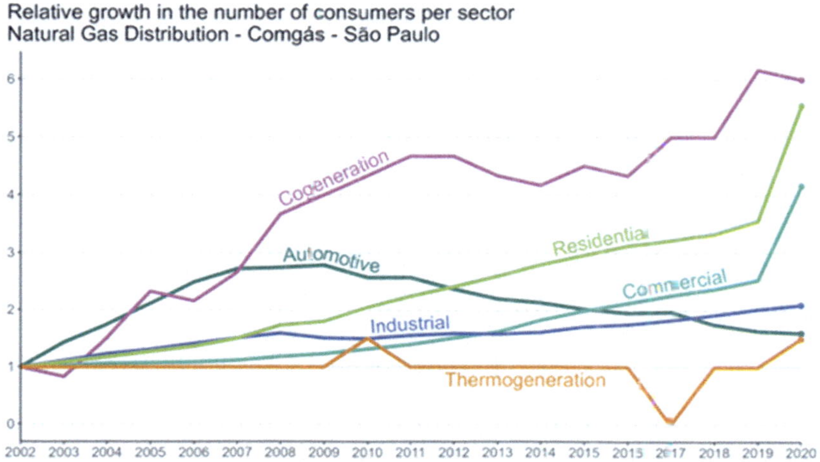


**Fig. 5.4** Evolution of the relative number of natural gas customers of COMGÁS by type of customer/application over 19 years

Therefore, in its strategic planning from 2022 to 2026, Petrobras presents several relevant goals to enable the use of gas from the Santos Basin.

Table 5.4 demonstrates the predicted evolution and goals defined by Petrobras for the volumes of natural gas that can be processed in treatment units in 2026 (an increase of 27%, evolving from 66 to 84 MMm$^3$/d). It also sets targets for regasification capacity in 2026 (an increase of 35%, evolving from 37 to 50 MMm3/d).

Additionally, Petrobras reports that it is moving on with its SEAP Project—Sergipe Waters Deep and the Route 3 Gas Pipelines project, which aim to expand the flow of natural gas from the projects now

**Table 5.4** Capacity of offshore natural gas treatment and liquefied natural gas regasification units in 2021 and 2026

| | *2021* | *2026* |
|---|---|---|
| NG Treatment Units | 66 MM m$^3$/d | 84 MM m$^3$/d |
| Regasification Terminals | 37 MM m$^3$/d | 50 MM m$^3$/d |

*Source* Petrobras (2021)

operating in the pre-salt area of Santos. The Route 3 gas pipeline is approximately 355 km, with a 307 km maritime stretch and a 48 km onshore stretch. The natural gases will flow from the Pre-Salt Pole of the Santos Basin to the Rio de Janeiro State Petrochemical Complex (Comperj) in Itaboraí, where the Natural Gas Processing Unit (UPGN Route 3) is located. The project has completed over 90% of the physical aspects and is scheduled to start operating in 2022. As a result, its capacity was expanded to 21 MM $m^3/d$.

Implementing a new gas flow system for the SEAP project (located in the Sergipe-Alagoas Basin, 100 km from the coast, at depths of up to 3,000 meters) provides a capacity of 18 MM $m^3/d$, but it is still in progress. The planning phase and the beginning of the operation are scheduled for after 2026. With investments planned in the Strategic Planning for 2022–2026, Petrobras will be able to significantly change the volumes of natural gas currently placed in the national market from *onshore* and *offshore* fields operated by Petrobras itself or by other companies (Fig. 5.5).

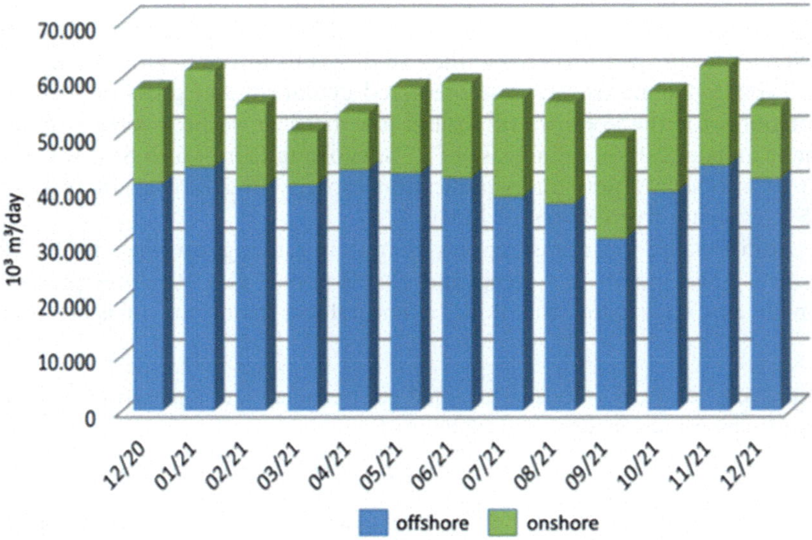


**Fig. 5.5** National availability of natural gas (*Source* ANP [2021])

In addition to the development of offshore gas, companies such as COMGÁS should seek even greater diversification and create alternatives that increase their gas supply's operational flexibility and robustness.

One of the possible alternatives for supplying the domestic market, specifically, is the import of LNG, which, in 2021, reached the level of 26 MMm3/d. The leading importer was Petrobras, and the main supplier country was the United States. In 2021, the liquefied natural gas was re-gasified in five waterway terminals: TRBA in Bahia (8 MM $m^3$/d); Pecém in Ceará (0.6 MM $m^3$/d); Guanabara Bay in Rio de Janeiro (14.5 MM $m^3$/d); Açu Natural Gas in Rio de Janeiro (0.9 MM $m^3$/d); Celse in Sergipe (2.1 MM $m^3$/d). There are plans to install other regasification terminals, such as Compass (from the same economic group as the distributor COMGÁS) seeks to install in Santos. The Floating Storage and Regasification Unit (FSRU) will be anchored in Largo do Caneu, near Bagres Island in Santos, São Paulo, and will be able to re-gasify up to 14 $MMm^3$/km long.

The relevance of LNG imports in 2021, marked by Brazil's water crisis and a higher demand for natural gas, can be noted in the total volume of imports reported by the ANP. There were, on average 46 $MMm^3$/d in 2021: 26 MM $m^3$/d of liquefied natural gas and 20 MMm $^3$/d of compressed natural gas imported from Bolivia through the Brazil-Bolivia gas pipeline (GASBOL).

GASBOL, which became fully operational more than a decade ago, was fundamental to the evolution of the natural gas market in Brazil. Operated by the Brazilian Transport Company Gasoduto Bolivia-Brasil S/A, TBG, this pipeline is 2593 km long in Brazil and 557 km long in Bolivia, crossing the states of Mato Grosso do Sul, São Paulo, Paraná, Santa Catarina, and Rio Grande do Sul. The pipeline has a capacity of 30 $MMm^3$/d. However, the Ministry of Mines and Energy (MME, 2020) has recently directed Petrobras to import only up to a maximum limit of 20 $MMm^3$/d. Such a move makes room for the import of the remaining capacity by other companies seeking to promote, especially in the State of São Paulo, the replacement of Bolivian gas by *offshore gas*.

However, in addition to this discussion involving Bolivian gas, imported liquefied natural gas, and offshore gas from the Campos and Santos Basins, another alternative involves fossil gas from *onshore* fields. The *onshore* fields have significant participation in the North and Northeast states. For example, the Azulão field in Amazonas produces natural gas. It liquefies it to be transported by cryogenic trucks to the Jaguatirica

II TPP in Roraima (1,100 km away). Likewise, the fields of the Parnaíba Basin in the state of Maranhão have a production capacity of 8 $MMm^3/d$ and directly supply the Parnaíba Complex TPPs. All these projects are from the integrated energy company Eneva. There are onshore fields in the Southeast and South states, though they are smaller in terms of volume, like those operated by the company Tradener (Portogente, 2018), which were granted authorization to explore a conventional field in the central region of Paraná which should produce 0.1 MM $m^3$/day at its total extraction capacity.

There are renewable natural gas options (also known as renewable natural gas) in addition to natural gas options with fossil fuel origins. These possibilities are being explored in Brazil and other markets, such as North America. A study by CIBIOGÁS (2021) indicated that the national crude biogas production potential calculated by ABiogás (Brazilian Biogas Association) is 82.58 billion cubic meters per year, considering the sugarcane, sanitation, animal protein, and agricultural production sectors. However, according to the same study, the current scenario of Brazilian biogas production of 1.83 billion cubic meters per year (5 MM m3/d) would correspond to only 2% of the estimated potential.

Biogas can also be used in its raw form or merely filtered to remove some of the more significant contaminants. However, to be injected into a pipeline network of a distributor such as COMGÁS, biogas would must still be adequately treated and purified to meet the minimum technical specifications defined by the ANP.

The following resolutions regulate the specifications of biomethane in Brazil:

- ANP Resolution no. 685/2017—establishes the rules for the approval of quality control and the specification of biomethane from sanitary landfills and sewage treatment stations intended for vehicular use and residential, industrial, and commercial facilities to be sold throughout the country.
- ANP Resolution no. 8/2015—applies to biomethane derived from agro-silvopastoral and commercial organic products and waste destined for vehicular use (CNG) and residential and commercial facilities.

ABEGÁS (2018) reported that in November 2018, "the Secretariat of Energy and Mining of São Paulo defined the mandatory minimum percentage of insertion of biomethane in the piped gas network, which will need to be met by the three São Paulo concessionaires.' Representatives of the government, industry, and academic community formed the São Paulo Biogas Committee. In the case of COMGÁS, the minimum percentage of biomethane would be 0.5% by the end of the third year of publication of the decree, increasing to 1% in the fourth year.

Specifically, in the case of São Paulo, there is evident potential for biomethane to be injected into the concession area of another distributor, Gas Brasiliano, where there are 66 sugar and alcohol plants less than 20 km from the pipeline. This distance between producers and the pipeline allows biomethane (produced by purifying biogas from sugarcane waste) to be directly injected into the network or more easily transported. As a result, the state of São Paulo has a production potential of 5.5 $MMm^3$/day of biogas and 2.9 million $MMm^3$/d of biomethane. In addition to the sugarcane industry, biogas in São Paulo may also come from landfills, sanitation, and agro-silvopastoral waste.

One of the possible sources of biomethane is the excess sludge produced in the treatment of effluents. As a result, sanitation firms have focused heavily on solid waste from treatment. To avoid restricting the example to the State of São Paulo, one can also take into account the history of Sanepar in Paraná. Sanepar has implemented sustainable solid waste management techniques during the treatment process, in addition to guaranteeing that the treated effluent enters the rivers in accordance with legal requirements.

A portion of the sludge from the stations is now being employed in agriculture (320 thousand tons since 2007). The United Nations Environment Program (UNEP) saw this as an example of ecologically responsible behavior as opposed to simply throwing it away. Sanepar then began to use part of the sewage sludge to generate electricity. The pioneering model was implemented at the Ouro Verde Sewage Treatment Station in Foz do Iguaçu. It was the first Brazilian plant for the distributed generation of electricity powered by biogas from sewage treatment to be registered with the National Electric Energy Agency (Agência Nacional de Energia Eletrica—ANEEL).

In the continuation of this initiative, the Belém STP, in the Metropolitan Region of Curitiba, began supplying sludge to be transformed into electricity by the company CS Bioenergy, which also uses

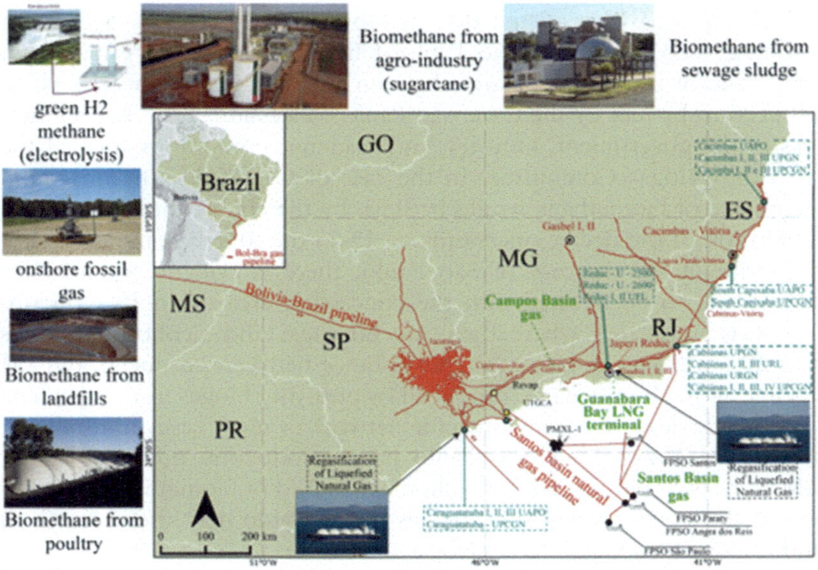


**Fig. 5.6** A map of the potential sources of natural gas for the COMGÁS distribution grid in the state of São Paulo (*Source* Adapted from COMGÁS [2021])

organic materials from other generators and has a generation power of 2.8 MW (AEN, 2021). However, with the expansion of the Belém STP, excess sludge can generate biomethane, which has been discussed between Sanepar and Companhia Paranaense de Gas—Compagas (AEN, 2021).

Figure 5.6 summarizes the various alternatives of natural gas sources for the distribution network of COMGÁS in the State of São Paulo.

## The Case of Renewal of COMGÁS Concession Contract

### *The Corporate Governance of COMGÁS*

Companhia de Gas de São Paulo, COMGÁS, is part of the Cosan Group, which has business in the energy and logistics segment with companies specializing in fuel distribution, sugar, ethanol, and electricity production, natural gas and lubricant distribution, rail transportation, port elevation, and storage. The group consists of the following companies Cosan SA, Cosan Logística, Rumo ALL, Raízen, COMGÁS, Moove, and Compass Gas & Energia. The energy segment of the group is structured under the companies Raízen and Compass Gas & Energy, under the control of which COMGÁS is located.

Compass Gas & Energy is controlled by Cosan, which holds 99.01% of the company's voting shares (Compass, 2021b). The latter divides its portfolio into four areas of activity: (i) infrastructure and gas origination, accessing the competitive supply of pre-salt gas and importing LNG (liquefied natural gas), (ii) commercialization, through the management of the supply and demand, (iii) gas thermal generation and trading of electric energy, through the transformation of gas into electricity, and (iv) distribution of natural gas, through COMGÁS, the largest piped gas company in Brazil (volume).[1]

### *The Corporate Governance and* Compliance *Standards Required in the 7th Addendum*

In brief, in September 2019, COMGÁS submitted a request for the extension of its concession contract no. CSPE 01/99, signed on May 31, 1999, between the company and the State of São Paulo, for twenty years, starting on May 31, 2029. Contract No. CSPE 01/99 has a term of thirty years and, therefore, will only reach its expiration date on 05/30/2029. In addition, for a single time, an extension is allowed in the Fifth Clause for an additional term of 20 (twenty) years. This contract also highlights that the company follows a formality of State Law no. 16.933/19 which guides requests for an early extension of public service concession contracts (arts. 3 to 7) in the State of São Paulo between piped gas distribution (art. 1, paragraph 1).

COMGÁS was able to make such a request, which meets the dictates of the law, because it (i) complies with the contract in operational, in both legal and financial aspects; (ii) meets the public interest from the economic point of view, from the advantage of the continuity of the

[1] To consult *Cosan* Business Portfolio: https://www.cosan.com.br/sobre-a-cosan/portfolio-de-negocios/ . To consult the *Compass Gás & Energia* Business Portfolio: https://www.compassbr.com/sobre-a-compass-gas-e-energia/portfolio-de-negocios/. Last access: July 21, 2021.

operator due to its expertise and quality; and (iii) continues and expands investments.

In 2021, Public Consultation no. 10/21 and Public Hearing no. 05/21 were opened, subjecting the 7th Amendment to the concession contract no. CSPE 01/99 to public scrutiny, seeking suggestions for its possible improvements.

It is appropriate to analyze the various elements of corporate governance provided in the 7th Addendum.. The governance mechanisms provided by this analysis are crucial because they encourage the execution and fulfillment of contractual deadlines in accordance with the normative framework of anticipated extensions. These governance mechanisms are primarily concentrated in Clause Nineteen and complementarily in the Second Sub-Clause of the Second Clause (transparency).

In Section Eight of Clause Nineteen, it is stipulated that policies governing transactions with Related Parties shall be developed and implemented. These policies must comply with the Brazilian Code of Corporate Governance and the regulations of B3's New Market, or subsequent standards recommended by the Securities and Exchange Commission of Brazil (Comissão de Valores Mobiliários—CVM), as applicable. Among the minimum (but not exhaustive) content provided are (i) criteria that must be met for transactions between COMGÁS and its related parties, requiring the observance of fair conditions compatible with market practice; (ii) procedures to assist in the identification of individual situations that may involve conflicts of interest and, consequently, determine the impediment of voting concerning shareholders or administrators of COMGÁS; (iii) procedures and those responsible for the identification of related parties and the classification of operations as transactions with related parties; (iv) indication of the instances of approval of transactions with related parties, depending on the amount involved or other relevant criteria; (v) requirement of conducting a competitive process with the market, according to rules approved by the management of COMGÁS, as a condition for contracting with related parties; and (vi) the duty of the ratio of COMGÁS to formalize, in a written document to be filed at COMGÁS headquarters, the justifications for the selection of related parties, at the expense of market alternatives.

These requirements are met by the current Policy of Transaction with Related Parties and Conflicts of Interest of COMGÁS. In this policy, the transactions with related parties (TPR) must be approved by the Board of Directors and may reject or suggest changes so that the deal is executed equitably and in the interest of COMGÁS and shareholders. The Board should analyze the following criteria: compliance with the *arm's length*, market conditions, and the Code of Conduct of COMGÁS. In addition, transactions should be demonstrated as the best available alternative based on economic and strategic reasons. For these conditions to be proven, an evaluation report may be required. In terms of disclosure, COMGÁS includes the TPRs in its periodic financial statements via the COMGÁS Reference Form.

Regarding the conflicts of interest, the same policy includes some examples, such as (i) a situation in which the particular interest (personal benefit) of the Employee or Director competes in a transparent or noncompetitive way with the interest of COMGÁS; (ii) a situation in which there are professional relationships that conflict with the performance of their functions in COMGÁS or that may be affected by such functions; and (iii) a situation in which friends and family are hired as employees or service providers of COMGÁS in an improper, covert manner and who are in disagreement with the Code of Conduct and policies of COMGÁS.

The Ninth Sub-Clause also requires that the concessionaire to regularly update the TPR policy. Another good governance practices is the periodic updating of internal company policies, allowing for reviews, changes, and improvements in the process.

### *Further Requirements Within the 7th Addendum*

Another duty of transparency is the need to disclose, on the COMGÁS website, one month after the conclusion of the contract with the related party and at least five working days before the beginning of the activities, the following information: (i) general information about the contracted Related Party; (ii) the object of the contract; (iii) the contract term; (iv) the general terms of payment and readjustment of the amounts related to the contracting; (v) the description of the transaction negotiated with the Related Party and the decision about the execution of the transaction; and (vi) the justification for contracting with the Related Party at the expense of market alternatives. Currently, COMGÁS does not individually disclose this information on the website, so the signature of the 7th Addendum will represent an essential evolution in its information disclosure structure.

The duties of transparency also serve as a deterrent to non-execution and delay, and the provisions throughout the 7th Addendum anticipate such possibilities. Among the excerpts, we highlight the Third Sub-Clause of the Second Clause, which has a voluntary rule for COMGÁS to undertake efforts in other business activities, providing, for this, the duty to do so by creating a new legal entity so as not to compromise the performance of existing businesses, as well as for the sake of transparency. In turn, the Ninth Sub-Clause of Clause Nineteen establishes transparency as a mandatory value and content of the policies indicated above, which COMGÁS must design, execute, and constantly improve.

The 7th Addendum will also include Clause Twenty-Three, which addresses the mandatory implementation of a *compliance* program within 720 days from the signing of the respective term. The First Sub-Clause requires that this program follows the parameters of Law No. 12,846/2013, the Anti-Corruption Law. It is important to note that, while not specifically addressed in the document, the sixteen instruments listed in Article 42 of Decree no. 8,420/2015, which convey the main elements of an integrity program, should also be observed. The Second Sub-Clause requires the sector to be responsible for the program implementation, with the requisite autonomy and independence for management.

Furthermore, COMGÁS and its controllers (direct and indirect) are committed to the quality of corporate governance and the socioenvironmental and economic impact of its activity management, which is consistent with ESG (environment, social, and governance) principles. This is evidenced by the Code of Conduct, governance, and compliance policies of COMGÁS and other companies of the Cosan group.

## Concluding Remarks

Natural gas may be required to ensure a safe transition from solid and liquid fossil fuels—coal and fuel oil—to renewable energy sources such as solar and wind. Brazil can make rational use of the fossil natural gas that it generates in offshore fields, notably those in the Santos Basin. Moreover, renewable natural gas sources can be exploited and developed from agricultural and livestock waste, urban waste, and sewage treatment units. The significance of natural gas prompted the establishment of Brazil's New Gas Market. It has also accelerated the discussion of concession renewal processes for gas distribution companies, such as COMGAS, in São Paulo.

Moving forward, it may be important to discuss the federalization of the gas market in Brazil. Piped gas exploration in Brazil is conducted at the state level, while other energy sources (eolic, thermal, hydroelectric, etc.) are handled at the federal level. But this change would require amendments to the Brazilian Constitution, since art. 25, § 2°, grants individual states the right to this exploration. In terms of a national energy strategy, it would be beneficial to centralize all energy source provisions in the Federal Government, as national plan coordination could improve the delivery of these services to individual states. However, the assessment of such a strategy goes beyond the scope of this chapter and would require further research.

Federal Law 14,134/2021 enacted the regulatory grounds for the gas sector in the country. This regulatory framework may foster further investments and exploration of national gas in the country because it will bring more legal certainty to the sector.

## References

ABEGÁS—Associação Brasileira das Empresas Distribuidoras de Gás Canalizado. (2018). *SP define percentual mínimo de bi metano na rede de gás*. November 5th. https://www.abegas.org.br/arquivos/69270 Accessed on July 25, 2021.

AEN—Agência Estadual de Notícias do Estado Paraná. (2021). Sanepar e Compagas estudam parceria para produção de biometano. https://www.aen.pr.gov.br/modules/noticias/article.php?storyid=113095. Accessed on July 25.

ANP—Agência Nacional do Petróleo, Gás Natural e Biocombustíveis. (2021). *Boletim da Produção de Petróleo e Gás Natural*, December, number 136. https://www.gov.br/anp/pt-br/centrais-deconteudo/publicacoes/boletins-anp/bmp/2021/2021-05-boletim.pdf. Accessed on July 25.

Bouckaert, S., Fernandez Pales, A., McGlade, C., Remme, U., Wanner, B., Varro, L., & Spencer, T. (2021). *Net zero by 2050-A roadmap for the global energy sector*.

Caineng, Z. O. U., Zhi, Y. A. N. G., Dongbo, H. E., Yunsheng, W., Jian, L., Ailin, J., & Shen, Y. (2018). Theory, technology, and prospects of conventional and unconventional natural gas. *Petroleum Exploration and Development, 45*(4), 604–618.

CIBIOGÁS—Centro Internacional de Energias Renováveis. (2021). *Panorama do Biogás no Brasil 2020*, Technical Note number 001/2021, March. https://abiogas.org.br/wp-content/uploads/2021/06/PANORAMA-DO-BIOGAS-NO-BRASIL-2020-v.8.0-1_1.pdf. Accessed on July 15

COMGÁS—Companhia de Gás de São Paulo S/A. (2021). Plano de Negócios – 4ª Revisão Tarifária. http://www.arsesp.sp.gov.br/BancoDadosAudienciasPublicasArquivos/OFCR132-19%20-%20PLano%20de%20Negocios%20Comgas.pdf. Accessed on July 15

Compass—Compass Gás e Energia. (2021a). *Relatório de Sustentabilidade de 2020.*
Compass—Compass Gás e Energia. (2021b). Shareholding composition. https://www.compassbr.com/governanca-corporativa/composicao-acionaria/. Accessed on July 21.
EPE—Empresa de Pesquisa Energética. (2018). Balanço Energético Nacional 2018. EPE, Rio de Janeiro. https://www.epe.gov.br/pt/publicacoes-dados-abertos/publicacoes/balanco-energetico-nacional-2018. Accessed on July 17.
Feijoo, F., Iyer, G. C., Avraam, C., Siddiqui, S. A., Clarke, L. E., Sankaranarayanan, S., Binsted, M. T., Patel, P. L., Prates, N. C., Torres-Alfaro, E., & Wise, M. A. (2018). The future of natural gas infrastructure development in the United States. *Applied Energy*, *228*, 149–166.
IEA—International Energy Agency. (2020). *Global Energy Review 2020*, IEA, Paris. https://www.iea.org/reports/global-energy-review-2020. Accessed on July 17, 2021.
IEA—International Energy Agency. (2021). *Global Energy Review 2021*, IEA, Paris. https://www.iea.org/reports/global-energy-review-2021. Accessed on July 17.
IEDI (2021). *Letter IEDI n. 1094—The 14th Chinese Five-Year Plan: transforming China into an industrial and technological power.*
Leal, D. S., Cabral, R. P. B., de Oliveira Pereira, K. R., & Cutrim, A. A. (2021). O uso do gás natural na geração termelétrica e os impactos causados pela pandemia.
MetronLab. (2021). *Blog*. https://www.metronlab.com/blog/overview-brazilian-market. Accessed on July 25.
MIT—Massachusetts Institute of Technology. (2011). *The future of Natural Gas.*
MME—Ministério de Minas e Energia. (2020). Ordinance of the Brazilian Ministry of Mines and Energy Number 282/2020. https://www.gov.br/mme/pt-br/acesso-a-informacao/legislacao/portarias/2020/portaria-n-282-2020.pdf/view#:~:text=11/2021%2012h33-,Portaria%20n%20282%2D2020.pdf,-%E2%80%94%20352%20KB. Accessed on July 20, 2021.
Oliveira da Silva, V., Gomes Relva, S., Mondragon, M., Bergsten Mendes, A., Nishimoto, K., & Peyerl, D. (2020). Building Options for the Brazilian Pre-salt: A technical-economic and infrastructure analysis of offshore integration between energy generation and natural gas exploration. *Resources Policy*. Volume 81, 2023, https://doi.org/10.1016/j.resourpol.2023.103305
Patric, S. M. (2021). *The EU Green Deal Just Raised the Bar on Climate Policy.* Project Syndicate.
PETROBRAS—Petróleo Brasileiro S/A (2021). *Strategic Plan for 2022–2026.* https://api.mziq.com/mzfilemanager/v2/d/25fdf098-34f5-4608-b7fa-17d60b2de47d/2f9ccf1c-e389-8ac0-16ad-3e74135b32d3?origin=1. Accessed on July 25.

Portogente. (2018). *Poços de gás do Paraná recebem licença ambiental de teste*. https://portogente.com.br/noticias/transporte-logistica/99948-pocos-de-gas-do-parana-recebem-licenca-ambiental-de-teste. Accessed on July 25, 2021.

Segal, M. (2021). *ESG Today. Japan to Boost Renewables to Largest Energy Source by 2030 in Bid to Meet Climate Goals*. Accessed on July 21.

Teixeira, C. A. N., Mendes, A. P. D. A., Costa, R. C. D., Rocio M. A. R., & Prates, H. F. (2021). *Gás natural: um combustível-chave para uma economia de baixo carbono*.

Townsend, A. F. (2019). *Natural Gas and the Clean Energy Transition*.

PART III

# Sustainable Frameworks and Solutions for Environmental Challenges in the Oil & Gas Industry

CHAPTER 6

# The Social License to Operate Across the Energy Industry: Lessons for Low-Carbon Energy from Oil and Gas

*Siân Stephens*

## Introduction

The Social License to Operate (SLO) broadly refers to the ongoing acceptance and approval of an operation (Parsons & Moffat, 2014), and the absence of an SLO may manifest in social, legal, and/or political objections which pose severe threats to the viability of exploration and extraction. The concept was originally developed for use in the oil and gas industry (Morrison, 2014), and substantial work has been made in both academia and the industry to develop useful models of the SLO that can be applied to identify the meaningful consent of local communities.

While traditional sources such as coal, oil, and gas continue to provide the majority of the world's energy, the contribution of low-carbon alternatives is increasing and likely to grow rapidly in the coming years. As the

S. Stephens (✉)
Middlesex University, London, UK
e-mail: s.stephens@mdx.ac.uk



T. Walker et al. (eds.), *Sustainability in the Oil and Gas Sector*,
https://doi.org/10.1007/978-3-031-51586-6_6

energy industry diversifies in pursuit of sustainability, many energy companies are seeking to expand their portfolio to include renewable sources. Despite their green credentials, new energy projects such as onshore wind farms, nuclear sites, and solar farms often face local opposition. In particular, onshore wind energy faces a significant amount of local resistance (Botetzagias et al., 2015; Horst, 2007) and, in some places, such as the UK, where local acceptance is required for the approval of new developments, local opposition has serious implications for the industry.

The SLO has proven to be of crucial importance to the oil and gas industry, because local support is necessary when dealing with geographically bound resources, and because the extraction process is particularly destructive. Resources can only be extracted in the area where they are situated; hence governments of resource-rich nations and oil and gas (O&G) businesses engaging in exploration and extraction must acquire the consent of nearby populations. While the renewable and low-carbon energy industries are arguably less geographically restricted than the extractive energy industries, they nonetheless encounter issues of local objection, and there is ample evidence of obstacles in relation to the siting of energy operations such as onshore wind farms, large-scale solar farms, and nuclear power and waste disposal sites. Research suggests that the primary concerns of communities that host oil and gas operations have to do with the immediate and local impacts of the operation, such as concerns with social and economic impacts, as was the case of the Baku-Tbilisi-Ceyhan and Southern Caucasus Pipeline projects (Jijelava et al., 2017). The salience of local concerns offers both warnings about the proposed projects and opportunities to turn to alternative renewable energy sources such as onshore and offshore wind and solar power. It can be inferred that the low-carbon impact of such initiatives on a global scale will not be sufficient to alleviate local damage, but local concerns can often be addressed with significant socio-economic investments, such as content policies and remuneration.

While the SLO remains most closely associated with extractive energy, the utility and applicability of the concept in other areas of operation have been demonstrated in numerous studies, ranging from the use of ocean-based resources (Kelly et al., 2017; Voyer et al., 2019) to thoroughbred horseracing (Heleski et al., 2020). Trust and legitimacy, the fundamental elements of the SLO, are proven to be of crucial value in any industry that either requires or benefits from the consent and support of local stakeholders. The necessity of an SLO does not appear to be limited to 'controversial' industries such as the oil and gas industry, or those with particularly well-known negative environmental impacts.

In this chapter, we argue that there are notable commonalities between the nature of local resistance and the conditions of local acceptance across the energy industries, and that the extant research relating to the SLO of O&G can offer valuable lessons to alternative sources of energy. Conversely, experiences in renewable and low-carbon energy industries such as wind, solar, and nuclear energies may provide some useful insights to the O&G industry. For example, evidence that the environmental credentials of newer forms of energy do not outweigh substantial community opposition suggests that where there is local resistance, it is likely due to more immediate, community-specific issues. A greater understanding of these concerns may inform and influence how the O&G industry approaches difficulties related to social acceptance, even if the industry is unable to compete with alternatives on the basis of sustainability. Such an understanding will be of great value to the O&G industry, as well as to low-carbon alternatives, as governments and industries seek diversified energy portfolios which make the most of our available resources. This chapter will consider the similarities and differences between the local acceptance challenges facing the O&G industry and renewable alternatives such as onshore wind and identify the key lessons which can be drawn and applied to other sources of energy.

## The Social License to Operate in Mining Oil and Gas

The SLO in the extractive energy sector is particularly fraught because the impact of exploration and extraction on local populations can be severe and consent may not be easy to obtain. Many of the direct consequences resulting from O&G operations are relatively unique to the industry. Such consequences include the relocation of local communities, the impact on the local environment of the operations themselves, and the socio-economic impacts of migratory work. Much academic attention has been paid to exploring the nature and consequences of these aspects of O&G operations, particularly in Africa (e.g., Arthuer et al., 2020; Baghebo et al., 2012; Ogwang & Vanclay, 2019; Udoh, 2013) and significant attempts have been made to address the worst of these consequences through provisions such as Free Prior and Informed Consent (FPIC) for indigenous communities.

Many of these industry-specific issues do not apply to renewable/low-carbon energy; the relevant resources are not geographically contingent in the same manner, such that while an onshore wind farm may be uncomfortably close to a community, it is unlikely to cause the relocation of a community. Renewable and low-carbon energy does not offer the same labor opportunities as traditional extractives and as such, creates neither significant employment opportunities nor significant changes in the local population. Nonetheless, there are valuable lessons to be drawn from the experience of the O&G industry which can be applied to the energy industry more broadly.

A majority of the theoretical development initiatives of the SLO concept have been undertaken with reference to the mining industry and then subsequently applied to the O&G, and, more recently, renewable and low-carbon energy industries. The prevalent finding in extant work is that the local context must be carefully considered and reflected in successful attempts to gain community consent. Robust extant literature reveals a diversity in relevant criteria for consent in differing national contexts, including Russia (Wilson, 2016), Greenland (Smits et al., 2017), Australia (Luke et al., 2018; Richert et al., 2015), North America (Gehman et al., 2016), and Uganda (Ogwang & Vanclay, 2019). In each of these cases, local factors are identified as key drivers of, or obstacles to, the SLO. For example, in Uganda Ogwang and Vanclay (2019) identify that tangible benefits must be made available to local stakeholders in order for a given operation to obtain an SLO, while in Greenland, Smits et al. (2017) argue that the language barrier between those working for the O&G companies and the local communities poses a challenge to good relations. The literature also identifies institutional factors, such as political and legal frameworks, along with the presence or absence of NGOs, as key determining criteria for precisely what the community will require in order to grant an SLO.

The literature contends that conceptual ambiguity is the primary obstacle which traditional extractive energy industries must overcome in order to successfully apply the SLO concept (e.g., Bice et al., 2017; Brueckner et al., 2018). Vagaries around the term's use lead to a lack of accountability when firms claim an SLO, and allow for companies to use it as a defensive mechanism rather than as a tool of collaborative stakeholder-engagement (Owen et al., 2013; Putten et al., 2018). From an industry perspective, the lack of conceptual clarity also poses challenges in terms of how to identify, interpret, and overcome potential stakeholder objections to lucrative projects, as it may not be obvious to the developers where to look for obstacles or what overcoming these may entail.

In response to these concerns, efforts have been made to clarify and establish a clear understanding of the concept and its application, including the development of a four-stage 'pyramid' model that depicts the four stages of SLO as follows: withheld/withdrawn, acceptance, approval, and psychological identification (Boutilier & Thomson, 2011). Subsequently, this model was refined in light of additional empirical research and re-conceptualized as a four-stage 'arrowhead' model (Boutilier & Thomson, 2011), which delineates economic legitimacy, socio-political legitimacy, interactional trust, and institutionalized trust as the four components of an SLO, operating along a continuum which culminates in institutionalized trust (but within which all four elements are necessary criteria). The model provides a framework for identifying the necessary sources of requisite trust and legitimacy while allowing for substantial contextual differences relating to, for example, the socio-economic context. This approach has been successfully applied to evaluate the SLO of the O&G projects in Georgia (Jijelava & Vanclay, 2017), demonstrating the utility of a formalized model in this sector.

In an attempt to provide a broader suite of consent, reflective of the multifaceted risks to viability operations may face, Bice et al. (2017) developed the Social, Actuarial, and Political (SAP) model. The SAP model identifies how mining and extractive industries must engage with stakeholders when seeking permission to proceed, and it reflects the three sources of consent required for a successful project. While the SAP model breaks the SLO into three categories, it is argued that stakeholder concerns regarding all three should, ideally, be properly addressed. It is also acknowledged that, in reality, the relationship between the stakeholder groups and the three sources of risk is complex, changeable, and unlikely to be balanced. The SAP model has been applied to investigate legitimacy gaps in the Australian extractive industry (Brueckner & Eabrasu, 2018), and it was found to be effective in drawing attention to the complexity of stakeholder risks and relations.

There is some tension between the two lessons identified above, as these identify a need for both a broadly applicable and widely recognized framework, and a contextually sensitive approach. However, the models outlined above provide frameworks for identifying and understanding local issues, and they also have been successfully applied in a variety of contexts. The conceptual issues presented here are applicable to any industry where local consent is both important and challenging to obtain, and are not exclusive to the O&G industry or to the industry-specific challenges previously discussed in this chapter, such as relocation.

## The Social License to Operate and Renewable and Low-Carbon Energy

There are notable differences between the social challenges facing the O&G industry and those facing the renewable energy industry, and renewable energy has a reputational advantage over O&G. Nonetheless, there is ample evidence of local objections to the siting of onshore wind and solar operations across national contexts. Nuclear energy is particularly controversial, but is often quietly supported by governments as the most efficient, readily available form of low-carbon energy and a necessary contributor to net-zero ambitions. It is therefore likely that there is much which can be learned by renewable energy operators from traditional energy operators who have been grappling with issues of local consent for much longer. The four primary sources of low-carbon energy globally are nuclear, hydropower, wind, and solar energy (Low Carbon Power, 2022). In this section, we shall consider the SLO of nuclear, onshore wind, and solar energy as these land-based operations are the most likely to directly affect communities and are therefore more likely to face community opposition. As will be discussed below, the community opposition faced by all three sources suggests that industries would benefit from a more concerted effort toward obtaining a SLO, and that while some academic attention has been given to this in relation to wind energy, the SLO for nuclear and solar operations has yet to be adequately considered in the academic literature.

## Nuclear Energy and the SLO

Nuclear energy is the most important form of low-carbon energy, notably in Europe, where nuclear power accounts for 25% of total electricity production (Low Carbon Power, 2022). Nuclear power is also one of the more controversial sources of low-carbon energy, and political appetite for energy diversification in this direction varies dramatically from country to country. Many governments moved away from nuclear power following the Fukushima disaster in 2011 (Wang & Kim, 2018), although more recently nuclear has regained favor, such as in the UK where the government is now planning for nuclear power to supply 25% of the country's energy by 2050 (Department for Business, Energy & Industrial Strategy, 2022). Despite high-profile accidents and opposition, the social license to operate for nuclear power remains understudied and unexplored. However, it is apparent that trust in public and private institutions is a crucial issue for the support of large-scale nuclear projects (Lehtonen et al., 2022) and much of the extant research addresses the importance of public faith in the government policies and practices which regulate the nuclear power industry, rather than in the industry itself. Within this research, it has been found that the governance processes are, on the whole, lacking. According to Richter et al. (2022), there is evidence of inadequacy in the procedures for obtaining consent for the placement of nuclear waste in the United States, as well as with the procedures for obtaining local approval for restarting a nuclear power plant in Japan (Nakazawa & Tatsumi, 2022). Moreover, Lehtonen et al. (2020) assert that the role of the state is of such particular importance to the management of the nuclear industry, due to the very long-term timescale of the risks of nuclear waste disposal, that state-related elements must be added to the Thomson and Boutilier model in order to better reflect the nature of the SLO for projects such as nuclear power operations.

## Solar Power and the SLO

Large-scale solar panel installations, known as 'solar farms' or photovoltaic power plants, provide power for the national grid (as opposed to smaller solar panel installations which might be used to produce power directly for homes or businesses). Despite the significant land requirements of these installations, there is relatively little research on whether communities support or oppose this type of renewable energy. The majority of the relevant research relates to community opposition to the siting of solar farms in North America, despite solar power accounting for only a small fraction (Low Carbon Power, 2022) of the energy produced there. While the extant literature does not explicitly relate the SLO concept to solar farms, there is evidence of community opposition to the solar industry in much the same way as exists for other energy operations. Although the majority of Americans support solar energy generally, the industry faces specific challenges when deciding where to locate farms (Carlisle et al., 2014), and local opposition exists on environmental grounds due to the ecological impacts of land redevelopment (Mulvaney, 2017), and the impact of solar farms on local property values (Carlisle et al., 2015).

Research suggests that organized opposition from small groups is the main threat to securing siting consent for solar farms. This opposition can have a disproportionate impact on the projects' progression, but it has been argued that such obstacles could be overcome by involving community earlier, in order to identify and mitigate the minority objections early in the siting process (Crawford et al., 2022; Susskind et al., 2022). The North American experience can be contrasted with findings of support for a proposed solar farm in Morocco, where there was a strong expectation of socio-economic benefit contributing to overall support for the initiative (Hanger et al., 2016). These findings support the notion that for onshore wind energy, socio-economic benefits are critical in the context of developing countries (Stephens & Robisnon, 2021).

## Onshore Wind and the SLO

Local opposition to onshore wind farms is particularly well publicized, and it may provide the most direct evidence that renewable energy faces much of the same local opposition as more traditional energy initiatives. The wind energy industry is well developed, and many national governments have championed wind energy as a key pillar in their country's carbon reduction efforts in recent years. However, the proliferation of onshore wind farms has sparked opposition in some countries, particularly in Europe, leading to an academic and policy interest in the methods in which an SLO could be obtained for onshore wind farms.

Much of the community opposition to onshore wind appears to be based on concerns/objections to the visual impact of the operations (e.g., Jones & Eiser, 2010; Hall et al., 2013; Phillips, 2015), which holds true in different national contexts. A further barrier to social acceptance is the lack of local consultation; local communities feel that the wind farms are being imposed on them without any consideration of, or consultation with, the community, and the SLO is generally lacking (D'Souza & Yiridoe, 2014). The value of local consultation links closely to the importance of trust which is fundamental to the SLO as obtained in the O&G industry; trust in the developers was shown to be a contributing factor to the SLO of wind farms in Tunisia (Hammami et al., 2016) and Australia (Hall et al., 2013), and trust in the local government was found to be an important aspect of the SLO for a proposed onshore wind farm in

England (Jones & Eiser, 2010). It can therefore be concluded that strong, trusted institutions will be conducive to obtaining the social license to operate for onshore wind.

Extant literature also demonstrates some effective tools for obtaining an SLO for visually intrusive wind farms. The success of some form of community ownership in obtaining an SLO has drawn some attention and has been shown to be successful in European countries (Musall & Kuik, 2011; Toke et al., 2008), in Scotland (Warren & McFadyen, 2010), and in South Africa (Stephens & Robisnon, 2021). However, in Denmark it was found to appeal only to those who were already supportive the operation, and opponents did not want to invest in something to which they were fundamentally opposed (Johansen & Emborg, 2018).

Discussion of the economic benefits of the onshore wind industry is conspicuously absent in the onshore wind literature; indeed, it has been shown that economic benefits are of little concern to affected local communities (Groth & Vogt, 2014). An emergent theme in the available data is the importance of very local concerns, rather than global (e.g., environmental) concerns. These local concerns are likely to have negative associations because wind energy neither provides many jobs, nor trickle-down investments. Furthermore, aspects such as the visual impact of the turbines, which may in turn lead to concerns regarding the impact on tourism and local-political concerns to do with the involvement of untrusted actors, may hinder the process of obtaining consent from local communities to build them. Onshore wind thus lacks an opportunity for support which is afforded O&G developments, which hold at least the promise of significant local and national economic benefit. It is also worth noting that the literature does not show that the macro-environmental advantages of renewable energy, such as wind, offer much in terms of incentivizing community consent. Opposition and acceptance are both based on local impact and local consultation and as such the O&G industry, which cannot capitalize on global environmental concerns, can similarly adopt very local approaches to obtaining consent.

## Conclusion

Across the literature relating to nuclear, solar, and onshore wind energy, there is evidence that the key findings from the O&G literature (the importance of conceptual clarity, the importance of institutional trust and legitimacy, and the context dependency of SLO criteria) are highly applicable to the renewable and low-carbon energy industries. There is also evidence of some consent challenges that are specific to renewable energy, such as the role of subsides and incentives (or the perception of subsidization or incentives), which may undermine the legitimacy of a project which is perceived to have an unfair competitive advantage (e.g., solar energy, Carlisle et al., 2015). There is more evidence that strong and trustworthy institutions facilitate an SLO for renewable operations than for O&G, but this may well reflect the developmental context of the operation and the research; i.e., there is more research on O&G in developing contexts and renewable energy in developed contexts, and it is likely that operations in countries with governance gaps attempt to bypass government in search of an SLO whereas operations in countries with more well-established political institutions can 'piggyback' on governmental legitimacy to gain the operational legitimacy.

However, the extant academic literature demonstrates that all energy sources face local opposition, and there are noteworthy commonalities in the nature of these oppositions. While O&G operations are frequently far more disruptive to lives and livelihoods than low-carbon alternatives, it is clear that affected communities may challenge any imposition which they deem counters their own interests. Therefore, while the specific interventions required of the O&G industry to such challenges may not be widely applicable (e.g., free, prior and informed consent in the case of relocation), the conceptual underpinnings of the SLO offer much to alternative energy sources. It is apparent that there is a need for a clear understanding of what an SLO is, what it covers, and what are the implications when a company claims such a license.

According to the literature reviewed above, local considerations are critical across nations and industries, and the most effective approach to community agreement is one which entails detailed consideration of the host communities. Relatively deprived communities are likely to place greater value on tangible benefits, whereas more affluent and/or rural communities may be less willing to compromise on the aesthetic consequences of developments such as solar and wind farms (Stephens & Robisnon, 2021). Beyond such generalizations, however, are a plethora of local concerns which will vary dramatically from community to community and which can only be identified through careful consultation. Trustworthy industry standards, which include provision for local content, community investment and extensive local consultation, are likely to ensure that companies with a solid track record benefit from a good reputation, engendering the goodwill of potential host communities. A formal process for demonstrating extensive local consultation may also serve to balance out any disproportionate opposition from small minority groups.

There are also lessons to be drawn from the experiences of nuclear, solar, and wind energy. The dominance of local concerns over global environmental concerns is notable and suggests an opportunity for high-carbon sources of energy in obtaining an SLO as companies in this field may be better resourced and able to offer more in terms of mitigating local environmental impact. Similarly, the evident concerns about the (lack of) local economic benefits offered by low-carbon energy sources do not apply to the more labor-intensive traditional energy operations, which will have more to offer in terms of employment and trickle-down investments. The provision of infrastructure and public goods such as health and education also offer an SLO-boosting 'offset,' and arguably, the more established energy companies with a strong local presence are in the best position to make these contributions effectively. The benefits of community ownership as demonstrated in the wind industry offer lessons that can be applied to all energy operators, and it has been established that local ownership goes a considerable way toward overcoming potential resistance to new energy projects. Community ownership polices must be carefully crafted to ensure maximum benefit and inclusion for the community while also taking into account the region's socio-economic conditions; for instance, optional buy-in is less likely to work in economically deprived contexts.

Overall, the literature reviewed here serves as a reminder of the significant challenges posed by energy production. The pervasive nature of local objections to energy operations, regardless of global environmental impact, suggests that the growing urgency of climate change and the race to net-zero has done little to persuade communities to tolerate unsightly and intrusive energy production sites, and attempts to obtain an SLO will continue to be fraught. As governments seek to address the combined dangers of climate change and energy security, the variety of communities with which energy companies must engage will expand considerably. As a result, an increasing number of communities will become both energy producers and consumers.

Some encouragement can perhaps be found in the consistency of local objections across the renewable and low-carbon energy sectors, which may be effectively addressed through close consultation with local stakeholders. The O&G industry may also discover that using their considerable resources to provide local benefits to communities might win them favor. There is considerable opportunity for further research into how solar and nuclear operations can gain an SLO, as well as lessons which can be applied from the onshore wind industry and O&G. More broadly, industry and academia would benefit from further consideration of the conditions under which the SLO was won, across industries and national contexts, so that lessons can be learned from best practice.

## References


Arthuer, J. L., & Amo-Fosu, A. (2020). Oil and gas exploitation in the Ghanaian context: The balance of benefits and challenges. *African Journal of Environmental Science and Technology, 14*(7), 177–182.

Baghebo, M., Samuel, U. P., & Nwagbara, E. N. (2012). Environmental damage caused by the activities of Multi National oil giants in the Niger delta region of Nigeria. *Journal of Humanities and Social Science, 5*(6), 09–13.

Bice, S., Brueckner, M., & Pforr, C. (2017). Putting social license to operate on the map: A social, actuarial and political risk and licensing model (SAP Model). *Resources Policy, 53*, 46–55.

Boutilier, R. G., & Thomson, I. (2011). *Modelling and measuring the social license to operate: Fruits of a dialogue between theory and practice.* Retrieved June 02, 2022, from http://socialicense.com/publications/Modelling%20and%20Measuring%20the%20SLO.pdf

Brueckner, M., & Eabrasu, M. (2018). Pinning down the social license to operate (SLO): The problem or normative complexity. *Resources Policy, 59*, 217–226.

Carlisle, J., Kane, S. L., Solan, D., & Joe, J. C. (2014). Support for solar energy: Examining sense of place and utility-scale development in California. *Energy Research & Social Science, 3*, 124–130.

Carlisle, J. E., Kane, S. L., Solan, D., Bowman, M., & Joe, J. C. (2015). Public attitudes regarding large-scale solar energy development in the U.S. *Renewable and Sustainable Energy Reviews, 48*, 835–847.

Crawford, J., Bessette, D., & Mills, S. B. (2022). Rallying the anti-crowd: Organized opposition, democratic deficit, and a potential social gap in large-scale solar energy. *Energy Research & Social Science, 90*, (online).

Department for Business, Energy & Industrial Strategy. (2022, April 7). *British energy security strategy.* Retrieved June 9, 2022, from https://www.gov.uk/government/publications/british-energy-security-strategy/british-energy-security-strategy#nuclear

D'Souza, C., & Yiridoe, E. K. (2014). Social acceptance of wind energy development and planning in rural communities of Australia: A consumer analysis. *Energy Policy, 74*, 262–270.

Gehman, J., Thompson, D. Y., Alessi, D. S., Allen, D. M., & Goss, G. G. (2016). Comparative analysis of hydraulic fracturing wastewater practices in unconventional shale development: Newspaper coverage of stakeholder concerns and social license to operate. *Sustainability, 8*(912), 1–23.

Groth, T. M., & Vogt, C. A. (2014). Rural wind farm development: Social, environmental and economic features important to local residents. *Renewable Energy*, (63), 1–8.

Gunningham, N., Kagan, R. A., & Thornton, D. (2004). Social license and environmental protection: Why businesses go beyond compliance. *Law & Soc Inquiry, 29*, 307–341.

Hall, N., Ashworth, P., & Devine-Write, P. (2013). Societal acceptance of wind farms: Analysis of four common themes across Australian case studies. *Energy Policy, 58*, 200–208.

Hall, N., Lacey, J., Carr-Cornish, S., & Dowd, A.-M. (2015). Social licence to operate: Understanding how a concept has been translated into practice in energy industries. *Journal of Cleaner Production, 86*, 301–310.

Hammami, S. M., Chtourou, S., & Triki, A. (2016). Identifying the determinants of community acceptance of renewable energy technologies: The case study of a wind energy project from Tunisia. *Renewable and Sustainable Energy Reviews*, (54), 151–160.

Hanger, S., Komendantova, N., Schinke, B., & Zejli, D. (2016). Community acceptance of large-scale solar energy installations in developing countries: Evidence from Morocco. *Energy Research & Social Science, 14*, 80–89.

Harper, M., Anderson, B., James, P. A., & Bahaj, A. S. (2019). Onshore wind and the likelihood of planning acceptance: Learning from a Great Britain context. *Energy Policy, 128*, 954–966.

Heleski, C., Stowe, J., Fielder, J., Peterson, M. L., Brady, C., Wickens, C., & MacLeod, J. N. (2020). Thoroughbred racehorse welfare through the lens of 'Social license to operate—With an emphasis on a U.S. perspective. *Sustainability, 12*(1706), 1–23.

Jijelava, D., & Vanclay, F. (2017). Legitimacy, credibility and trust as the key components of a social license to operate: An analysis of BP's projects in Georgia. *Journal of Cleaner Production, 140*, 1077–1086.

Johansen, K., & Emborg, J. (2018). Wind farm acceptance for sale? Evidence from the Danish wind farm co-ownership scheme. *Energy Policy* (117), 413–422.

Jones, C. R., & Eiser, J. R. (2010). Understanding 'local' opposition to wind development in the UK: How big is a backyard? *Energy Policy*, 3106–3117.

Kelly, R., Pecl, G. T., & Fleming, A. (2017). Social licence in the marine sector: A review of understanding and application. *Marine Policy, 81*, 21–28.

Lehtonen, M., Kojo, M., Tuija, J., Litmanen, T., & Kari, M. (2020). The roles of the state and social licence to operate? Lessons from nuclear waste management in Finland, France, and Sweden. *Energy Research & Social Science, 61*, 1–12.

Lehtonen, M., Prades, A., Espluga, J., & Arapostathis, S. (2022). Introduction to the special issue "Trust, mistrust, distrust, and trust-building in the nuclear sector: Historical and comparative experience from Europe." *Journal of Risk Research, 25*(5), 547–561.

Lombard, A., & Ferreira, S. (2014). Residents' attitudes to proposed wind farms in the West Coast Region of South Africa: A social perspective from the South. *Energy Policy, 66*, 390–399.

Low Carbon Power. (2022, June 13). Retrieved from low carbon power: https://lowcarbonpower.org/

Luke, H., Brueckner, M., & Emmanouil, N. (2018). Unconventional gas development in Australia: A critical review of its social license. *The Extractive Industries and Society, 5*, 648–662.

Morrison, J. (2014). *The social license: How to keep your organization legitimate*. Palgrave Macmillan.

Mulvaney, D. (2017). Identifying the roots of green civil war over utility-scale solar energy projects on public lands across the American Southwest. *Journal of Land Use Science, 12*(6), 493–515.

Musall, F. D., & Kuik, O. (2011). Local acceptance of renewable energy - A case study from Southeast Germany. *Energy Policy, 39*, 3252–3260.

Nakazawa, T., & Tatsumi, T. (2022). Disagreeing with 'local agreement': A survey of public attitudes toward restarting the Hamaoka nuclear power plant. *Journal of Environmental Planning and Management, 65*(1), 150–167.

Nelson, J. (2006). Social license to operate. *International Journal of Mining Reclamation and Environment, 20*, 161–162.

Ogwang, T., & Vanclay, F. (2019). Social impacts of land acquisition for oil and gas development in Uganda. *Land, 8*, 109, 1–15.https://doi.org/10.3390/land8070109

Owen, J. R., & Kemp, D. (2013). Social license and mining: A critical perspective. *Resources Policy, 28*, 29–35.

Parsons, R., & Moffat, K. (2014). Constructing the meaning of social license. *Social Epistemology: A Journal of Knowledge, Culture and Policy, 28*(3–4), 340–363.

Phillips, J. (2015). A quantitative—based evaluation of the environmental impact and sustainability of a proposed onshore wind farm in the United Kingdom. *Renewable and Sustainable Energy Reviews, 49*, 1261–1270.

Putten, I. E., Cvitanovic, C., Fulton, E., Lacey, J., & Kelly, R. (2018). The emergence of a social license necessitates reforms in environmental regulation. *Ecology and Society, 23*(3), 24.

Richert, C., Roberts, A., & Burton, M. (2015). Measuring the extent of a social license to operate: The influence of marine biodiversity offsets in the oil and gas sector in Western Australia. *Resources Policy, 43*, 121–129.

Richter, J., Bernstein, M. J., & Farooque, M. (2022). The process to find a process for governance: Nuclear waste management and consent-based siting in the United States. *Energy Research & Social Science, 87*, (online).

Smits, C. C., van Leeuwen, J., & van Tatenhove, J. P. (2017). Oil and gas development in Greenland: A social license to operate, trust and legitimacy in environmental governance. *Resources Policy, 53*, 109–116.

Stephens, S., & Robisnon, B. M. (2021). The social license to operate in the onshore wind energy industry: A comparative case study of Scotland and South Africa. *Energy Policy, 148 Part B*, (online).

Susskind, L., Chun, J., Grant, A., Hodgkins, C., Cohen, J., & Lohmar, S. (2022). Sources of opposition to renewable energy projects in the United States. *Energy Policy, 165*, (online).

Thomson, I., & Boutilier, R. G. (2011). Social license to operate. In P. Darling (Ed.), *SME Mining Engineering Handbook* (pp. 1779–1796) Society for Mining.

Toke, D., Breukers, S., & Wolsink, M. (2008). Wind power deployment outcomes: How can we account for the differences? *Renewable and Sustainable Energy Reviews,* (12), 1129–1147.

Udoh, I. A. (2013). Oil, migration, and the political economy of HIV/AIDS prevention in Nigeria's Niger delta. *International Journal of Health Services, 43*(4), 681–697.

Voyer, M., & van Leeuwen, J. (2019). 'Social license to operate' in the Blue Economy. *Resources Policy, 62*, 102–113.

Wang, J., & Kim, S. (2018). Comparative analysis of public attitudes toward nuclear power energy across 27 European countries by applying the multilevel model. *Sustainability, 10*, 1–21.

Warren, C. R., & McFadyen, M. (2010). Does community ownership affect public attitudes to wind energy? A case study from south-west Scotland. *Land Use Policy, 27*, 204–213.

Wilson, E. (2016). What is the social license to operate? Local perceptions of oil and gas projects in Russia's Komi Republic and Sakhalin Island. *The Extractive Industries and Society, 73–81*(3), 73–81.

Botetzagias, I., Malesios, C., Kolokotroni, A., & Moysiadis, Y. (2015). The role of NIMBY in opposing the siting of wind farms: evidence from Greece. *Journal of Environmental Planning and Management, 58*(2), 229–251. https://doi.org/10.1080/09640568.2013.851596

Dan, van der Horst. (2007). NIMBY or not? Exploring the relevance of location and the politics of voiced opinions in renewable energy siting controversies. *Energy Policy, 35*(5), 2705–2714. https://doi.org/10.1016/j.enpol.2006.12.012

CHAPTER 7

# Carbon-Negative Crude Oil

*Steven Bryant*

## Introduction

"Carbon-negative crude oil" may sound like an oxymoron, but the choice of words is deliberate. The use of carbon-negative crude oil could result in the net removal of carbon from the atmosphere, which would in turn mitigate climate change. The phrase "crude oil" distinguishes this material from oils and liquid hydrocarbon fuels such as bio-oil, pyrolysis oil, bio-crude, renewable diesel, biodiesel, sustainable aviation fuel, which are derived from non-fossil sources such as biomass, $CO_2$, and hydrogen.

Carbon-negative crude oil has the same chemical composition as conventional crude oil and can be transported, refined, and consumed just like crude oil, because it *is* crude oil. What distinguishes carbon-negative crude oil from other oil is the way it is produced. Here, the term refers to combining reservoir engineering and extracting $CO_2$ from the atmosphere into a process in which more carbon is removed from the air and stored in the reservoir than is emitted during the production and consumption of the oil and its associated gas. The result is that the atmosphere contains less $CO_2$ after the production and consumption

S. Bryant (✉)
University of Calgary, Calgary, AB, Canada
e-mail: steven.bryant@ucalgary.ca



T. Walker et al. (eds.), *Sustainability in the Oil and Gas Sector*,
https://doi.org/10.1007/978-3-031-51586-6_7

of this oil than it would have contained otherwise, which is what makes it "carbon-negative." Carbon-negative processes are also categorized as "negative emissions" technologies.

That $CO_2$ is removed from air is a crucial aspect of carbon-negative crude oil. It distinguishes the process from a more widely discussed process which uses $CO_2$ captured from an industrial source. The latter process, commonly referred to as CCUS (carbon capture, utilization and storage), stores the captured $CO_2$ in oil reservoirs and thereby avoids emissions from the industrial source (Azzolina et al., 2015; Bachu, 2016; Hares, 2020; Lake et al., 2018; Núñez-López & Moskal, 2019). While this outcome is a beneficial one, the overall process is necessarily carbon-positive, because emissions from the production, refining, and burning of oil still enter the atmosphere.

Regardless of the $CO_2$ source, it is possible to manage the operation of the reservoir so that it contains more carbon in the form of $CO_2$ at the end of the process than the amount of carbon produced in the form of oil. As discussed below, such a management strategy is necessary for producing carbon-negative crude oil. It is not necessary for a CCUS project, but it obviously enables operators to increase the amount of avoided industrial emissions. In the context of mitigating climate change, however, the frame of reference for assessing whether the produced oil is carbon-negative is the atmosphere, not the reservoir used for storage.

Figure 7.1 illustrates a possible process for carbon-negative crude oil production. This example uses direct air capture (DAC), a process in which carbon is removed from the atmosphere using machines which extract $CO_2$ from the air, typically by bringing air into contact with liquid or solid sorbents (McQueen et al., 2021; Sandalow et al., 2018). The captured $CO_2$ is compressed and injected into the reservoir, where it occupies space previously occupied by reservoir fluids. Oil and associated gas are produced, marketed, and used in the existing infrastructure without modification. Brine is also produced along with oil and gas. In the case shown here, the produced brine is injected into other deep formations containing only brine. The produced brine could be used in other oilfield operations such as maintaining pressure in nearby reservoirs, and depending on its salinity, it could even be treated to become suitable for irrigation. The key difference from common oilfield practices is that much less produced brine is re-injected into the reservoir. The net removal of more brine from the reservoir frees more space for storing $CO_2$, which in turn makes the produced oil and associated gas more carbon negative.

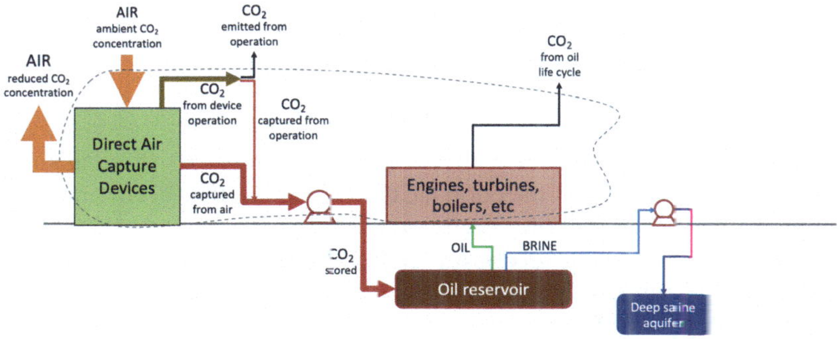


**Fig. 7.1** Carbon-negative crude oil can be produced by removing more $CO_2$ from the atmosphere, in this illustration by means of direct air capture devices, and storing it along with device process emissions in an oil reservoir (red arrow), than is emitted while operating the capture machines and while extracting, transporting, refining, and combusting oil and gas produced from that reservoir (black arrows). Brine is produced along with the oil (blue arrow). Instead of re-injecting the brine into the oil reservoir, as is commonly done in $CO_2$ enhanced oil recovery, it is injected into other deep formations containing brine (second blue arrow). The brine extraction is necessary to make enough room in the reservoir to store the volume of $CO_2$ required for carbon-negativity. The dashed curve illustrates the carbon balance of the process with respect to the atmosphere: more $CO_2$ leaves (thick red arrow) than enters (thin black arrows)

With this definition in place, we next describe the carbon accounting within the reservoir and over the full life cycle of the oil. These accounts determine whether the oil is in fact carbon negative. We then use extensive field data to evaluate the feasibility of producing carbon-negative crude oil. Finally, we survey the challenges of implementing carbon-negative crude oil as a sustainable way to use petroleum resources and simultaneously to address the need for $CO_2$ removal at scale.

## Carbon Accounting for Carbon-Negative Crude Oil

### *Reservoir Volumetrics*

The production of carbon-negative crude oil is similar to the enhanced recovery of oil by $CO_2$ injection ($CO_2$ EOR) as has been practiced commercially for the last fifty years, except when it comes to the source of $CO_2$. The simplest process for carbon-negative crude oil captures $CO_2$ directly from the atmosphere. In contrast, commercial $CO_2$ EOR was developed with $CO_2$ extracted from natural reservoirs and delivered by pipeline to regions such as the Permian Basin in Texas and New Mexico. These projects produce carbon-positive crude oil, because any $CO_2$ stored is not sourced from the atmosphere, and the oil production and consumption emits $CO_2$ into the atmosphere. Recently, projects have begun to use $CO_2$ captured from existing industrial processes such as power generation, steam-methane reforming, and fermentation. If the captured $CO_2$ is "fossil $CO_2$," i.e., the product of fossil fuel combustion, such projects avoid emissions but are not carbon-negative, as explained above. If the captured $CO_2$ is not from a fossil source, the EOR project could be carbon-negative, as long as the overall process removes more $CO_2$ from the atmosphere than it emits. For example, producing biomass then burning it to produce energy while capturing $CO_2$ from the flue gas (BECCS) can yield a net removal of $CO_2$ from the atmosphere, if suitably designed (Brack & King, 2020).

Operationally, producing carbon-negative crude oil is an exercise in volumetrics. For present purposes, it is useful to treat the volume of a reservoir as constant during the injection of $CO_2$ and the production of fluids. This assumption simplifies calculations: though the volume occupied by each fluid in the reservoir—$CO_2$, brine, oil—changes over the course of the process of producing carbon-negative crude oil, the sum of these volumes is constant during the process.

As illustrated in Fig. 7.2, before the process begins, the reservoir contains brine and oil.[1] $CO_2$ removed from the atmosphere is injected

[1] In practice, a gas phase may also be present. Extending the analysis to this situation is straightforward.

into the reservoir, and both brine and oil are produced.[2] Some of the produced brine may be re-injected, and the net production of brine is the difference between the total brine produced and the volume of brine which is re-injected. At the end of the process, as equation 7.1 below shows, the volume occupied by $CO_2$ in the reservoir is the volume in the reservoir previously occupied by oil and brine:

$$V_{\text{stored}CO_2} = V_{\text{netbrine}} + V_{\text{removedoil}}. \tag{7.1}$$

Note that $V_{\text{removedoil}}$ is the volume the oil occupied in the reservoir, not its volume at surface conditions. The distinction between surface and reservoir conditions is discussed below.

The carbon account for producing carbon-negative crude oil compares the mass of carbon removed from the atmosphere by the capture devices with the total mass of carbon in the emissions associated with the oil life cycle. The mass of carbon removed from the atmosphere by the capture devices is the mass of carbon captured from the atmosphere, denoted $M_c$, less the mass of any carbon emitted to the atmosphere while operating those devices, cf. Fig. 7.1. Operating emissions could arise if fossil fuels were burned to generate power or provide process heat for the devices. These emissions would be proportional to the mass of $CO_2$ captured from air and are thus denoted $\varepsilon M_c$. Burning the produced oil, $V_{\text{removedoil}}$, will emit the mass of carbon in that volume of oil, commonly referred to as "downstream" emissions. Additional $CO_2$ emissions arise from production operations, such as the generation of power for compressors and the delivery of heat to process equipment, and from transportation and refining. These "upstream" and "midstream" emissions are typically proportional to the amount of oil produced. Mathematically, carbon-negativity requires that at the end of the process, the mass of carbon removed (left hand side of Eq. [7.2]) exceeds the mass of carbon emitted (right-hand side of Eq. [7.2]):

$$M_c - \varepsilon M_c > w_{\text{oil}} \rho_{\text{oil}} V_{\text{removedoil}} + w_{CO_2} E_{u+m} V_{\text{removedoil}}, \tag{7.2}$$

[2] Injected $CO_2$ may eventually make its way to production wells, where it is produced along with brine and oil. This happens routinely in conventional $CO_2$ EOR. The $CO_2$ is separated in surface facilities and re-injected into the reservoir. The re-injection of $CO_2$ will also be necessary for carbon-negative crude oil. For simplicity, the production and re-injection of $CO_2$ are not shown in Fig. 7.2.

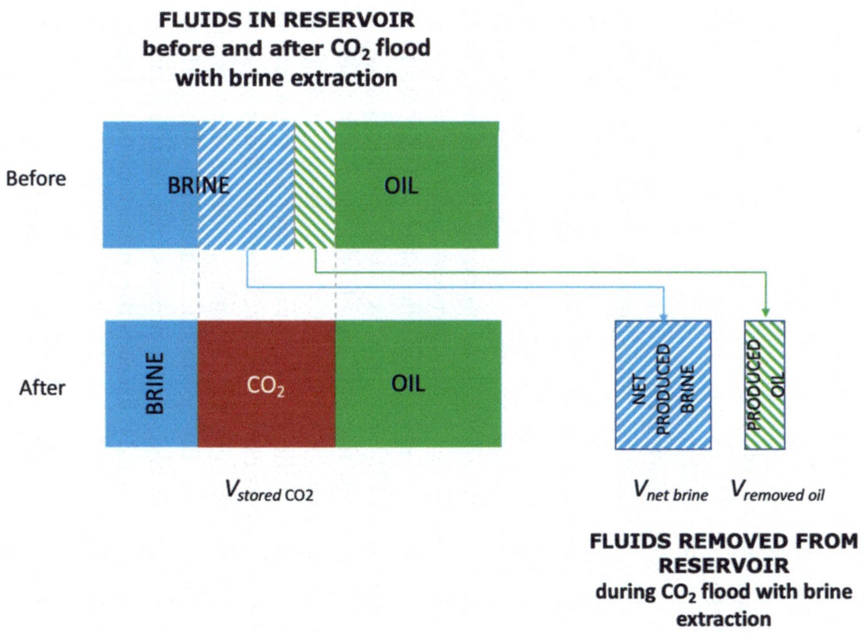


**Fig. 7.2** Before $CO_2$ enhanced oil recovery (EOR), the reservoir contains brine and oil. After $CO_2$ EOR, the reservoir contains $CO_2$, along with some of the initial oil and brine. The reservoir volume occupied by $CO_2$ is equal to the volume previously occupied by the produced oil plus the volume of net produced brine (Net produced brine is the difference between the total volume of produced brine and the volume of brine re-injected). Producing carbon-negative crude oil requires net production of large volumes of brine relative to the volume of oil produced

where $w_{CO_2}$ and $w_{\text{oil}}$ are the weight fractions of carbon in $CO_2$ and oil, respectively; $\rho_{\text{oil}}$ is the density of oil at the temperature and pressure of the reservoir; and $E_{u+m}$ is the mass of $CO_2$ emitted during upstream and midstream operations to produce a unit reservoir volume of oil.

As noted above, capture devices may produce $CO_2$ during operation. The devices may be designed to captured some of that produced carbon, which could be stored along with the $CO_2$ captured from air, cf. Fig. 7.1. Denoting this mass $\sigma M_c$, the total mass of carbon stored as $CO_2$ in the reservoir is $M_s = M_c + \sigma M_c$. This mass is proportional to the volume of stored $CO_2$:

$$M_s = w_{\text{CO}_2} \rho_{\text{CO}_2} V_{\text{storedCO}_2}, \tag{7.3}$$

where $\rho_{\text{CO}_2}$ is the density of $CO_2$ at the temperature and pressure of the reservoir. Combining Eq. (7.1)–(7.3) determines the volume of brine that must be removed from the reservoir to achieve carbon-negativity for a given volume of oil removed from the reservoir:

$$V_{\text{netbrine}} / V_{\text{removedoil}} > \frac{w_{\text{oil}} \rho_{\text{oil}} + w_{\text{CO}_2} E_{u+m}}{w_{\text{CO}_2} \rho_{\text{CO}_2} \frac{1-\varepsilon}{1+\sigma}} - 1. \tag{7.4}$$

When the ratio of brine removed to oil removed is equal to the right-hand side of Eq. (7.4), the oil will be "zero carbon," that is, just as much carbon will have been removed from the atmosphere as will have been produced during the production and consumption of the oil. When net brine production exceeds this threshold, the overall process will yield carbon-negative crude oil.

### *Carbon Densities of Reservoir Fluids*

Equation 7.4 relates the volumetrics of producing carbon-negative crude oil to the mass of $CO_2$ produced by operating the capture device (parameters $\varepsilon$ and $\sigma$, , which depend on the device design and energy sources), to the carbon densities of the reservoir fluids, and to the upstream + midstream emissions associated with the oil. The product $w\rho$ is the "carbon density" of a fluid in units of kg carbon per $m^3$ of fluid at reservoir temperature and pressure.

The weight fraction of carbon in $CO_2$ is 12/44. For reservoirs deeper than about 800 m, $CO_2$ exists as a supercritical phase, and its density (~700 kg/m$^3$) is much greater than that of gas phase $CO_2$. Thus, carbon-negative crude oil is not practical in shallow (<800 m) reservoirs. The density of supercritical $CO_2$ varies only slightly with reservoir temperature and pressure. A typical carbon density of stored $CO_2$ is therefore 190 kg C/m$^3$.

The carbon density of a given crude oil at reservoir conditions can be calculated from its routinely measured characteristics. Rather than consider specific oils, we determine carbon densities for typical ranges of these characteristics. The weight fraction of carbon in crude oils in the reservoir, $w_{\text{oil}}$, depends on the weight fraction of carbon at surface conditions, typically between 0.83 and 0.87, and $R_s$, the amount of gas dissolved in the oil in the reservoir. Dissolved gas is released and separated from the oil during processing at surface. Assuming all dissolved gas is produced and burned, whether in a flare, as fuel gas for field operations or by a purchaser, it is convenient to incorporate its contribution to emissions into the oil carbon density. Gas molecules have smaller weight fraction carbon (methane is smallest at 0.75), so oil in the reservoir has smaller weight fraction carbon than at surface conditions.

The density of oil in the reservoir, $\rho_{\text{oil}}$, depends mainly on its density at surface conditions and on $R_s$. The density of crude oil at surface conditions varies with composition. We consider ranges, with "light" oil between 825 and 875 kg/m$^3$ (30 < API gravity[3] < 40) and "medium" oil between 875 and 930 kg/m$^3$ (20 < API < 30). Dissolved gas decreases the density of oil. Consequently, a unit volume of crude oil at surface conditions (the "stock tank barrel," or STB, is the industry convention) occupies more volume when it is in the reservoir.[4]

Ranges of carbon densities of crude oils at reservoir conditions, $w_{\text{oil}}\rho_{\text{oil}}$, were calculated for light and medium oils, i.e., for the above ranges of API gravity, across typical ranges of temperature, pressure, $R_s$

[3] API gravity is defined as (141.5/SG)—131.5, where SG is the specific gravity of the fluid measured at a temperature of 60 °F.

[4] The ratio of reservoir volume occupied to the volume occupied in a tank at surface conditions is denoted $B_0$. This ratio is used extensively in this work to relate commonly used measures of oil volumes (STB) to the volumes relevant to producing carbon-negative crude oil.

and gas gravity using empirical correlations[5] derived from hundreds of reservoirs (Vasquez & Beggs, 1980).

Equations of state were used to calculate densities of natural gas, $CO_2$, and propane. The range of carbon density corresponds to the variation in temperature and pressure with depth, assuming typical gradients of 25 °C/km and 1 MPa/km, respectively, for depths between 1 and 4 km.

Figure 7.3 summarizes the results. In the reservoir, hydrocarbons in the liquid state, whether pure propane (shown for reference), gas condensate, or crude oil, have considerably greater carbon density (black dashed outlines) than $CO_2$. That this is the case guarantees that the right-hand side of Eq. (7.4) will be a positive number, even before accounting for upstream and midstream emissions or capture device emissions. This fact has important implications: it is not enough to simply replace the reservoir volume occupied by oil with $CO_2$ removed from the atmosphere in order to produce carbon-negative oil. Rather, a volume of reservoir brine determined by Eq. (7.4) must also be produced and discarded, and the vacated reservoir volume must be occupied by $CO_2$ removed from the atmosphere.

### *Upstream and Midstream Emissions*

The carbon density of the oil in the reservoir sets a lower bound on the net brine production required for carbon-negative crude oil. The actual required net brine production must offset the upstream and midstream emissions as well as the downstream emissions. The quantity $E_{u+m}$ in Eq. (7.4) is routinely expressed in terms of oil or refined product volumes at surface conditions.[6] For reference, a typical value of upstream emissions for a wide range of light and medium oils is 40 kg $CO_2e$/STB (Carnegie Endowment for International Peace, 2015). Using $CO_2$ for enhanced oil recovery is relatively energy intensive, however, and this process results in larger upstream emissions, with estimates ranging from 60 to 165 kg

[5] For reference, dissolved gas content $R_s$ was varied from 100 to 2000 standard cubic feet per stock tank barrel. The correlations also estimate $B_o$ to range from 1.07 to 1.5 for $100 < R_s < 1000$, and from 1.5 to 2.0 for $1000 < R_s < 2000$.

[6] Many field operations are powered by gas produced along with the oil. The analysis presented here double-counts the gas combustion in these fields, because the carbon density of the oil, Fig. 7.3, includes the dissolved gas. The consequent overestimation of emissions does not qualitatively alter our conclusions.

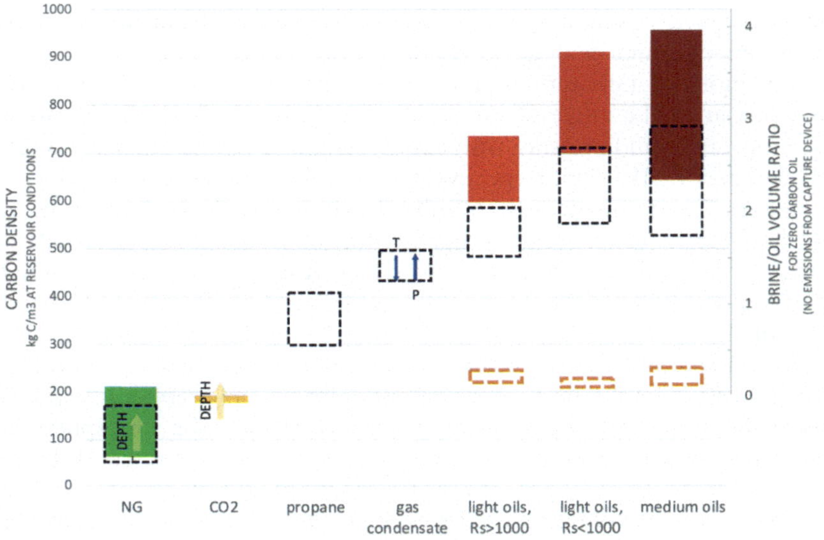


**Fig. 7.3** *Left axis*: Carbon density of fluids (kg of carbon per $m^3$ of fluid) at typical reservoir conditions is convenient for the carbon accounting of producing carbon-negative crude oil. Fluids are natural gas (NG), $CO_2$, and propane (shown for reference) in reservoirs at depths between 1 and 4 km, with gradients of temperature and pressure of 25 °C/km and 1 MPa/km, respectively; a representative gas condensate (composition C1 = 0.0366; C2 = 0.0547; C3 = 0.2507; i-C4 = 0.0675; n-C4 = 0.3009; i-C5 = 0.0579; n-C5 = 0.0948; and C6+ = 0.1369; $T$ between 60 and 122 °F; $P$ between 500 and 4000 psi); and crude oils with two ranges of density (light: 30 < API < 40; medium 20 < API < 30) and with dissolved gas concentration $R_s$ ranging from 100 to 2000 standard cubic feet of gas per stock tank barrel of oil, at temperatures between 80 and 220 °F. Black dashed outlines account for combustion emissions only; colored rectangles account for full life cycle emissions. Colored dashed outlines for oils account for upstream and midstream emissions only, relevant when oil used as feedstock rather than fuel. Arrows show direction of increasing depth, temperature or pressure. *Right axis*: ratio of volume of net produced brine to volume of produced oil measured at reservoir conditions for which the mass of $CO_2$ removed from the atmosphere equals the mass of $CO_2$ emitted during production, transportation, refining, and combustion of the oil. The ratio is calculated assuming the capture devices produce no $CO_2$ emissions (see text)

$CO_2e$/STB (Cooney et al., 2015; Jaramillo et al., 2009). These emissions may be ~35% smaller if the operating strategy seeks to increase $CO_2$ storage (Cooney et al., 2015). Similarly, midstream emissions for North American crude oils range from less than 20 kg $CO_2e$/STB for non-EOR production (Carnegie Endowment for International Peace, 2015) to ~55 kg $CO_2e$/STB for conventional $CO_2$ EOR (Cooney et al., 2015; Jaramillo et al., 2009).

For illustration, we consider a value of 125 kg $CO_2e$/STB for the combined upstream and midstream emissions. We incorporate these emissions into the carbon density of the oil at reservoir conditions, for convenience. The resulting ranges of effective carbon density, which include all emissions associated with the oil, are shown as colored rectangles in Fig. 7.3. As the right-hand axis of Fig. 7.3 shows, the ratio of net produced brine volume to oil volume required for zero-carbon crude oil ranges from 2 to 4, depending on the oil characteristics, when the capture device produces zero emissions ($\varepsilon = \sigma = 0$). The required ratios are larger when capture device emissions are stored and/or emitted. For example, the range is from 4 to 9 when $\varepsilon = 0.25$ and $\sigma = 0.5$ tonne C emitted by and captured from device operation, respectively, per tonne C captured from air. Ratios greater than these ranges result in carbon-negative crude oil.

### *How to Produce Carbon-Negative Natural Gas*

The carbon density of $CO_2$ is greater than that of natural gas (NG) at reservoir conditions (black dashed outline in Fig. 7.3), and as much as three times greater for reservoirs ~1 km deep. Thus, simply replacing the reservoir volume occupied by natural gas with $CO_2$ removed from the atmosphere can be sufficient to produce carbon-negative natural gas, as long as upstream and midstream emissions from production and transmission operations are modest. Because methane has much larger global warming potential than $CO_2$, leakage associated with natural gas production and distribution has a disproportionate effect. Consequently upstream + midstream emissions range quite widely, from as little as 3–4 g $CO_2e$/MJ (Liu et al., 2021) to more than 30 g $CO_2e$/MJ (International Energy Agency, 2021a). We consider for illustration a value of 15 g $CO_2e$/MJ and treat this value as an increment to the effective carbon density of natural gas in the reservoir, yielding the green rectangle in Fig. 7.3. Deep reservoirs have similar effective carbon density to $CO_2$

and can thus produce near-zero-carbon NG, but only relatively shallow reservoirs can produce significantly carbon-negative NG.

## Feasibility of Producing Carbon-Negative Crude Oil

The preceding discussion shows that producing carbon-negative crude oil requires net removal of significantly more brine than oil from the reservoir. The feasibility of this process thus hinges on brine management.

Field data from three dozen commercial $CO_2$ EOR projects (Lake et al., 2018), as can be seen in Fig. 7.4, show that in practice, net brine removal routinely exceeds oil removal. The data are expressed in "HCPV," which means that reservoir condition volumes are normalized by the volume of oil originally in the reservoir. At the end of about half of the projects, the ratio $V_{netbrine}/V_{removedoil}$ was between two and four. In this range of values, the mass of carbon stored equals the mass of life cycle carbon emissions for oils typical of these projects (cf. Fig. 7.3, right axis). The ratio was even larger in the early stages (less than 0.05 HCPV oil produced) of most projects. This is because $CO_2$ EOR typically is implemented when oil production is accompanied by very high rates of brine production after extensive waterflooding (the injecting of water to displace oil). During waterflooding, much of the produced brine is re-injected. When $CO_2$ EOR commences, less brine is injected so that $CO_2$ can be injected to mobilize oil that cannot be displaced by brine. Typically, there is a lag between $CO_2$ injection and an increased rate of oil production, which explains the steepness of most curves in Fig. 7.4 at early stages.

The projects in Fig. 7.4 were not operated with the intention to store $CO_2$. Nevertheless, many of them would have removed enough brine to produce carbon-negative crude oil, had the $CO_2$ been sourced from the atmosphere via a device with zero or low emissions ($0 < \varepsilon + \sigma < 0.3$). The question of feasibility of carbon-negative crude oil then hinges upon whether larger values of $V_{netbrine}/V_{removedoil}$ can be achieved. The data for brine and oil production from these projects, as seen in Fig. 7.5, shows that brine production exceeds oil production by a factor of five for the entire duration of nearly all projects and by a factor of ten for many

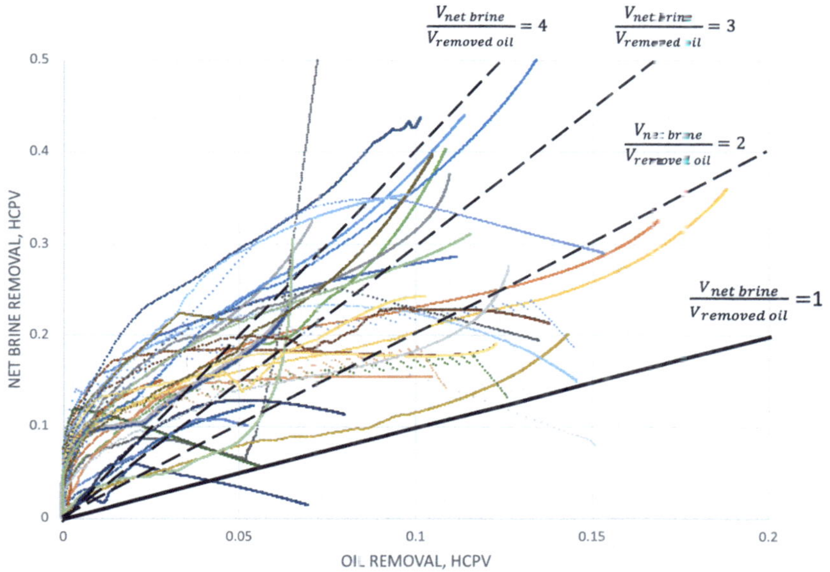


**Fig. 7.4** Plots of cumulative net brine and oil production from commercial $CO_2$ EOR projects (Lake et al., 2018) almost always fall above $\frac{V_{\text{netbrine}}}{V_{\text{removedoil}}} = 1$ (thick black line) throughout the project life. Indeed, the net volume of brine removed from the reservoir (i.e., produced but not re-injected) is usually more than twice the volume of oil extracted (cf. dashed black lines). Each set of colored points corresponds to one project. Volumes are corrected to reservoir conditions, as required for Eq. (7.1)–(7.4), and are expressed as fractions of HCPV, the volume originally occupied by oil in the reservoir

projects. This behavior is not specific to $CO_2$ EOR; rather, it is characteristic of mature conventional reservoirs. In most projects, more than 80% of the produced brine was re-injected, and for this reason the net brine removal ranged from 0.1 to 0.4 HCPV (cf. Fig. 7.4) even though brine production typically exceeds 1 HCPV (Fig. 7.5). Consequently, the option to increase $V_{\text{netbrine}}/V_{\text{removedoil}}$ exists during typical operations. For example, an operating strategy that disposes of half of the produced brine, e.g., by injecting it into disposal wells, and re-injecting the other half into the reservoir, would yield $V_{\text{netbrine}}/V_{\text{removedoil}} > 5$ for the entire duration of almost all of these field projects and $V_{\text{netbrine}}/V_{\text{removedoil}} > 8$ in many of them. This strategy may require additional surface facilities, e.g., flowlines to disposal wells, but because all $CO_2$ EOR strategies will inject all produced brine into subsurface formations, producing carbon-negative crude oil would incur essentially the same operating costs for injection as conventional $CO_2$ EOR.

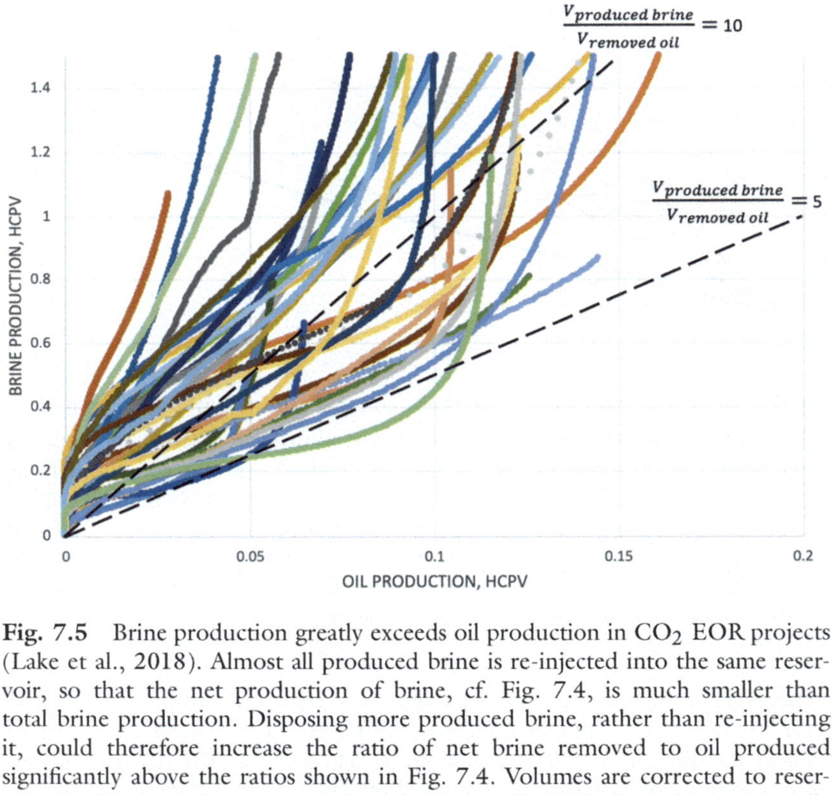


**Fig. 7.5** Brine production greatly exceeds oil production in $CO_2$ EOR projects (Lake et al., 2018). Almost all produced brine is re-injected into the same reservoir, so that the net production of brine, cf. Fig. 7.4, is much smaller than total brine production. Disposing more produced brine, rather than re-injecting it, could therefore increase the ratio of net brine removed to oil produced significantly above the ratios shown in Fig. 7.4. Volumes are corrected to reservoir conditions and are expressed as fractions of HCPV, the volume originally occupied by oil in the reservoir

## Scalability of Producing Carbon-Negative Crude Oil

The scales needed to describe pathways to net zero $CO_2$ emissions are daunting: replacing several sources of tens of exajoules of energy per year with new sources, mitigating emissions of gigatonnes of $CO_2$ per year, and accomplishing all this in one to three decades (DeAngelo et al., 2021; Fuss et al., 2018; International Energy Agency, 2021b; National Academies of Sciences, Engineering, and Medicine, 2019; Rogelj et al., 2018; The Royal Society, 2018; Yergin, 2021). Oil and its use in the transportation sector play a very large role in net zero pathways. Even with the rapid replacement of oil by alternative energy sources for transportation in the IEA's Net Zero Emissions pathway (NZE), oil consumption in the next three decades will be measured in tens of millions of barrels per day (International Energy Agency, 2021b). The goal of producing carbon-negative crude oil is not just to decarbonize transportation, but also to provide a near-term, scalable negative emissions technology. The NZE calls for 2 Gt/y of energy-related CDR by 2050, and other pathways call for 5–15 Gt/y by 2050 (International Energy Agency, 2021b).

Consider the production of one million barrels of carbon-negative crude oil per day (1 MMBOPD) from reservoirs containing oils of effective carbon density less than 700 kg C/Rm$^3$ and operated at $V_{netbrine}/V_{removedoil} = 5$. If the capture device produces zero-carbon emissions, this rate of carbon-negative crude oil production would remove 150–250 Mt $CO_2$/y from the atmosphere. The same operations with a low emissions capture device, for which $\varepsilon + \sigma < 0.3$ t $CO_2$/t $CO_2$ captured from air, would remove 50–100 Mt $CO_2$/y. However, a high emissions capture device, for example $\varepsilon = 0.25$ and $\sigma = 0.5$ t $CO_2$/ t $CO_2$ captured from air, would result in net positive emissions of $CO_2$ under these operating conditions. Increasing the brine removal to $V_{netbrine}/V_{removedoil} = 8$ enables larger rates of CDR for oils with larger effective carbon density. For example, producing 1 MMBOPD by coupling the low emissions capture device to reservoirs containing oils up to 850 kg C/Rm$^3$ would remove 100–300 Mt $CO_2$/y. Coupling the example high emissions capture device to reservoirs containing oils up to 700 kg C/Rm$^3$ would remove 50–100 Mt $CO_2$/y. These ranges of removal rates correspond to 5–10% of the NZE forecast need for $CO_2$ removal in 2050.[7]

Though 1 MMBOPD is only ~1% of global oil consumption in 2019 (BP P.L.C., 2021), it is not obvious whether sufficient reservoirs with oils of appropriate carbon densities exist to support this rate of carbon-negative crude oil production. For example, many reservoirs are at depths less than 1 km, where the density of stored $CO_2$ is too small. Achieving sufficiently large rates of $CO_2$ injection into tight reservoirs may prove difficult. Furthermore, in other reservoirs, oil is too viscous. Though not all reservoirs are candidates for producing carbon-negative crude oil, more detailed screenings of existing reservoirs for storing $CO_2$ during EOR support the potential for material rates of $CO_2$ removal, even though the economic intentions of these screenings were to avoid emissions, rather than to achieve negative emissions. Total $CO_2$ EOR production was 0.5 MMBOPD in 2019 (International Energy Agency, 2019), constrained primarily by availability of $CO_2$. Hares (2020) estimated that as much as 0.25 MMBOPD could be produced in Alberta via CCUS with favorable economics. Kuuskraa et al. (2011) estimated 2 MMBOPD could be produced by current state of the art $CO_2$ EOR in the United States. Thus, producing carbon-negative crude oil could contribute materially both to decarbonizing transportation and to removing $CO_2$ from the atmosphere, regardless of the actual path taken to achieve net zero.

## Challenges for Implementing Carbon-Negative Crude Oil

The advantage of producing carbon-negative crude oil is that it makes use of existing energy infrastructure (oil and gas production, processing and distribution; industrial, business and residential users; vehicle fleets and manufacturing facilities, especially heavy vehicles), decades of experience

[7] If each barrel of carbon-negative crude oil substitutes for a barrel of oil that would otherwise have been produced by existing methods, this would eliminate 175–250 Mt/y of $CO_2$ emissions. Though not a contribution to CDR, replacing the consumption of conventional oil in this way would slow the consumption of the remaining carbon budget, i.e., the amount of $CO_2$ that can still be emitted while preserving a chance to limit global warming below a target value.

in $CO_2$ EOR, and established global energy markets. As such, carbon-negative crude oil has a head start over other methods for achieving large rates of CDR.

The challenges of producing carbon-negative crude oil can be categorized into technical, market, and political uncertainties. All these challenges are heightened by the time scale for action: To be effective, many efforts to mitigate climate change must be implemented rapidly and simultaneously. The pace would be daunting even in a stable, predictable world. Sustaining that pace in the face of instability and uncertainty will require the resilience of both of technologies and societies.

### *Technical Uncertainties*

There is little field experience of $CO_2$ EOR at large (>4) ratios of net brine removal to oil removal for long periods of time. The re-injecting of produced brine, and the corresponding operation at small net brine removal rates, mitigates the tendency of injected $CO_2$ to flow through regions previously swept by injected $CO_2$. As $CO_2$ enters new unswept regions, oil production tends to increase. The disposal, rather than re-injection, of brine, and therefore the operation of the reservoir procedures at larger rates of net brine removal, may reduce the production of carbon-negative crude oil while increasing $CO_2$ production. The $CO_2$ produced would have to be re-injected, which would in turn reduce the rate at which $CO_2$ newly captured from the atmosphere could be stored. Alternatives to water injection, such as increasing the viscosity of the $CO_2$, exist but have not been widely deployed under the economics of conventional $CO_2$ EOR.

Producing one million barrels per day of carbon-negative crude oil would require capturing hundreds of Mt of $CO_2$ per year from the atmosphere. This process in turn would require replicating the largest direct air capture project under development in 2022 several hundred times. While replication appears feasible, the energy requirements for DAC are substantial. For example, a midrange estimate from an analysis (National Academies of Sciences, Engineering, and Medicine, 2019) of NG-fueled liquid sorbent capture is 15 GJ per net tonne $CO_2$ removed from the atmosphere by the overall process.[8] Direct capture of 500 Mt $CO_2$/y by

[8] The majority of NG combustion in this process yields a pure stream of $CO_2$ which is assumed to be stored. The remaining combustion emissions are assumed to be vented,

this device (enabling ~1 MMBOPD of carbon-negative crude oil and 50–100 Mt/y of CDR) would thus require power equivalent to 20 BCFD of natural gas. For reference, in 2021 the four most prolific basins in North America each produced 10–25 BCFD (C.E.R., 2023; EIA, n.d.). While existing energy infrastructure is therefore sufficient to power $CO_2$ removal at material rates, regions with large capacities for both EOR and gas production, such as the Permian Basin, the Western Canadian Sedimentary Basin, and the Middle East are advantageous locations for producing carbon-negative crude oil.

The use of existing gas production speeds up production of carbon-negative crude oil at scale, but also places a premium on reducing the energy required by the air capture device. The supplying of that energy via natural gas combustion produces $CO_2$ which must be avoided (captured and stored along with the $CO_2$ removed from the atmosphere) or emitted. The former increases the amount of brine that must be net produced to achieve a given amount of $CO_2$ removal. The latter reduces the rate of $CO_2$ removal. The consequences of either of these possibilities are significant. The example high emissions device ($\varepsilon = 0.25, \sigma = 0.5$) yields two to three times less CDR than a low emissions device ($\varepsilon + \sigma < 0.3$) for the same reservoir operating conditions. Thus the pace of development of scalable low emissions air capture devices will strongly influence the scale of carbon-negative crude oil's contribution to CDR.

## *Market Uncertainties*

### *Oil Demand for Transportation*

The anticipated wholesale shift to electricity and hydrogen for transportation will reduce oil demand by a factor of ten. Surely this makes investment in carbon-negative crude oil unwise? The answer to this question depends on how quickly this shift occurs. On the one hand, reducing oil consumption very rapidly, as envisioned in the IEA NZE, will still incur ~200 Gt $CO_2$ emissions from oil by 2050. Those emissions would consume a substantial fraction of the remaining carbon budget. This outcome suggests it would be unwise *not* to use carbon-negative crude oil to abate these emissions during the shift. On the other hand, the elimination of oil use also requires building infrastructure for zero-carbon energy

and these are subtracted from the amount of $CO_2$ removed from the atmosphere. The values used in the high emissions device example are drawn from this analysis.

generation and distribution. The scale of this infrastructure for transportation will be comparable to the current scale for gasoline, diesel, aviation fuel, etc. All net zero pathways call for this infrastructure to be built simultaneously with new infrastructure at a similar scale to replace other applications of fossil fuels. The longer it takes to build this infrastructure, the more valuable carbon-negative crude oil becomes for meeting climate targets.

The NZE pathway serves to illustrate the pace of this transition of infrastructure. Annual growth rates for projected wind and solar energy consumption from 2020 until 2050 derived from the NZE are plotted against the annual consumption of each energy source in Fig. 7.6. While recent growth rates for wind and solar are indeed large, current annual consumption is small, less than 10 EJ each, whereas oil, gas, and coal are well over 100 EJ each. Figure 7.6 shows that after consumption of any of world's dominant energy sources reaches 10 EJ, annual growth rates for that source are usually less than 5%, and the durations of sustained larger growth rates become shorter. Above this consumption threshold, no energy source has sustained 10% growth per annum for longer than three years. Only oil and gas have sustained more than 5% per annum for more than a decade, and that era ended in the mid-1970s. During the last fifty years, only coal sustained more than 5% growth per annum, and this rate lasted less than a decade. As the NZE example shows, adopting zero-carbon energy sources such as solar and wind fast enough to meet climate targets requires unprecedented sustained growth rates for these new sources.[9]

The influences on these historical trends are numerous, complicated and interdependent, not least because consumption requires coordination between generation, distribution, and end-user infrastructure. Many influences are unexpected or unpredictable, others apparent only in hindsight. To the extent that a similarly complex array of events pushes near-term wind and solar growth below the NZE pathway, decarbonization of transportation will be delayed, and carbon-negative crude oil will become increasingly useful to meet net zero targets on time.

[9] This pathway proposes unprecedented growth rates for wind and solar for 15–20 years followed by historically feasible growth rates for 10–15 years. For comparison, distributing growth uniformly across 30 years would reduce the annual rates to ~10%; sustaining that pace of growth for decades would also be unprecedented.

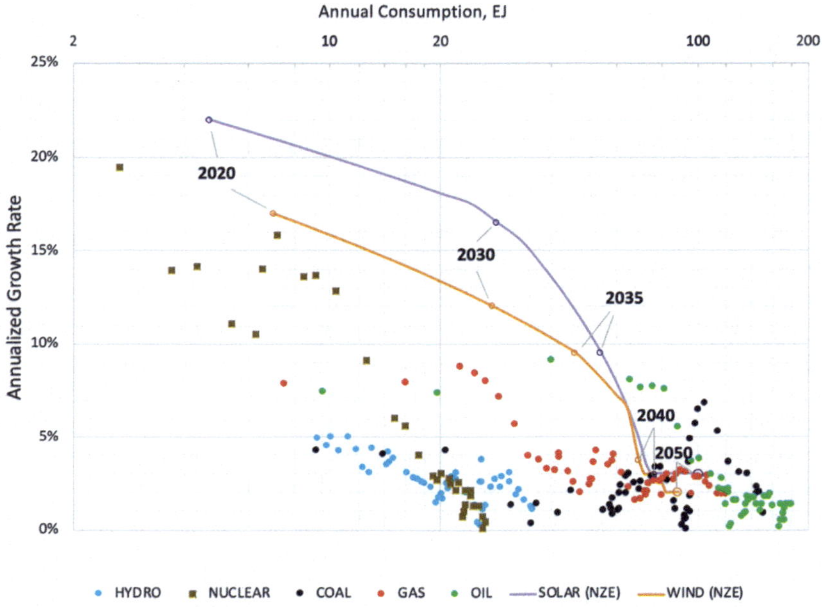


**Fig. 7.6** Historically, the growth rate of consumption of energy from a particular source decreases as the amount of consumption increases. *Filled symbols*: growth rates of the five largest global energy sources annualized over 5 y intervals vs consumption during first year of each interval (fossil fuels consumption pre-1965 from [Ritchie et al., 2020], all other consumption post-1965 from [BP P.L.C., 2021]; consumption less than 2 EJ per year not shown). Negative growth rates omitted for clarity. *Curves with open symbols*: annual growth rates of solar and wind consumption consistent with IEA NZE pathway from 2020 to 2050 (IEA, 2021b)

*Oil Demand, Non-transportation*

Non-combustion uses of crude oil, e.g., as a feedstock for petrochemicals, are independent of the demand for it as transportation fuel. The demand for non-combusted oil anticipated in the NZE in 2050 exceeds 10 million barrels per day, suggesting a significant opportunity for CDR via carbon-negative crude oil during the transition and beyond. Only the combustion of associated gas and the upstream + midstream emissions from $CO_2$ EOR operations contribute to the effective carbon density of non-combusted oil, making it comparable to the carbon density of

$CO_2$ at reservoir conditions, cf. colored dashed outlines in Fig. 7.3. Thus carbon-negative crude oil can be produced for use as a feedstock with much smaller ratios of net brine to oil removal. This means material contributions to CDR can be achieved even under current $CO_2$ EOR practice for brine handling. For example, producing one million barrels of non-combusted oil per day at $V_{netbrine}/V_{removedoil} = 3$, a ratio routinely observed in the projects in Fig. 7.4, would remove 50–100 Mt $CO_2$ from the atmosphere annually, depending on emissions from the capture device. Operating at $V_{netbrine}/V_{removedoil} = 5$ would remove 100–200 Mt $CO_2$/y. Because current refining capacity is designed to produce liquid fuels at about ten times the rate of petrochemicals production, a key question will be how to preserve and repurpose enough refining capacity to meet feedstock demand while decommissioning most existing capacity. A related question will be how to use the molecules which are prevalent in crude oil but will no longer be destined for liquid fuels.

*$CO_2$ Removal Demand*

Direct air capture is a convenient technology for the production of carbon-negative crude oil, but it is not the only means of removing $CO_2$ from the atmosphere. Nature-based solutions, hybrid technologies, and energy-producing alternatives such as BECCS (Griscom et al., 2017; McQueen et al., 2020; Sagues et al., 2019; Sandalow et al., 2020) can likely be implemented at lower costs than carbon-negative crude oil. However, none of these alternatives have been demonstrated at scale, some will be difficult to verify, others may not keep the removed carbon out of the atmosphere long enough, and some may have negative consequences on other parts of the environment, such as land and water. Thus, the key question is whether other approaches to carbon dioxide removal can reach material rates in time to meet climate targets. Because sufficient infrastructure for storage (oil reservoirs, wells) and energy supply for capture (gas production) already co-exist at scale, carbon-negative crude oil could make material contributions to $CO_2$ removal relatively rapidly. The larger question to ask will be that of how much society is willing to pay for CDR in any form alongside the costs of eliminating and avoiding emissions.

*Demand for Natural Gas*

The energy required to produce carbon-negative crude oil is large because capturing $CO_2$ from the atmosphere is inherently energy intensive.

Supplying this energy with natural gas would use existing infrastructure, which is often co-located with oil production, and would thereby accelerate the mitigation benefits of carbon-negative crude oil. A challenge to this process is that adding a substantial new consumer of natural gas further complicates the dynamics of fuel switching in net zero pathways. For example, some pathways call for increased natural gas consumption in the near-term to displace coal, and a new consumer could drive prices up or encourage new exploration and production for gas. Another new consumer sector may soon emerge which converts natural gas to hydrogen. In the longer term, all pathways anticipate steady reduction in gas consumption, and a new consumer which is also carbon-negative could be welcome. On the other hand, the production of gas in some regions is capital-intensive and may not survive a long-term decline in global demand. Finally, the major uses of natural gas, e.g., electricity generation and industrial processes, differ from the major use of oil, which is for transportation. Moreover, unlike crude oil, natural gas combustion emissions can be mitigated, e.g., by CCS at large fixed consumers and by decarbonization of the gas itself. Thus, on a pathway to net zero the demand for natural gas may become more decoupled from demand for oil, complicating its potential availability for producing carbon-negative crude oil.

### *Political Uncertainties*

#### *Fossil Fuel Dependency*

Some stakeholders may focus on the "crude oil" aspect of carbon-negative crude oil. Those who view elimination of fossil fuel consumption as a core element of the net zero transition may oppose carbon-negative crude oil altogether, regardless of whether it might be useful as a negative emissions technology. For example, it can be argued that in practice, the effect of CDR will be merely to prolong the consumption of fossil fuels (cf. Asayama [2021] and references therein), and given the imperative for action to address climate change, some object to any action that has this effect. Though carbon-negative crude oil is presented here as a near-term, scalable option for CDR, the explicit link to oil consumption may reinforce objections to it. To the extent that the objections are addressed to the *combustion* of fuels derived from oil, rather than to the oil itself, considering the non-combustion uses of oil could be important, as producing carbon-negative crude oil for this purpose could make even larger contributions to CDR. Meanwhile, other stakeholders, who benefit from tax revenues, royalty payments, dividends, wages, or profits from oil production and consumption, may support carbon-negative crude oil regardless of how it is used. Still other stakeholders will focus on the "carbon-negative" aspect of carbon-negative crude oil. These stakeholders may differ on the merits of this form of CDR relative to others (Kreuter & Lederer, 2021; Madhu et al., 2021). They may also differ on the need for and cost of negative emissions vs avoided and eliminated emissions.

Balancing these perspectives in a democratic society will not be simple, but seeking to do so will nonetheless be important because any form of $CO_2$ removal will require substantial investment. In order to encourage stakeholders to invest in carbon-negative crude oil, policymakers will have to provide a framework which accommodates the diversity of stakeholder perspectives and which is robust over the long term (Meckling & Biber, 2021).

*Transportation Pricing*

One way in which carbon-negative crude oil is advantageous compared to other forms of CDR, is in its production of a commodity that can be sold into an existing global market. Fuels refined from carbon-negative crude oil will provide exactly the same benefits as current fuels in terms of fuel efficiency, engine operation, maintenance, etc. However, the energy input to produce carbon-negative crude oil is larger than that of producing conventional crude oil, so the cost of producing carbon-negative crude oil will be correspondingly larger. Carbon-negative crude oil would thus occupy an unusual position in carbon markets: It would be more expensive than, but functionally equivalent to, conventional oil. As such, it would presumably be subject to taxes and policies intended to discourage $CO_2$ emissions, yet it would be operationally equivalent to other negative emissions technologies for which incentives such as carbon credits or fuel standards may be available.

As with other $CO_2$ mitigation strategies, a key question to ask is that of how the financial benefits and costs of carbon-negative crude oil are shared. Transportation end-users are unlikely to adopt carbon-negative crude oil fuels unless they are competitively priced relative to existing fuels in the near-term and relative to low-to-zero-carbon fuels in the longer term. In many jurisdictions, end-user fuel prices already include substantial levies or taxes, so there is both precedent and need for policy to play a crucial role in determining the price the consumer sees. In contrast, companies whose carbon footprint is dominated by transportation may be willing to pay a premium for the same fuels. Because oil producers could offset or eliminate their Scope 3 emissions at source with carbon-negative crude oil, they may attach additional intrinsic value to producing it. Revenue from carbon-negative crude oil and the ability to use existing infrastructure are likely to give its producers a competitive advantage over developers of other CDR technologies. Whether equity markets, lenders and governments will attach value to these considerations remains to be seen. A satisfactory price structure for carbon-negative crude oil is likely to be complicated, to say the least.

## Conclusion

Pathways to net zero now call for negative emissions (the removal of $CO_2$ from the atmosphere) in addition to the avoidance and elimination of emissions (e.g., capturing $CO_2$ from flue gas, replacing gasoline and diesel with electricity from renewable sources). In addition to mitigating hard-to-eliminate transportation emissions, carbon-negative crude oil could contribute a substantial portion of the needed negative emissions more rapidly and at lower cost than other technologies. Decades of field experience with $CO_2$ EOR confirm that the necessary reservoir operations are feasible, and a commercial scale demonstration of a technology that removes $CO_2$ from air is currently under construction.

Carbon-negative crude oil thus appears technically feasible, but as with many aspects of reaching net zero emissions, the more difficult challenges faced by carbon-negative crude oil are social, not technical. Issues such as how much carbon-negative crude oil will cost, who will bear that cost, and who will profit, can help or hinder its development. It is also important to ask whether we can establish coherent policies, regulations, incentives, and taxes so that capital is deployed at a scale sufficient for carbon-negative crude oil to help meet climate targets; whether or not removing one tonne of $CO_2$ from the atmosphere via carbon-negative crude oil is more or less desirable than other methods of removing that ton; whether or not it makes sense to use existing fossil fuel infrastructure and vehicles to remove $CO_2$ from the atmosphere, even as we are phasing out that infrastructure; and, whether or not it is possible to encourage carbon-negative crude oil use without discouraging the transition to electricity and hydrogen for transportation.

The period of time within which meaningful action must be taken is short, especially considering the magnitude of action needed in order to limit warming to 2 °C or less. Will carbon-negative crude oil merely perpetuate fossil fuel consumption, or is it a smart hedge against the possibility that renewable energy capacity does not get built fast enough to meet net zero targets? What will be the cost of *not* producing carbon-negative crude oil, if other ways of removing $CO_2$ do not get built to scale fast enough? Should we use carbon-negative crude oil to abate emissions from oil that will be consumed along the way to net zero, or should we accept those emissions as inevitable and attempt to manage the diminished carbon budget by other means?

The same time scale is long in terms of election cycles. Here, the social challenges go well beyond the particulars of carbon-negative crude oil, decarbonizing transportation and Negative Emissions Technologies. Is it possible to sustain the policy/regulation/incentives framework needed for deploying methods of eliminating emissions, avoiding emissions *and* removing $CO_2$ from the atmosphere for three decades—all while simultaneously adapting to the climate changes already underway?

The production of carbon-negative crude oil raises many challenges and questions. However, as far as the overarching challenge of addressing climate change is concerned, the more options available to mitigate it, the better, and carbon-negative crude oil puts another much-needed option on the table.

## References

Asayama, S. (2021). The oxymoron of carbon dioxide removal: escaping carbon lock-in and yet perpetuating the fossil status quo? *Frontiers in Climate, 3*, 72. https://doi.org/10.3389/fclim.2021.673515

Azzolina, N. A., Nakles, D. V., Gorecki, C. D., Peck, W. D., Ayash, S. C., Melzer, L. S., & Chatterjee, S. (2015). $CO_2$ storage associated with $CO_2$ enhanced oil recovery: A statistical analysis of historical operations. *International Journal of Greenhouse Gas Control, 37*, 384–397. https://doi.org/10.1016/j.ijggc.2015.03.037

Bachu, S. (2016). Identification of oil reservoirs suitable for $CO_2$-EOR and $CO_2$ storage (CCUS) using reserves databases, with application to Alberta, Canada.

*International Journal of Greenhouse Gas Control, 44*, 152–165. https://doi.org/10.1016/j.ijggc.2015.11.013

BP P.L.C. (2021). *Statistical review of world energy*. Retrieved (n.d.), from https://www.bp.com/content/dam/bp/business-sites/en/global/corporate/xlsx/energy-economics/statistical-review/bp-stats-review-2021-all-data.xlsx

Brack, D., & King, R. (2020). *Net zero and beyond: What role for bioenergy with carbon capture and storage?* Chatham House/The Royal Institute of International Affairs. https://www.chathamhouse.org/2020/01/net-zero-and-beyond-what-role-bioenergy-carbon-capture-and-storage-0/beccs-carbon-negative.

Carnegie Endowment for International Peace (CEIP). (2015). *Oil Climate Index: Profiling emissions in the supply chain*. Retrieved March 4, 2022, from https://oci.carnegieendowment.org/#supply-chain

Cooney, G., Littlefield, J., Marriott, J., & Skone, T. J. (2015). Evaluating the climate benefits of $CO_2$-enhanced oil recovery using life cycle analysis. *Environmental Science & Technology, 49*(12), 7491–7500. https://doi.org/10.1021/acs.est.5b00700

DeAngelo, J., Azevedo, I., Bistline, J., Clarke, L., Luderer, G., Byers, E., & Davis, S. J. (2021). Energy systems in scenarios at net-zero $CO_2$ emissions. *Nature Communications, 12*. https://doi.org/10.1038/s41467-021-26356-y

Energy Information Administration (EIA). (n.d.). *Natural gas explained: Where our natural gas comes from*. Retrieved October 18, 2022, from https://www.eia.gov/energyexplained/natural-gas/where-our-natural-gas-comes-from.php

Fuss, S., Lamb, W. F., Callaghan, M. W., Hilaire, J., Creutzig, F., Amann, T., Beringer, T., de Oliveira Garcia, W., Hartmann, J., Khanna, T., Luderer, G., Nemet, G.F., Rogelj, J., Smith, P., Vicente, J. L. V., Wilcox, J., del Mar Zamora Dominguez, M., & Minx J. C. (2018). Negative emissions-Part 2: Costs, potentials and side effects. *Environmental Research Letters, 13*(6). https://doi.org/10.1088/1748-9326/aabf9f

Government of Canada, C.E.R. (2023, February 22). *Markettable natural gas production in Canada*. Retrieved October 18, 2022, from https://www.cer-rec.gc.ca/en/data-analysis/energy-commodities/natural-gas/statistics/marketable-natural-gas-production-in-canada.html

Griscom, B. W., Adams, J., Ellis, P. W., Houghton, R.A., Lomax, G., Miteva, D. A., Schlesinger, W. H., Shoch, D., Siikamäki, J. V., Smith, P., Woodbury, P., Zganjar, C., Blackman, A., Campari, J., Conant, R. T., Delgado, C., Elias, P., Gopalakrishna, T., Hamsik, M. R., Herrero, M., Kiesecker, J., Landis, E., Laestadius, L., Leavitt, S. M.., Minnemeyer, S., Polasky, S., Potapov, P., Putz, F. E., Sanderman, J., Silvius, M., Wollenberg, E., & Fargione, J. (2017). Natural climate solutions. *Proceedings of the National Academy of Sciences of the United States of America*, *114*(44), 11645–11650. https://doi.org/10.1073/pnas.1710465114

Hares, R. (2020). *Feasibility of CCUS to $CO_2$-EOR in Alberta* (Unpublished master's thesis). University of Calgary. https://hdl.handle.net/1880/112625

International Energy Agency (IEA). (2019). *Can $CO_2$-EOR really provide carbon-negative oil?* Retrieved (n.d.), from https://www.iea.org/commentaries/can-co2-eor-really-provide-carbon-negative-oil

International Energy Agency (IEA). (2021a). *Methane Tracker 2021*. Retrieved (n.d.), from https://www.iea.org/reports/methane-tracker-2021.

International Energy Agency (IEA). (2021b). *Net zero by 2050—A roadmap for the global energy sector*. https://www.iea.org/reports/net-zero-by-2050

Jaramillo, P., Griffin, W. M., & McCoy, S. T. (2009). Life cycle inventory of $CO_2$ in an enhanced oil recovery system. *Environmental Science and Technology*, *43*(21), 8027–8032. https://doi.org/10.1021/es902006h

Kreuter, J., & Lederer, M. (2021). The geopolitics of negative emissions technologies: Learning lessons from REDD+ and renewable energy for afforestation, BECCS, and direct air capture. *Global Sustainability*, *4* https://doi.org/10.1017/sus.2021.24

Kuuskraa, V. A., Van Leeuwen, T., & Wallace, M. (2011). *Improving domestic energy security and lowering $CO_2$ emissions with "Next Generation" $CO_2$-Enhanced Oil Recovery ($CO_2$-EOR)*. (DOE/NETL-2011/1504). U.S. Department of Energy. https://www.netl.doe.gov/sites/default/files/netl-file/NextGen_CO2_EOR_06142011.pdf

Lake, L., Lotfollahi, M., & Bryant, S. (2018, October 21–26). *Fifty years of field observations: Lessons for $CO_2$ storage from $CO_2$ enhanced oil recovery* (Paper Presentation). 14th Greenhouse Gas Control Technologies Conference 2018, Melbourne, Australia. https://doi.org/10.2139/ssrn.3366254

Liu, R. E., Ravikumar, A. P., Bi, X. T., Zhang, S., Nie, Y., Brandt, A., & Bergerson, J. A. (2021). Greenhouse gas emissions of Western Canadian natural gas: Proposed emissions tracking for life cycle modeling. *Environmental Science & Technology*, *55*(14), 9711–9720. https://doi.org/10.1021/acs.est.0c06353

Madhu, K., Pauliuk, S., Dhathri, S., & Creutzig, F. (2021). Understanding environmental trade-offs and resource demand of direct air capture technologies through comparative life-cycle assessment. *Nature Energy*, *6*(11), 1035–1044. https://doi.org/10.1038/s41560-021-00922-6

McQueen, N., Kelemen, P., Dipple, G., Renforth, P., & Wilcox, J. (2020). Ambient weathering of magnesium oxide for $CO_2$ removal from air. *Nature Communications*, *11*, 3299. https://doi.org/10.1038/s41467-020-16510-3

McQueen, N., Vaz Gomes, K., McCormick, C., Blumanthal, K., Pisciotta, M., & Wilcox, J. (2021). A review of direct air capture (DAC): Scaling up commercial technologies and innovating for the future. *Progress in Energy*, *3*. https://doi.org/10.1088/2516-1083/abf1ce

Meckling, J., & Biber, E. (2021). A policy roadmap for negative emissions using direct air capture. *Nature Communications, 12*(1). https://doi.org/10.1038/s41467-021-22347-1

National Academies of Sciences, Engineering, and Medicine. (2019). *Negative emissions technologies and reliable sequestration: A research agenda*. The National Academies Press. https://doi.org/10.17226/25259

Núñez-López V., & Moskal, E. (2019). Potential of $CO_2$-EOR for near-term decarbonization. *Frontiers in Climate, 1*. https://doi.org/10.3389/fclim.2019.00005

Ritchie, H., Roser, M., & Rosado, P. (2020). *Energy*. Retrieved (n.d.), from https://ourworldindata.org/energy

Rogelj, J., Shindell, D., Jiang, K., Fifita, S., Forster, P., Ginzburg, V., Handa, C., Kheshgi, H., Kobayashi, S., Kriegler, E., Mundaca, L., Séférian, R., & Vilariño, M. V. (2018). *Mitigation pathways compatible with 1.5°C in the context of sustainable development* (Masson-Delmotte, V., Zhai, P., Pörtner, H.-O., Roberts, D., Skea, J., Shukla, P. R., Pirani, A., Moufouma-Okia, W., Péan, C., Pidcock, R., Connors, S., Matthews, J. B. R., Chen, Y., Zhou, X., Gomis, M. I., Lonnoy, E., Maycock, T., Tignor, M., & Waterfield, T., Eds.). Cambridge University Press. https://doi.org/10.1017/9781009157940.004

Sagues, W. J., Park, S., Jameel, H., & Sanchez, D. L. (2019). Enhanced carbon dioxide removal from coupled direct air capture–bioenergy systems. *Sustainable Energy & Fuels, 3*(11), 3135–3146. https://doi.org/10.1039/C9SE00384C

Sandalow, D., Friedmann, J., McCormick, C., & McCoy, S. (2018). *Direct air capture of carbon dioxide*. ICEF Roadmap 2018. https://www.icef.go.jp/pdf/summary/roadmap/icef2018_roadmap.pdf

Sandalow, D., Aines, R., Friedmann, J., McCormick, C., & Sanchez, D. (2020). *Biomass Carbon Removal and Storage (BiRCS) Roadmap* (No. LLNL-TR-815200). U. S. Department of Energy. Retrieved (n.d.), from https://doi.org/10.2172/1763937

The Royal Society. (2018). *Greenhouse gas removal*. Royal Academy of Engineering. https://royalsociety.org/-/media/policy/projects/greenhouse-gas-removal/royal-society-greenhouse-gas-removal-report-2018.pdf

Vasquez, M., & Beggs, H. (1980). Correlations for fluid physical property prediction. *Journal of Petroleum Technology, 32*(6), 968–970. https://doi.org/10.2118/6719-PA

Yergin, D. (2021, November). Why the energy transition will be so complicated. *The Atlantic*. https://www.theatlantic.com/international/archive/2021/11/energy-shock-transition/620813/

CHAPTER 8

# HydroFlame and Gas-Assisted Gravity Drainage: Two Technologies That Enable Environmental Sustainability in the Oil & Gas Industry

*Dandina N. Rao and Bikash D. Saikia*

## Introduction

Capturing carbon dioxide from the burning of fossil fuels and sequestering it safely from the atmosphere is a twenty-first-century grand challenge posed by the National Academy of Engineering (NAE). Hydroflame technology tackles two major environmental challenges facing the oil and gas industry while simultaneously yielding the additional economic benefit of significantly improving oil recovery from remote and marginal oil fields in the United States and elsewhere. The novel HydroFlame

D. N. Rao (✉) · B. D. Saikia
Craft and Hawkins Department of Petroleum Engineering, Louisiana State University, Baton Rouge, LA, USA
e-mail: dnrao@lsu.edu

B. D. Saikia
e-mail: bsaiki1@lsu.edu



T. Walker et al. (eds.), *Sustainability in the Oil and Gas Sector*,
https://doi.org/10.1007/978-3-031-51586-6_8

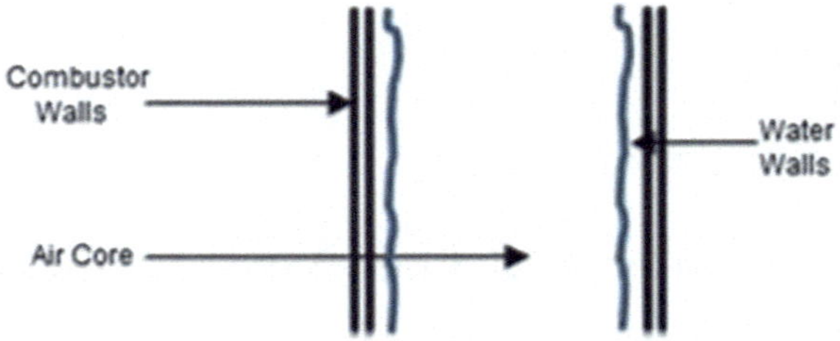


**Fig. 8.1** Illustration of air core surrounded by water walls inside combustor

process, in which a flame is in direct contact with feed water, provides an innovative solution to the major two-fold environmental problem of flared gas and produced water recycling. This is achieved by creating rotating films of the feed water so as to cover the combustor's inner walls and igniting a flame within the air core of the rotating body of water. Figure 8.1 illustrates this concept. The combustor walls are only exposed to the incoming water temperature, thereby eliminating thermal stresses that result in combustor failure.

The core design of the HydroFlame (HF) heat transfer process, originally implemented in the HF direct contact steam generator, is a high intensity flame always surrounded by two films of rotating water (the flame is in direct contact with the water). Feed water is tangentially injected at the base of the combustion chamber, forming along the interior surface of the container a continuous, inertially rotating liquid vortex flow of spiraling water which contains a substantially liquid free core within the chamber. High intensity flames are generated in the liquid free core within the chamber by injecting air and fuel at the top of the combustion chamber. A tangential supply of air creates a vortex recirculation zone where hot gases from the flame are recirculated to the base of the flame, thereby providing a continuous source of ignition of the injected fuel. Figure 8.2 shows the dimensions of a 1 MMBtu/h combustor, and a photograph of it in operation where the solid metal combustion chamber has been replaced with a polycarbonate plastic tube to demonstrate the flame-in-water concept. Two films of rotating water protect the combustion chamber walls from the flame in the middle of the chamber. Experiments conducted at the HydroFlame test facility in Baton Rouge have shown that the combustion chamber wall temperatures do not rise above 120 °F (48.9 °C) even when there is a 2500 °F

(1371 °C) flame in the core. Due to this cooling of walls by water films, there is no thermal degradation of the combustion chamber walls due to thermal stresses and cracking. This internal cooling of combustor walls by injected water also enables the use of poorer quality waters than conventional heaters. This aspect is currently being tested. The hydrodynamic stability of the rotating body of water and the aerodynamic stability of the flame complement each other, resulting in an elegant solution to the ancient problem of combustion containment.

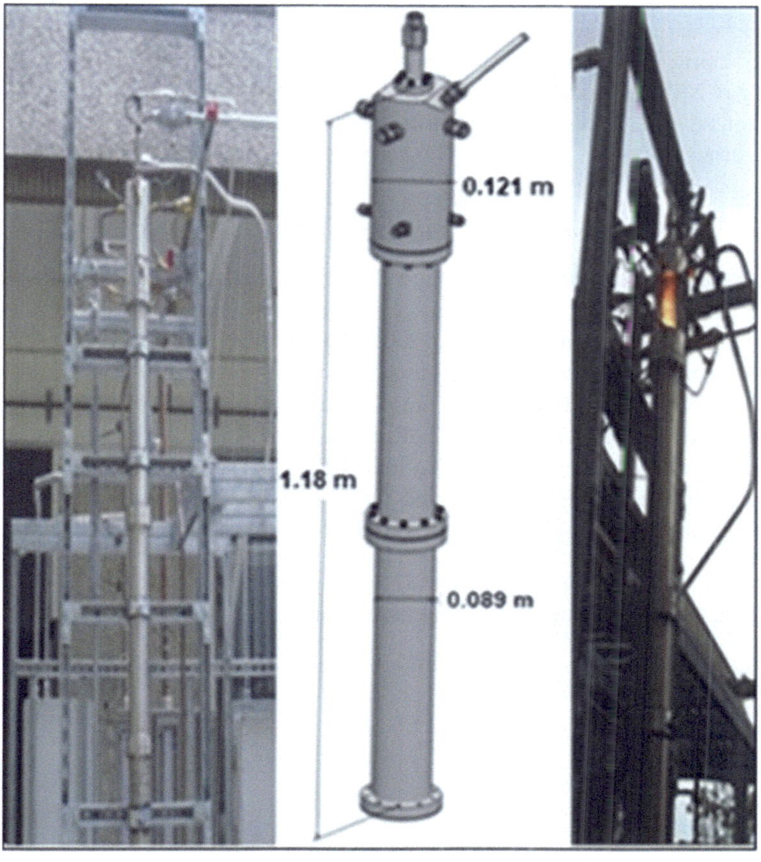


**Fig. 8.2** Dimensions and photograph of 1 MMBtu/h HydroFlame combustor

This revolutionary concept enables the capture of natural gas that is currently flared from stranded oil fields (conventional, unconventional, and shale), resulting not only in energy waste, but also in significant $CO_2$ emissions. This otherwise-wasted natural gas can be utilized as fuel for the HydroFlame process where it burns in a vortex water stream to generate a mixture of flue gas and steam (or hot water). The thermal energy can be used to run a turbine which operates a compressor to compress the air required for combustion, which improves operational efficiency. The thermal energy of combustion can also be used to remove scale-forming salts (calcium and magnesium sulfates and carbonates) from produced water, creating a significant supply of softened water that can be used for fracking in tight (shale) oil reservoirs or for agricultural purposes. The flue gas is then injected into the oil field to carry out gas injection-based Enhanced Oil Recovery operations thereby eliminating $CO_2$ emissions altogether.

## Development of HydroFlame Technology

The HydroFlame concept has been developed (as a hot water and steam generator) through several stages of testing (as shown in Table 8.1)—from research to bench-scale models to pilot demonstrations to oil field deployments—and can be considered to be at the technology readiness level (TRL) of 6–7. The HydroFlame combustors have been designed and tested at four different levels of heat duties. The operating pressures, heat duties, and by-products are shown in Table 8.1. Table 8.1 also shows that the HydroFlame unit can be scaled up to the desired capacity depending on the particular requirements of the field.

**Table 8.1** HydroFlame technology development progress

| *Model #* | *Capacity (Btu/h)* | *Operating pressure (psig)* | *Product* |
|---|---|---|---|
| 1 | 340,000 | 15 | Hot water |
| 2 | 750,000 | 50 | Steam + flue gas |
| 3 | 1,000,000 | 100 | Steam + flue gas (pilot + lab scale) |
| 4 | 5,000,000 | 500 | Steam + flue gas (field tested scale) |

**Table 8.2** Mass and energy balances of several tests of Model #1

| *Run #* | *119* | *118* | *201* | *203* |
|---|---|---|---|---|
| $\Phi$ | 0.889 | 0.937 | 0.999 | 1.040 |
| $\Delta H_{gen}(MJ/h)$ | 192.84 | 185.57 | 150.58 | 143.77 |
| Vaporization(%) | 1.59 | 1.65 | 0.84 | 0.86 |
| $\Delta H_{water}(MJ/h)$ | 143.45 | 143.45 | 135.13 | 130.13 |
| $\Delta H_{evap}(MJ/h)$ | 30.92 | 32.08 | 16.24 | 16.71 |
| $\Delta H_{CO}(MJ/h)$ | 5.98 | 4.34 | 0.90 | 1.08 |
| $\Delta H_{gas}(MJ/h)$ | 4.77 | 4.69 | 3.03 | 2.97 |
| $\Delta H_{total}(MJ/h)$ | 185.11 | 184.56 | 155.30 | 150.89 |
| Error(%) | 4.01 | 0.54 | −3.13 | −4.95 |
| $\frac{\Delta H_{water}}{\Delta H_{total}}(\%)$ | 77.49 | 77.73 | 87.01 | 86.24 |
| $\frac{\Delta H_{evap}}{\Delta H_{total}}(\%)$ | 16.70 | 17.38 | 10.46 | 11.07 |
| $\frac{\Delta H_{CO}}{\Delta H_{total}}(\%)$ | 3.23 | 2.35 | 0.58 | 0.72 |
| $\frac{\Delta H_{gas}}{\Delta H_{total}}(\%)$ | 2.58 | 2.54 | 1.95 | 1.97 |
| Massin(g/s) | 18.41 | 18.32 | 15.13 | 15.08 |
| Massout(g/s) | 19.01 | 18.82 | 15.33 | 15.40 |
| Error(%) | −3.29 | −2.72 | −1.33 | −2.15 |

Preliminary mass and energy balances were carried out for the smallest combustor designed (Model #1) and the error percentage was observed to be below < ± 5% as indicated in Table 8.2.

## Testing of 5-MMBtu/h HydroFlame Combustor

Based on the results from the 1 MMBtu/h model, a 5-MMBtu/h skid-mounted HydroFlame combustor (shown in Fig. 8.3) with fully automated operation and equipped with data acquisition capability was designed, constructed, and tested successfully at Louisiana State University's Well Facility in Baton Rouge, LA. The combustor operated continuously for 48 hours without human intervention. Figure 8.4 shows the temperature profiles that were captured throughout the testing. The temperatures of combustion chamber wall and the expansion chamber wall were always less than 100 °F throughout the run—demonstrating the effectiveness and uniqueness of the HydroFlame concept. The steam

**Fig. 8.3** 5-MMBtu/h—600 psi HydroFlame steam generator on a skid-mounted trailer

output temperature was measured as 425 °F at 500 psig which was in close agreement with the steam table properties. The flame temperature was measured to be 2200 °F.

## Field Operation of 5-MMBtu/h HydroFlame Unit in a Louisiana Oil Field

The first field test of the 5-MMBtu/h steam generator was conducted in a heavy oil field in Louisiana during February–April, 2012. Reservoir depth and oil gravity were 1100 feet, and 16.8° API, respectively. Figure 8.5 shows the 5-MMBtu/h–500 psi HydroFlame steam generator in operation at an oil field in Louisiana. The test well, last produced in 1985 at 5 BOPD, had declined to 2 BOPD and been shut-in. Production attempts were made in 2006 which failed to produce any oil. When steam and flue gas from the surface were injected into this well—using the 5-MMBtu/h

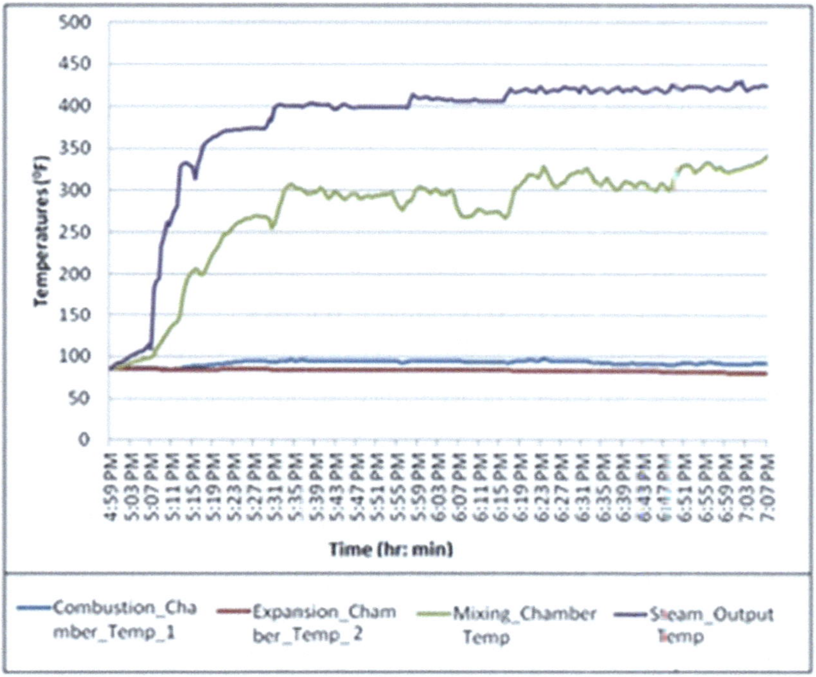


**Fig. 8.4** Example temperature profiles recorded during the 48-hour continuous test of a 5-MMBtu/h HydroFlame combustor

HydroFlame steam generator in a Cyclic Steam Simulation (CSS) process, a total of 1153 bbls of oil were produced over a few months when the well was put into production after a week of steam injection/soaking. In April–May 2014, a second cycle of steam injection was started on the same well for one week. The well tested at 14 BOPD when placed on production in mid-May 2014. It accumulated 1698 bbls of oil as of October 2014, and, as per the previous report from the Producing Company, it was still continuing to produce at 9 BOPD. These two field tests clearly demonstrated the continuous automated operating capability of the HydroFlame combustor with data acquisition, and the immense benefit of combustion flue gases injected with the steam in maintaining reservoir pressure, and pushing the heated oil out of the reservoir for extended periods of production. Similar benefits of combustion flue gas injection with steam have been documented and reported in the existing literature (Fox & Donaldson, 1985; Mohsenzadeh et al., 2012).

Table 8.3 provides a summary of the findings from downhole steam generator field tests carried out in the 1980s. When compared to conventional steam alone tests, the steam/oil ratio in the Midway Sunset field tests dropped by 30–50% using the downhole steam generator. This result can be attributed to the injection of combustion flue gases along with steam.

## HydroFlame Process for Produced Water Treatment

Produced water, which is produced with the oil and gas, is a byproduct of the oil and gas industry. Enormous volumes of produced water are generated on a daily basis from both conventional and unconventional reservoirs, either as a result of the regular production process or during the flow back following hydraulic fracturing. The shale boom that nearly doubled the US oil production has also significantly increased the generation of produced water. This is because shale boom thrives on hydraulic fracturing, which consumes tons of water in the form of frac water, and subsequently generates prolific amounts of produced water. Handling produced water is a growing environmental and economic concern of the oil and gas sector. There is also a growing regulatory pressure on the twin challenges of flaring and handling produced water. For instance, Pennsylvania regulations prohibit disposal wells, forcing produced water to be trucked to an injection well, which can be time consuming and very expensive. Outside of Pennsylvania, in Texas for example, many local jurisdictions now require that produced water be recycled. While regulatory pressures encourage operators to recycle flared gas and produced water, so too are there economic benefits to this recycling, especially as operators gain operational experience in shales. For example, in Marcellus Shale play (PA), due to dwindling water resources and the realization that frac water does not need to be pristine to begin with, operators are turning to recycling produced water. Sub-surface disposal of produced water typically costs them $4/barrel, including trucking. Gradually, however, recycling is becoming increasingly economically viable due to the limited availability of fresh water. The Marcellus Shale extends more than 34,000,000 acres with estimates of recoverable gas at 50 Tcf (Belvalkar & Oyewole, 2010;

**Fig. 8.5** 5-MMBtu/h—500 psi HydroFlame steam generator in operation at an oil field in Louisiana

**Table 8.3** Summary of downhole steam generator field tests (Fox & Donaldson, 1985)

| *Field* | *Wilmington (CA)* | *Midway Sunset (TX)* | | *Medina County (TX)* |
|---|---|---|---|---|
| Depth (ft) | 2000–2500 | 1200 | | 900 |
| Thickness (ft) | 8–120 | 500 | | 7–40 |
| API gravity | 12–16° | 14° | | 22° |
| Oil viscosity (cp) | 280 @ 115 °F | 165 @ 100 °F | | 200 @ 80 °F |
| Operating data | #z1-44: 4 MM Btu/h @ 1400 psi for 6 months<br>#J-113: 3.5 MM Btu/h @ 1800 psi for 6 months<br>#z1-37: 2 month Cyclic Steam Stimulation (graph) | Cyclic stimulation | | 7 wells cyclic stimulation |
| SOR (conventional) | – | #73: 1.67 | #102: 1.96 | – |
| SOR (DHSG) | Excellent results—operation expanded | #73: 1.16 | #102: 0.99 | 1.18–1.33 |

Hayes, 2010). Two significant challenges facing the development of this shale play are:

i. The availability of water for drilling and hydraulic fracturing, and
ii. The disposal of frac flowback and produced water.

Hydraulic fracturing is a necessary step in the completion of shale gas wells in order to achieve economic well performance. The average total volume of fluid injected per well for hydraulic fracturing in the Marcellus has been about 2.8 million gallons (Gaudlip & Paugh, 2008). The cost of the water obtained from public water supplies must be covered by shale gas developers. The reuse of the treated frac flowback water and of produced water could reduce the need for fresh water and also cut costs associated with obtaining fresh water from public water sources. Hence, it is necessary to develop a cost-effective process for treating both produced water and flowback water, which would be extremely advantageous for the oil and gas industry both economically and environmentally.

Oil-field produced waters that can be used without extensive pre-treatment are made possible by the HydroFlame concept's distinctive reversal in the direction of heat transfer. Figure 8.6 shows a schematic presentation of a conventional shell-and-tube heat transfer process and Figure 8.7 compares it with HydroFlame's direct contact combustion system, where the produced water is directly injected along the combustion chamber walls thereby avoiding heat transfer through metallic walls. In the shell-and-tube system, the heat transfer occurs through metal walls where scale-forming solid deposits may adhere to the heat exchanger's inner walls as the produced water is heated to higher temperatures. However, since the solid deposits of scales are carried through the water films along the walls, the HydroFlame concept's direct contact heat transfer enables HydroFlame combustors to use produced water directly as feed water without much pre-treatment.

A major Canadian heavy oil producer's produced water composition was used to carry out the produced water testing on the 1 MMBtu/h HF unit. This produced water contained ions of sodium, chlorides, magnesium, bicarbonate, potassium, calcium, and sulfate with a TDS of 1600 ppm. The original tool design, which included the following sections—burner head, heat transfer zone, and spray quench zone—was modified for this test. Figure 8.8 shows the original tool setup of DCSG with spray quench zone.

The spray quench section, where the hot combustion products and the feed water are mixed, was replaced with a long heat transfer section which is in fact a continuation of the heat transfer zone. The purpose

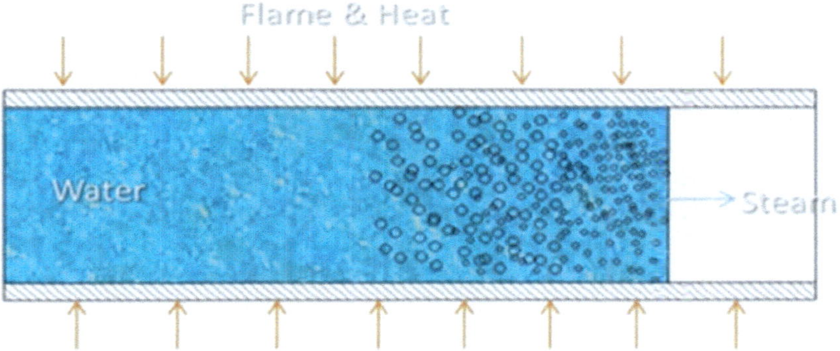


**Fig. 8.6** Indirect shell-and-tube heat exchange in conventional once-through steam generators

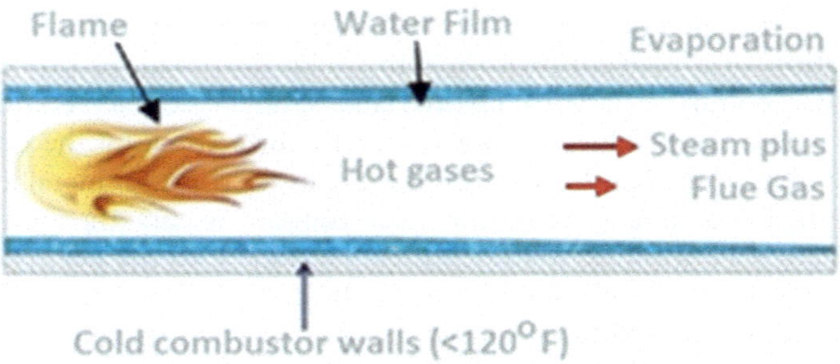


**Fig. 8.7** Direct contact heat transfer in HydroFlame devices

of this elongated heat transfer section is to induce film wise evaporation of the water, rather than droplet evaporation (which occurs in the spray quench section). This new design ensures that the water is not entrained in the gases as droplets, but rather exists as a film on the pipe wall. Thus, the salts are held in solution in the water film preventing precipitation and deposits, i.e., scaling. The testing also involved reconfiguring some of the systems in order to run the water in a batch mode to allow mixing of the salts. During the testing, two water tanks were used to hold simulated produced water and to allow a continuous run of the tool for two hours. Figure 8.9 shows the modified tool setup of DCSG with a longer heat transfer section.

Two scale coupons were inserted into the flow system—one close to the end of the steam generator, and the other in the horizontal exhaust pipe section. At the end of the test period, there was no visible scale on either coupon. The coupons were sent to the lab for further analysis, where X-Ray Diffraction (XRD) and Energy Dispersive X-Ray (EDX) analyses were performed on both. There was no detectable amount of scale on the coupon in the horizontal exhaust pipe section. The coupon inserted into the steam generator had some minor scale deposits (although not visible to the naked eye) primarily composed of calcium, phosphorus, and oxygen. However, the amount of scale was insufficient and below the quantifiable limit. The success of the test affirmed the versatility of the unit to operate with produced water with minimal to no pre-treatment. Therefore, recycling the produced water for re-injection into the well through the use of the HydroFlame tool may provide an

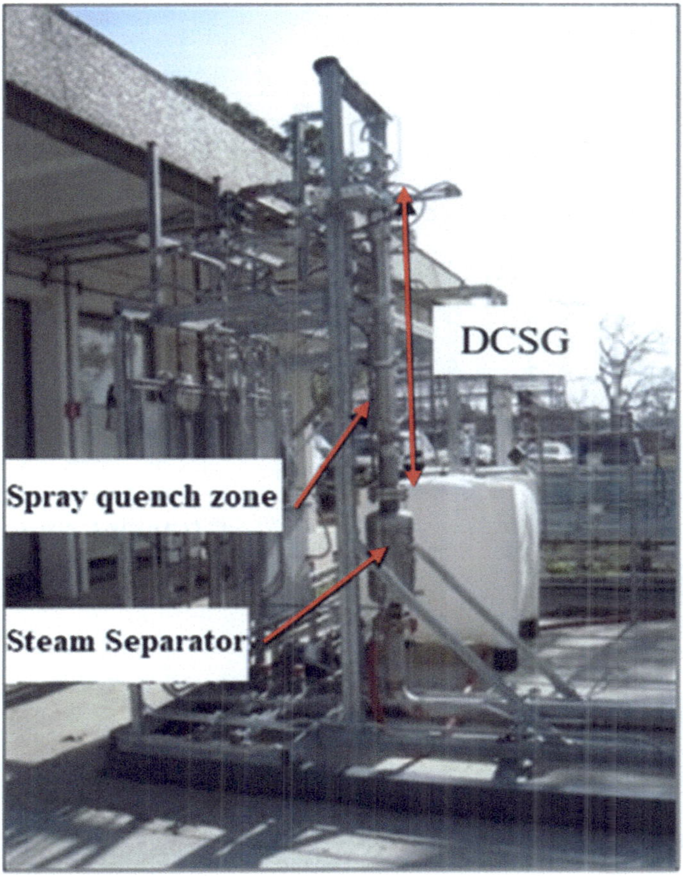


**Fig. 8.8** Original tool setup of DCSG with spray quench zone

alternative to hauling the produced water to disposal wells for underground dumping. Such an alternative would be significantly beneficial to the environment, and also be cost-effective.

**Fig. 8.9** Modified tool setup of DCSG for produced water treatment

## GAGD Process for Incentivizing $CO_2$ Sequestration

Nearly seven years have passed since the Paris Climate Agreement, but carbon emissions continue to trend upward. Global $CO_2$ emissions were at their highest level in history in 2021 (IEA, 2022), despite a Covid-19 induced drop in 2020. Before that, 2019 saw an increase over 2018 numbers by 250 megatons, with total emissions for 2019 at 37.08 gigatons. Also in 2019, the combined total of yearly Carbon Capture and Storage (CCS) activity was 31.5 megatons, of which 3.7 megatons came from geological sequestration (Fajardy et al., 2019). Thus, the year-to-year increase in $CO_2$ emissions worldwide grossly dwarfs the combined total of yearly global CCS activity. This should force us to rethink our CCS strategy so that we are able to meet the scale and pace needed to meet this massive climate challenge. Rapidly ramping up geological $CO_2$ sequestration is one of the time-tested ways that could match the scale and pace needed for us to combat this challenge. That would surely require having the oil industry as a meaningful partner in this endeavor, rather than just a scapegoat. Notwithstanding getting singular blame, perhaps unfairly, for the rapidly deteriorating climate, the industry does possess adequate resources to quickly reduce $CO_2$ emissions to mitigate the climate crisis. As the CEO of the Bank of America Brian Moynihan rightly pointed out during the World Economic Forum, global financial institutions need to stay with the oil & gas industry and not run away from it, since it alone has the wherewithal to tackle the problem of $CO_2$ emissions (Fuchs, 2020). In an ideal world, the oil and gas industry would take initiative to reduce its $CO_2$ emissions unprompted. In reality, however, this industry will require an appropriate profit incentive along with financial and, more importantly, technological support. We strongly believe that our process can provide the technology necessary to harness the power of capitalism and mitigate this global challenge facing humankind by massively scaling up geological $CO_2$ sequestration through $CO_2$ Enhanced Oil Recovery (EOR).

According to Kuuskraa et al. (2013), the continental US is home to an estimated ~400 billion barrels of stranded conventional oil (67% of the total Original Oil in Place) that requires newer technologies for its production. With the advent of shale boom in 2010, which catapulted US oil production, trillions of additional crude oil barrels have been added to the US oil resource base. However, the recovery factors in these newer shale plays are even worse ranging in single digits (around 3–7%), that would leave behind trillions of additional barrels of unrecovered oil with current recovery methods. The so called size of prize for EOR is therefore considerably enormous using more advanced technologies.

Gas injection EOR—the most popular EOR method in US conventional oil—long relied on Continuous Gas Injection (CGI) and Water-Alternating-Gas (WAG) processes using pure $CO_2$ gas as the primary injection. Although commercially profitable, the recoveries range from 5 to 10% of the remaining oil, based on many commercial field projects conducted worldwide (Christensen et al., 2001). Figure 8.10 shows a WAG process as depicted in Department of Energy (DOE) website (Enhanced Oil Recovery.Energy.gov). If the process were to operate as described in Figure 8.10, we would expect a 100% recovery efficiency.

Based on commercial field recovery range of 5–10% of remaining oil, there seems to be significant disconnect in the visualization of the process through Figure 8.10. It is thus more likely that the alternative visualization as shown in schematic in Figure 8.11 depicts a realistic picture of a WAG flood where much of the reservoir volume remains unswept by the injected gas due to gravity override.

Gas-Assisted Gravity Drainage (GAGD), a process developed with support from the US Department of Energy (DOE) and patented by LSU (Rao, 2012), has been described as one of the state-of-the-art technologies over current commercial practices. Figure 8.12 shows the schematic

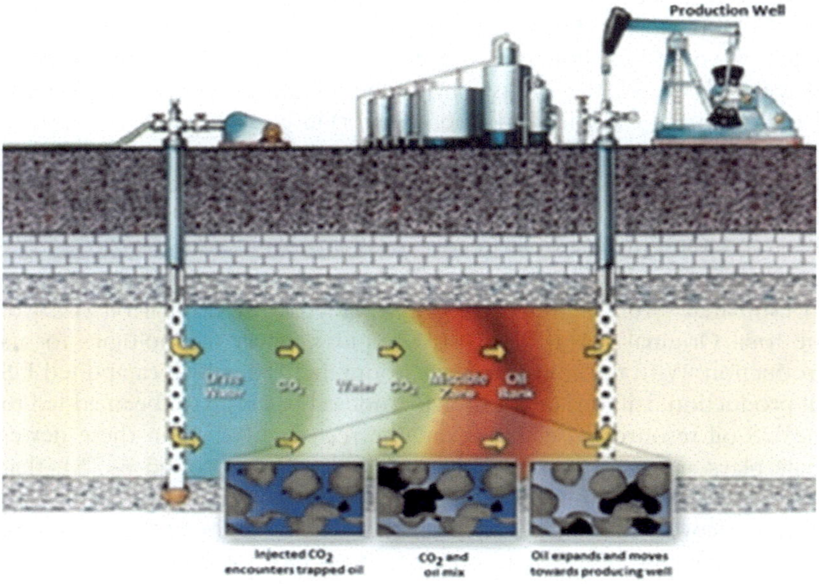


**Fig. 8.10** Conceptual view of a Water Alternating Gas (WAG) process as depicted by the Department of Energy (DOE)

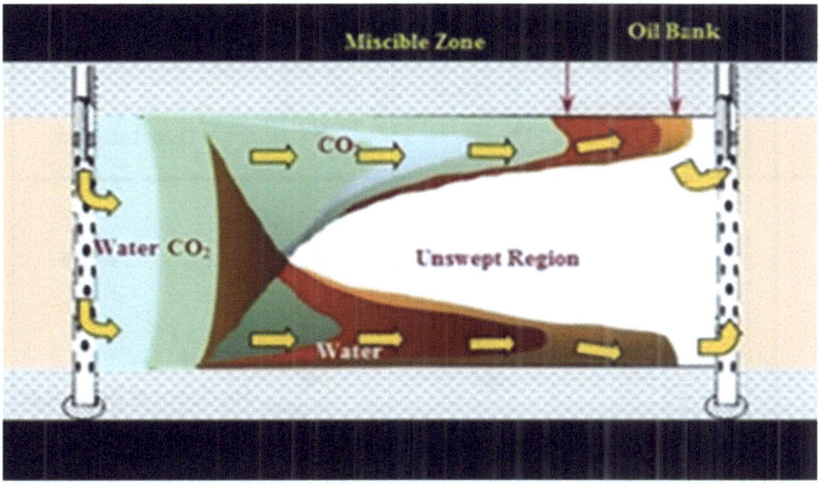


**Fig. 8.11** Alternative and more realistic view of the WAG process based on reported field recovery efficiency of just 5–10% of the remaining oil (Rao, 2012)

of a GAGD process, where $CO_2$/flue gas is injected through top vertical wells and production is tapped via the bottom horizontal lateral. GAGD has demonstrated significantly higher recoveries from 65 to 95% in realistic reservoir condition laboratory experiments. Another advantage of GAGD is that it does not require pure $CO_2$ for its operations.

Figures 8.13 and 8.14 show the GAGD performance in case of an immiscible and miscible mode, respectively. It can be clearly seen that the secondary GAGD floods demonstrate faster oil recovery rates than their tertiary counterparts. However, the ultimate recoveries for all the immiscible floods are comparable. It is interesting to note that the worst GAGD flood recovery (47.3% ROIP) is more than four times the best average miscible WAG flood recoveries. A significant finding was that all the GAGD miscible floods (Fig. 8.14), irrespective of the flood characteristics, such as fractured core, gravity stable displacement history (GSDH) or non-gravity stable displacement history (NSDH), reservoir model fluid systems; recovered almost all of the residual oil.

This demonstrates that the effect of various operating parameters on miscible GAGD performance has little to no significance. Furthermore, even in immiscible GAGD experiments at reservoir conditions (Fig. 8.13),

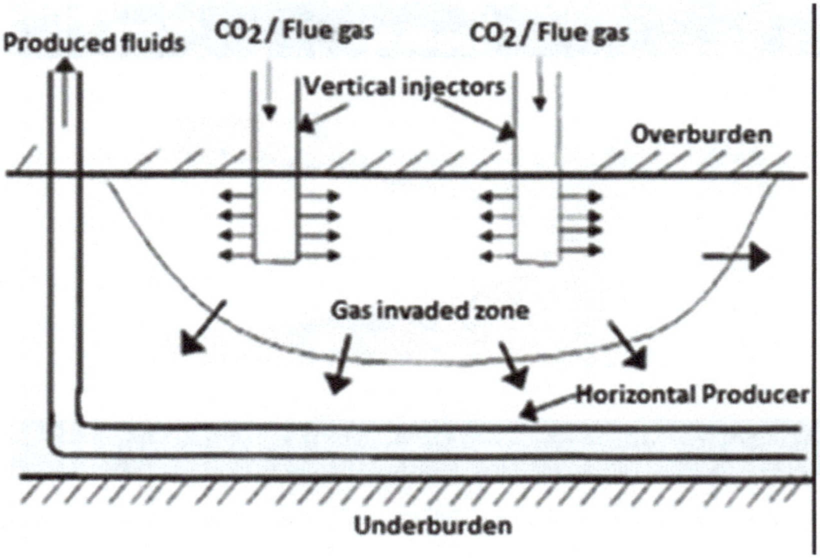


**Fig. 8.12** Schematic of a GAGD process showing $CO_2$/flue gas injected through vertical wells at the top of the reservoir; oil is produced through the horizontal lateral (Rao, 2012)

the recovery range in secondary mode gas injection was 62–88%. This is a very significant result in that it demonstrates that miscibility between the injected gas and the reservoir crude oil is not necessarily a requirement in GAGD process. This is what enables GAGD process to yield much higher recoveries, in excess of 60%, while using flue gas which, being a mixture of nitrogen (88%) and carbon dioxide (12%), is expected to be immiscible with the majority of reservoir crude oils at typical ranges of operating pressures in the fields.

For GAGD implementation in a depleted reservoir in northern Louisiana, a field-scale reservoir characterization and compositional reservoir simulation were conducted at LSU. A 3-D static reservoir model was built and its porosity and permeability distributions were populated using geo-statistical techniques with data derived from available core and log analyses. A good match of the reservoir model with historical production data was obtained using relative permeability data derived from reservoir

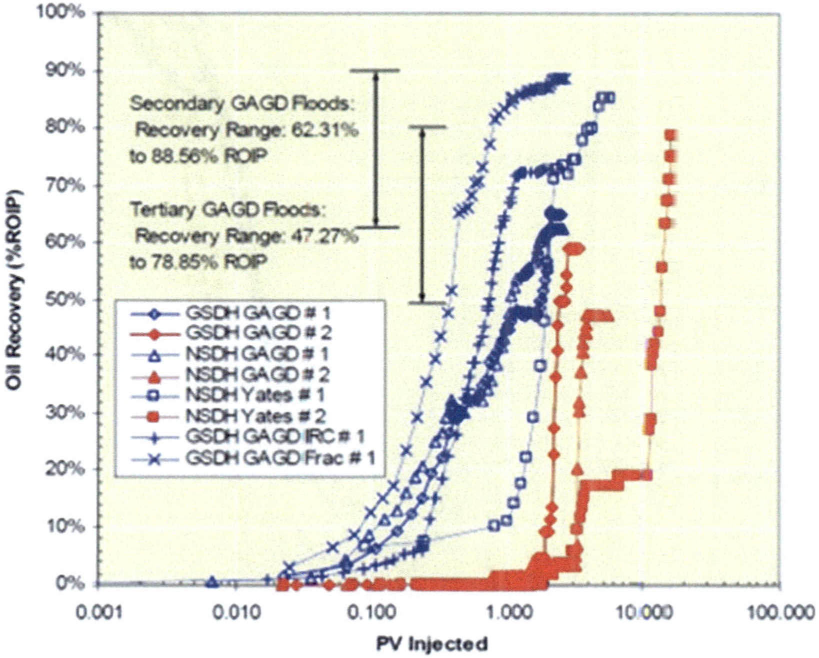


**Fig. 8.13** Immiscible GAGD flood performance (Kulkarni, 2005)

condition core floods conducted using native reservoir cores and fluids (Figs. 8.15 and 8.16).

Different scenarios and strategies were undertaken on this reservoir model to understand the reservoir fluids distribution over time and placement of the horizontal well over the oil-water contact. The well placements of both injection and producing and gas injection rates were optimized for highest GAGD recovery performance. The reservoir simulation study indicated a GAGD recovery of 65% OOIP (eqv. ~90% ROIP). The simulation results matched well with previous physical model and core flow tests. Based on the simulation results a GAGD field test in northern Louisiana was attempted.

A compositional reservoir simulation study was conducted to compare GAGD process with that of other conventional processes, namely Continuous Gas Injection (CGI) and Water Alternating Gas (WAG) to evaluate

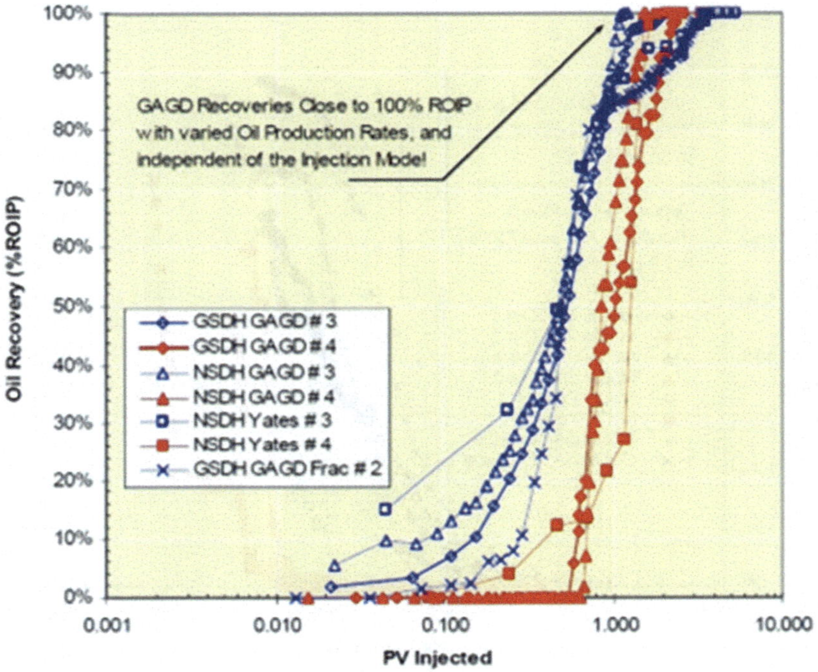


**Fig. 8.14** Miscible GAGD flood performance (Kulkarni, 2005)

their relative field recovery performance (Al-Mudhafar, 2016). The giant south Rumaila oil field in Iraq was selected for this study, and the reservoir was modeled through rigorous geo-statistical reservoir modeling. A satisfactory history match was obtained for oil rates, cumulative production, water injection rates and cumulative injection for the entire field. A 10-year simulated prediction run indicated that the GAGD process had significantly higher recoveries than its peers. The cumulative oil recovery at the end of the prediction period was 4.58 Bbbls in contrast to just 4.35 and 4.33 Bbbls for CGI and WAG respectively. Figure 8.17 depicts the results of this comparative study.

A GAGD version was field pilot tested in 2017 in an offshore Vietnam field around 180 km SE of Ho Chi Minh city (Dinh et al., 2017). The field was 6 km long and 3 km wide with 1.5 km thick oil-bearing basement rock comprised mainly of highly fractured granite. The reservoir

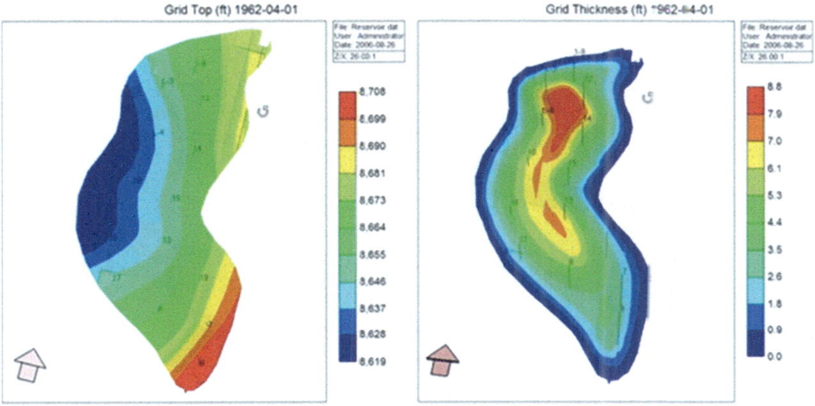


**Fig. 8.15** Grid top and grid thickness maps for the Buckhorn Field, LA (Rao, 2006)

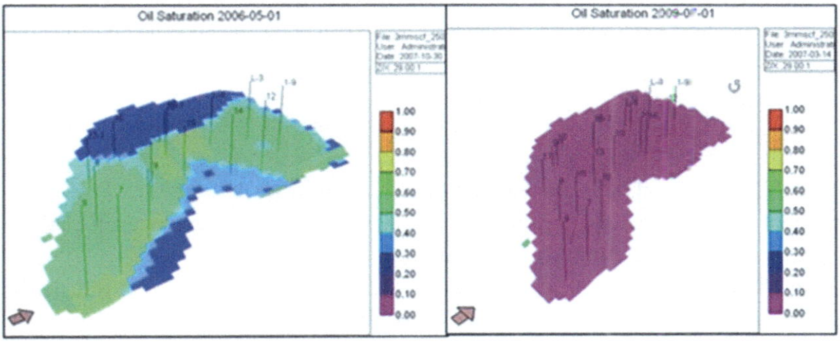


**Fig. 8.16** Initial and final oil saturation maps upon simulation runs (Rao, 2006)

had a favorable porosity (~13%) and medium permeability (15–20 mD). The reservoir crude was of medium gravity (35.1° API) with a bubble point pressure of 1465 psia, and with Rs of 258 scf/STB. The reservoir pressure was 4,400 psia at 2800 m TVDss and reservoir temperature was 130 °C. The pilot study consisted of 4 cycles of around 4–5 months of duration, produced respectively for the four cycles 5600, 7100, 2000, and

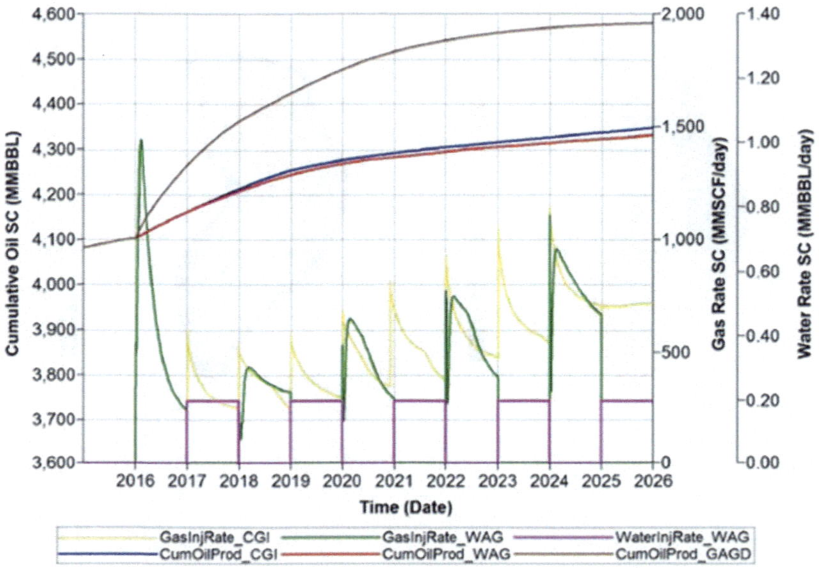


**Fig. 8.17** Comparative cumulative oil production for the GAGD, CGI, and WAG processes (Al-Mudhafar, 2016)

5000 STBO of oil, which was a significant economic benefit. The operation of the cycles was simple and non-expensive and the overall project was considered a technical and economic success.

As a result, the oil and gas industry is becoming more interested in the GAGD process. In the unconventional shale plays, industry has concentrated mainly on Huff-and-Puff gas injection process, as most other industry standard EOR methods have failed to demonstrate their applicability. Huff-and-Puff is a cyclical process involving intervening periods of well closure, meaning that the well is not producing for more than half of the project duration. In contrast, the GAGD process allows for Continuous Gas Injection and oil production, which has the potential to significantly boost oil production rates and recovery factors from shale plays.

The supply crunch of $CO_2$ is one of the major bottlenecks facing $CO_2$ EOR projects, with the majority of these projects requiring pure $CO_2$ for their operations. The $CO_2$ needed for these projects is mostly tapped from underground resources, defeating the "sequestration" benefit of $CO_2$ EOR, which is touted as its secondary advantage. Furthermore, 293.2 Billion cubic feet of natural gas was flared/vented from just the Permian shale oil basin last year in 2019 and this number has been steadily trending upward over the past 3 years (Abramov & Bertelsen, 2019). This gas is flared rather than piped to gas hubs for sale as a result of the lack of compression/pipeline infrastructure (Rassenfoss, 2019). Small to medium operators do not have the economic wherewithal to invest in these capital-intensive infrastructures and are content in selling the oil, which fetches a higher market price, in preference to gas. In the current tight oil production scenario, there is no economic incentive for the operators to not flare or vent the associated gas, which explains the upward trend in flaring and venting over the years. By collaborating with the HydroFlame process, the GAGD (which doesn't need pure $CO_2$ for its operation) can help further eliminate flaring and venting. This natural gas would be diverted to a HydroFlame unit instead of being flared or vented, which would use the energy content of the natural gas for its operations and use the burned gases in a subsequent GAGD process. This would help mitigate the colossal amount of flaring and venting ongoing in the shale plays. The following section illustrates this holistic concept of produced water treatment, recycling and elimination of flaring in a self-contained process.

## The Environmental and Economic Advantages of the HydroFlame-GAGD Concept

The impacts and benefits of HydroFlame process compared to current oil-field practices are:

1. *Reduction in Greenhouse Gas (GHG) Emissions and Efficient $CO_2$ Sequestration*

Natural sequestration of $CO_2$ occurs when all combustion reaction exhaust gases are injected into the reservoir. When combined with GAGD process, the EOR-based sequestration process is much more efficient because of the gravity stable nature of $CO_2$ displacement front in GAGD, unlike conventional EOR techniques that are currently practiced for $CO_2$EOR/sequestration. This has a tremendous implication in terms of amount of $CO_2$ sequestered in the sub-surface formations.

2. *Elimination of Vented and Flared Gas in Remote Oil-Fields*

The large quantities of natural gas that are currently being vented and flared, due to the lack of pipeline infrastructure in remote oil fields, will be used to generate flue gas for injection into the same oil field for prolonged production by pressure maintenance and gas injection EOR. This would eliminate the emission of flared gas (predominantly $CO_2$ and unburnt natural gas) and natural gas, which is 25 times more greenhouse potent that $CO_2$ into the atmosphere. Thus, by employing the HydroFlame process, net negative GHG emission are in fact possible.

3. *Pressure Maintenance*

Reservoir pressure declines, as fluids are produced from the reservoir. As a result, the production rate declines and eventually stops when the reservoir pressure is depleted. At this point, mechanisms to improve production such as artificial lift (pumps), water injection, or gas injection are implemented. In the application of the HydroFlame DHSG, flue gases (carbon dioxide and nitrogen) are injected into the reservoir along with the steam. These flue gases rise to the top of the reservoir and form a blanket. The reduction in reservoir pressure, when fluids are withdrawn, is offset by the increase in pressure when these gases are injected thereby maintaining the reservoir pressure or significantly lowering the pressure decline rate. This enables higher production rates, longer production times, and improved recoveries—without the need for additional pumping equipment.

4. *Smaller Footprint*

Since flame is in direct contact with water, very high heat transfer coefficients are achieved which render the HydroFlame devices quite compact and highly efficient heat transfer systems. The entire HydroFlame process skid could be mounted on a trailer and mobilized to its operating location thanks to its small size. This would facilitate accessing remote, far flung areas, where the majority of the flaring and venting is taking place.

5. *Reduced Water Treatment*

Water of lower quality can be used in this process, as opposed to water used in surface steam generators, because the heat transfer between the hot combustion gases and the water in the HydroFlame combustor are direct and no heat conduction materials are required. In situations where scaling ions (carbonates and sulfates) are present in the produced water in high concentrations, scale inhibitors can be injected with the water to prevent scaling. Less stringent water quality requirements mitigate the need for expensive water treatment.

## Conclusions

The twin technology scheme of HF and GAGD will help provide an integrated solution to the multi-dimensional and complex problems of greenhouse gas (GHG) emissions from oilfields and at-scale sequestration of GHG, while simultaneously providing adequate economic incentive to the oil and gas industry to willingly partake in this massive effort through sustainable energy production. The cost viability of any project, including the one to tackle the challenge of carbon sequestration, is key to its success. It is imperative that the oil and gas industry, which has the requisite resources and knowhow in the sub-surface domain, be enthusiastic to reduce its ecological impact; an outcome which will only be possible if inherent economic concerns are addressed when new technological solutions are proposed. The HF-GAGD combination, through its unique advantages such as its smaller footprint, portability, compliant at-scale sequestration, higher recovery, alleviating of produced water treatment, does just that, and can potentially usher in at-scale GHG sequestration to combat climate change.

**Acknowledgements** The authors would like to thank Arthur Cooper, Dinaker Deshini, Mayuri Murugesu, Paul Rodriguez, and Samarth Rao of HydroFlame Technologies, LLC.

## References

Abramov, A., & Bertelsen, M. (Con.). (2019). *Permian gas flaring reaches yet another high*. Rystad Energy—Energy Knowledge House. Retrieved July 25, 2022, from https://www.rystadenergy.com/newsevents/news/press-releases/permian-gas-flaring-reaches-yet-another-high/

Al-Mudhafar, W. J. M. (2016). *Statistical reservoir characterization, simulation, and optimization of field scale-Gas Assisted Gravity Drainage (GAGD) process with uncertainty assessments* (LSU Doctoral Dissertations. 3097). https://digitalcommons.lsu.edu/gradschool_dissertations/3097 (dissertation).

Belvalkar, R., & Oyewole, S. (2010). *Development of Marcellus Shale in Pennsylvania*. In SPE Annual Technical Conference and Exhibition (SPE 134852), Florence, Italy.

Christensen, J. R., Stenby, E. H., & Skauge, A. (2001). *Review of the WAG field experience*. SPE Reservoir Evaluation & Engineering (SPE 71203).

Dinh, H. K., Le, N. V., Peter, M. G., Dang, T. S., Nguyen, V. Q., Hoang, N. D., Truong, T. A., Tran, H. M., & Nguyen, K. B. N. (2017). *Gas-Assisted Gravity Drainage GAGD huff n puff application for fractured basement reservoir—Case study*. SPE/ATMI Asia Pacific Oil & Gas Conference (SPE 186210), Jakarta, Indonesia.

Enhanced Oil Recovery. Energy.gov., Retrieved July 25, 2022, from https://www.energy.gov/fe/science-innovation/oil-gas-research/enhanced-oil-recovery

Fajardy, M., Köberle, A., Dowell, N. M., & Fantuzzi, A. (2019). *BECCS deployment: A reality check* (Grantham Institute Briefing paper No 28).

Fox, R. L., & Donaldson, A. B. (1985). *Production of heavy crude oil using downhole steam generators*. In 3rd International Conference on Heavy Crude and Tar Sands, Long Beach, CA, USA.

Fuchs, E. (2020). *Bank of America CEO: We should lend to oil companies, not divest from them*. Yahoo! Finance. Retrieved July 25, 2022, from https://finance.yahoo.com/news/bank-of-america-brian-moynihan-on-climate-change-140826633.html

Gaudlip, A. W., & Paugh, L. O. (2008). *Marcellus Shale water management challenges in Pennsylvania*. SPE Shale Gas Production Conference (SPE 119898), Fort Worth, Texas.

Hayes, T. (2010). *Produced water research projects*. RPSEA Unconventional Gas Conference, Golden, Colorado (GTI).

Home. *NAE website*. Retrieved July 25, 2022, from https://www.nae.edu/

IEA. (2022, March 8). *Global $CO_2$ emissions rebounded to their highest level in history in 2021—News*. IEA. Retrieved July 25, 2022, from https://www.iea.org/news/global-CO2-emissions-rebounded-to-their-highest-level-in-history-in-2021

Kulkarni, M. M. (2005). *Multiphase mechanisms and fluid dynamics in gas injection enhanced oil recovery processes* (LSU Doctoral Dissertations 62). https://digitalcommons.lsu.edu/gradschool_dissertations/62

Kuuskraa, V. A., Godec, M. L., & Dipietro, P. (2013). $CO_2$ utilization from 'next generation' $CO_2$ enhanced oil recovery technology. *Energy Procedia, 37*, 6854–6866.

Mohsenzadeh, A., Escrochia, M., Afraz, M. V., Al-Wahaibi, Y., & Ayatollahi, S. (2012, June 12–14). *Experimental investigation of heavy oil recovery from fractured reservoirs by secondary steam—Gas assisted gravity drainage*. In SPE Heavy Oil Conference Canada Held in Calgary, Alberta, Canada. http://onepetro.org/SPECHOC/proceedings-pdf/12IHOC/All-12IHOC/SPE-157202-MS/1656383/spe-157202-ms.pdf/1

Rao, D. N. (2006). *A new gravity-stable $CO_2$-injection process for enhancing oil recovery from depleted reservoirs*. In PTTC Technology Connections Workshop, Shreveport, Louisiana.

Rao, D. N. (2010). *Direct combustion steam generator* (United States patent 7,780,152 B2).

Rao, D. N. (2012). *Gas-assisted gravity drainage process for improved oil recovery* (United States patent 8,215,392 B2).

Rassenfoss, S. (2019). Natural gas flared in just two major US Shale plays exceeded the amount of gas consumed last year in Colombia and Israel. *Journal of Petroleum Technology*.

CHAPTER 9

# Achieving the UN Sustainable Development Goals in the Oil and Gas Sector Through Risk Management

*Salim Ghettas*

## Introduction

The oil and gas sector plays a significant role in achieving the UN SDGs (United Nation's Sustainable Development Goals) and in implementing their ideals. This process involves ensuring sustainable industrialization, adopting sustainable energy sources, building resilient infrastructure, and providing decent and safe working conditions, among other things (United Nations, 2022). In this chapter, we suggest that this can be achieved through risk management and provide an analysis of the particular risks which may hinder the achievement of the SDGs.

This chapter is organized as follows: The first section introduces the hazards and risks surrounding the oil and gas sector; The next section discusses risk control measures and management strategies that

S. Ghettas (✉)
Rochester Institute of Technology, Rochester, New York, USA
e-mail: sg6129@g.rit.edu



T. Walker et al. (eds.), *Sustainability in the Oil and Gas Sector*,
https://doi.org/10.1007/978-3-031-51586-6_9

are already established; and the last section projects some future directions and necessary improvements to the industry such that the UN SDGs might be met. For a better understanding of these goals, Appendix 1 outlines a selection of actions and indicators of the UN SDGs that are relevant to the social, economic, and environmental aspects of activities in the oil and gas sector. Blamed for being a major contributor to climate change, major companies in the sector have adopted initiatives for the sustainable development of their activities, taking into account the preservation of the environment and the prevention of pollution, the promotion of safe and healthy working conditions for their employees, and the establishment of projects in small communities. The sector has also increased its investment in renewable energy production such as green hydrogen, and advanced technologies like zero routine flaring in an effort to mitigate its Green House Gas (GHG) emissions. In social-related sustainability, the implementation of voluntary programs to promote the well-being and safety of employees in the workplace as well as the health and safety of communities has become a common action.

However, even with these actions, high hazards and inherent risks resulting from exploration, extraction, transportation, processing, and distribution remain prevalent (Schneider et al., 2013). Throughout each of these phases, a poor control of risks and hazards can lead to devastating disasters that involve human, economic, and environmental losses. The occurrence of such disasters results in the disruption of energy supplies, human injuries and fatalities, economic losses for corporations and/or governments, environmental pollution, unemployment, and recessions in local community micro-economy. As these consequences are all directly related to one or many of the UN SDG goals, risk management is imperative.

One of the most significant incidents in the sector in the past decade was the British Petroleum (BP) Gulf of Mexico oil spillage, also known as the Deepwater Horizon oil spill, which occurred on April 20, 2010 at the Macondo well in the Gulf of Mexico, 48 miles off of the coast of Louisiana in the United States (Environment Protection Agency, 2022).[1]

[1] On April 20, 2010, during the final stage of the process of temporary well abandonment of the Macondo well (an exploratory well into the Deepwater oil reservoir in the Gulf of Mexico), a well control situation occurred due to a wrong decision and escalated. This caused hydrocarbons to escape accidently from the wellbore after the failure of existing barriers on the Macondo well, and unsuccessful attempts to re-establish control

The oil spillage and subsequent explosions and fires resulted in direct human, financial, and material losses, along with negative environmental, economic, and social impacts to local communities and sea habitats. Eleven workers lost their lives and seventeen crewmembers were injured and four million barrels of crude oil leaked into the ocean in the span of 87 days. BP suffered direct financial losses as they were fined an estimated 5.5 billion USD as a penalty for the violation of the Clean Water Act. The event also incurred some 8.8 billion dollars in natural resource damages (Environmental Protection Agency, 2022), as well as 61.6 billion dollars in clean-up activities (BBC, 2016). Additionally, BP and other parties were ordered to pay other bills for economic damages, medical compensations, and class action lawsuit settlements.

According to the report to the US President of the National Commission on the BP Deepwater Horizon oil spill (2011), this disaster could have been prevented if hazard and risk controls had been effectively implemented. Nonetheless, the commission found that the tragedy involved complex systematic failures, and entailed some risks and hazards that the sector and government could not have been prepared for.

Unfortunately, the BP Deepwater Horizon oil spill was not an exception. Similar disasters have occurred with many of the same root causes. In their periodic report on the largest losses in the oil and gas sector, Marsh (2020) detail the hundred most devastating events in the world over the span of 30 years (1979–2019). According to this report, there was an alarming increase in the number of large loss-events in the periods of 1988–1989 (six events) and 2018–2019 (four events). In fact, these four events resulted in a cumulative loss of 2800 million USD in property damage alone (Marsh, 2020).

Furthermore, many of the UN SDGs and actions imply the implementation of plans to ensure access to sustainable clean energy and control measures by the entities in the oil and gas sector. For instance, fulfilling Target 8.8 of Goal 8 on protecting labor and promoting safe workplaces requires companies in the sector to set and implement risk management processes and management systems to control workplace risks and hazards (Table 9.1).

of the well. The released hydrocarbons ignited which led to an explosion and fire, and continued to flow from the wellbore throughout the following 87 days. The offshore rig sunk after 36 hours from the incident, and 36% of the federal water of the Gulf of Mexico was contaminated and closed to fishing.

**Table 9.1** Selected UN SDGs relevant to the oil and gas sector (United Nations, 2022)

| *Goal* | *Target* | *Indicator* |
|---|---|---|
| #3 Ensure healthy lives and promote well-being for all at all ages | Target *3.4* By 2030, reduce by one third premature mortality from non-communicable diseases through prevention and treatment and promote mental health and well-being | 3.4.1 Mortality rate attributed to cardiovascular disease, cancer, diabetes, or chronic respiratory disease |
| | Target *3.6* By 2020, halve the number of global deaths and injuries from road traffic accidents | 3.6.1 Death rate due to road traffic injuries |
| | Target *3.9* By 2030, substantially reduce the number of deaths and illnesses from hazardous chemicals and air, water and soil pollution, and contamination | 3.9.1 Mortality rate attributed to household and ambient air pollution<br>3.9.2 Mortality rate attributed to unsafe water, unsafe sanitation, and lack of hygiene (exposure to unsafe Water, Sanitation and Hygiene for All (WASH) services) |
| #6 Ensure availability and sustainable management of water and sanitation for all | Target *6.3* By 2030, improve water quality by reducing pollution, eliminating dumping and minimizing release of hazardous chemicals and materials, halving the proportion of untreated wastewater and substantially increasing recycling and safe reuse globally | 6.3.1 Proportion of domestic and industrial wastewater flows safely treated<br>6.3.2 Proportion of bodies of water with good ambient water quality |

(continued)

**Table 9.1** (continued)

| *Goal* | *Target* | *Indicator* |
|---|---|---|
| | Target *6.4* By 2030, substantially increase water-use efficiency across all sectors and ensure sustainable withdrawals and supply of freshwater to address water scarcity and substantially reduce the number of people suffering from water scarcity | 6.4.1 Change in water-use efficiency over time<br>6.4.2 Level of water stress: freshwater withdrawal as a proportion of available freshwater resources |
| #7 Ensure access to affordable, reliable, sustainable and modern energy for all | Target 7.1 By 2030, ensure universal access to affordable, reliable, and modern energy services | 7.1.1 Proportion of population with access to electricity |
| | | 7.1.2 Proportion of population with primary reliance on clean fuels and technology |
| | *Target 7.2* By 2030, increase substantially the share of renewable energy in the global energy mix | 7.2.1 Renewable energy share in the total final energy consumption |
| | *Target 7.a* By 2030, enhance international cooperation to facilitate access to clean energy research and technology, including renewable energy, energy efficiency and advanced and cleaner fossil fuel technology, and promote investment in energy infrastructure and clean energy technology | 7.a.1 International financial flows to developing countries in support of clean energy research and development and renewable energy production, including in hybrid systems |

(continued)

**Table 9.1** (continued)

| *Goal* | *Target* | *Indicator* |
|---|---|---|
| | Target *7.b* By 2030, expand infrastructure and upgrade technology for supplying modern and sustainable energy services for all in developing countries, in particular least developed countries, small island developing States, and land-locked developing countries, in accordance with their respective programs of support | 7.b.1 Installed renewable energy-generating capacity in developing countries (in watts per capita) |
| #8 Promote sustained, inclusive and sustainable economic growth, full and productive employment and decent work for all | Target *8.2* Achieve higher levels of economic productivity through diversification, technological upgrading and innovation, including through a focus on high-value added and labor-intensive sectors | 8.2.1 Annual growth rate of real GDP per employed person |
| | Target 8.4 Improve progressively, through 2030, global resource efficiency in consumption and production and endeavor to decouple economic growth from environmental degradation, in accordance with the 10-Year Framework of Programs on Sustainable Consumption and Production, with developed countries taking the lead | 8.4.1 Material footprint, material footprint per capita, and material footprint per GDP<br>8.4.2 Domestic material consumption, domestic material consumption per capita, and domestic material consumption per GDP |

(continued)

**Table 9.1** (continued)

| *Goal* | *Target* | *Indicator* |
|---|---|---|
| | Target 8.5 By 2030, achieve full and productive employment and decent work for all women and men, including for young people and persons with disabilities, and equal pay for work of equal value | 8.5.1 Average hourly earnings of female and male employees, by occupation, age and persons with disabilities<br>8.5.2 Unemployment rate, by sex, age and persons with disabilities |
| | Target 8.8 Protect labor rights and promote safe and secure working environments for all workers, including migrant workers, in particular women migrants, and those in precarious employment | 8.8.1 Fatal and non-fatal occupational injuries per 100,000 workers, by sex and migrant status |
| # 9 Build resilient infrastructure, promote inclusive and sustainable industrialization and foster innovation | Target 9.4 By 2030, upgrade infrastructure and retrofit industries to make them sustainable, with increased resource-use efficiency and greater adoption of clean and environmentally sound technologies and industrial processes, with all countries taking action in accordance with their respective capabilities | 9.4.1 $CO_2$ emission per unit of value added |
| # 12 Ensure sustainable consumption and production patterns | Target 12.2 By 2030, achieve the sustainable management and efficient use of natural resources | 12.2.1 Material footprint, material footprint per capita, and material footprint per GDP<br>12.2.2 Domestic material consumption, domestic material consumption per capita, and domestic material consumption per GDP |

(continued)

**Table 9.1** (continued)

| *Goal* | *Target* | *Indicator* |
|---|---|---|
| | Target 12.4 By 2020, achieve the environmentally sound management of chemicals and all wastes throughout their life cycle, in accordance with agreed international frameworks, and significantly reduce their release to air, water and soil in order to minimize their adverse impacts on human health and the environment | 12.4.2 (a) Hazardous waste generated per capita; and (b) proportion of hazardous waste treated, by type of treatment |
| | Target 12.5 By 2030, substantially reduce waste generation through prevention, reduction, recycling and reuse | 12.5.1 National recycling rate, tons of material recycled |
| | Target 12.6 Encourage companies, especially large and transnational companies, to adopt sustainable practices and to integrate sustainability information into their reporting cycle | 12.6.1 Number of companies publishing sustainability reports |
| # 13 Take urgent action to combat climate change and its impacts | Target 13.1 Strengthen resilience and adaptive capacity to climate-related hazards and natural disasters in all countries | 13.1.1 Number of deaths, missing persons and directly affected persons attributed to disasters per 100,000 population |
| | | 13.1.2 Number of countries that adopt and implement national disaster risk reduction strategies in line with the Sendai Framework for Disaster Risk Reduction 2015–2030 |
| | Target 13.2 Integrate climate change measures into national policies, strategies, and planning | 13.2.2 Total greenhouse gas emissions per year |

## Risks and Hazards in the Oil and Gas Sector

In this second section, we present the main risks and hazards related to the oil and gas sector as well as to geoengineering and its feasibility to overturn climate change. The second section of the chapter details the risk controls and management strategies applied currently in the sector. Finally, we recommend some future directions and improvements to fulfill the UN SDGs.

Before discussing the main hazards and risks of the oil and gas sector, it is important to define the terms "hazard" and "risk" and explain how one is different from the other. Many people use these terms interchangeably although each one has a precise meaning. The term "risk" itself is defined in different ways by various sources. The International Organization of Standardization (ISO) (2018) defines risk broadly as "the effect of uncertainty on objectives." Many experts and organizations, however, define risk simply as the measure of likelihood (probability) and subsequent level of consequence of exposure to a hazard or hazardous material (Center for Chemical Process Safety, 2022; National Fire Protection Association, 2021). In the same sense, a hazard is simply defined as any material, object, or source of potential harm, loss, or adverse health effect (Canadian Center for Occupational Health & Safety, 2022). For the context of this chapter, since the objective is to ensure a safe and sustainable process, a hazardous release is any event that disturbs that objective. Risk is defined as the likelihood that this disruption would occur.

### *Risks and Hazards in the Oil and Gas Sector*

Activities in the oil and gas sector entail many hazards that may cause harm to humans, property, and the environment. These hazards can be grouped into five main classes: physical hazards, ergonomic and organizational hazards, chemical hazards, radioactive hazards, and environmental hazards.

- Physical hazards: These arise from the processing of energy and include dangers such as pressure, extreme temperatures, process aging, vibration, noise, confined spaces, wet floors.
- Ergonomic and organizational hazards: These include workloads, repetitive motions, heavy loads, and extended shift lengths, are present in many aspects of the sector's activities.

- Chemical hazards: These are associated with the inherent characteristics of hydrocarbons, byproducts, and the chemicals used throughout the hydrocarbon's value chain, being flammable, corrosive, explosive, toxic, etc.
- Radioactive hazards: These arise from the use of radioactive elements during some operations such as well logging and non-destructive tests or from the natural occurring radioactive materials that are a component of the extracted crude oil in some regions of the world.
- Environmental hazards: These relate to the hazardous effects of the extraction and production of oil on the soil, fauna, and flora. Spillage of crude oil or petroleum products into the environment result in significant environmental impacts, which may last for years as we have explained above in the case of the Deepwater Horizon incident.

Although their work is limited to occupational hazards and risks, Benson et al. (2021) exhaustively analyze the most common occupational hazards and relate health risks in the oil and gas sector. Similarly, we attempt to investigate the main risks linked to one or more of the above hazards.

The risk of fire is one of the major risks encountered in the oil and gas sector. This is due to the flammability of hydrocarbons and of other materials involved in the sector's activities. Hydrocarbons can be highly flammable and can enter into an oxidation reaction in the presence of an oxidant (like oxygen) and an ignition source. Fire causes human and material losses. Manan and Lee (2005) estimate that fires are often caused by leakages from hydrocarbon storage vessels and process components. In fact, besides the technological advancement in process design and operation, major oil and gas companies reported in their annual sustainability performance reports that large oil spill incidents are still being recorded (Schneider et al., 2013). Some of these fire incidents escalated to explosions, due to a failure to control them in a timely manner (Marsh, 2020).

Another risk often linked to that of fires is that of explosions. Explosion risks are associated with the ignition of a pressurized gas, flammable vapors, or solid explosives under certain conditions such as the physical status of flammable material, the geometry of the vessel, the immediate or delayed ignition of the flammable material, etc. The Center for Chemical Process Safety (2022) defines an explosion as "a release of energy that causes a pressure discontinuity or blast wave." Various explosion phenomena arise in the upstream and downstream activities of hydrocarbon products. Figure 9.1 summarizes the main types of explosion events that are recorded in the oil and gas sector.

These events can also be classified into two major categories depending on the velocity of the flame wave (Nolan, 2011): The first, deflagration, is the explosion that yields a flame propagation velocity below the local sound speed, and the second, detonation, is an explosion with supersonic flame velocities. Although researchers do not yet understand the transition well enough to predict it, under certain circumstance, a deflagration explosion may escalate to a detonation in the presence of obstacles or in partial confinement, resulting in an acceleration of the flame wave to supersonic levels.

The accidental release of hydrocarbons is another significant risk that is incurred when safety barriers fail to confine the hydrocarbon within its intended vessel and/or space. These leakages might form clouds of flammable, toxic vapors, gases, mists, or cause liquid spillages on the soil (Nolan, 2011). The released hydrocarbons can explode or ignite and/or cause environmental damage such as soil contamination, loss of sea habitat. Schneider et al. (2013) confirmed that subsequently, "It is common for companies to be fined for violations as well as be responsible for clean-up costs" (p. 111). The loss of hydrocarbon's confinement could be the consequence of a corrosion or a physical shock on vessels. Corrosion issues can be prevented if adequate protection is in place and rigorous process inspection plans are implemented. Unfortunately, Marsh (2020) found that a lack of inspection remained the second major cause of large losses in the sector, after comparing the underlying causes of major losses in the 1980s to those in the 2010s. Thus, the achievement

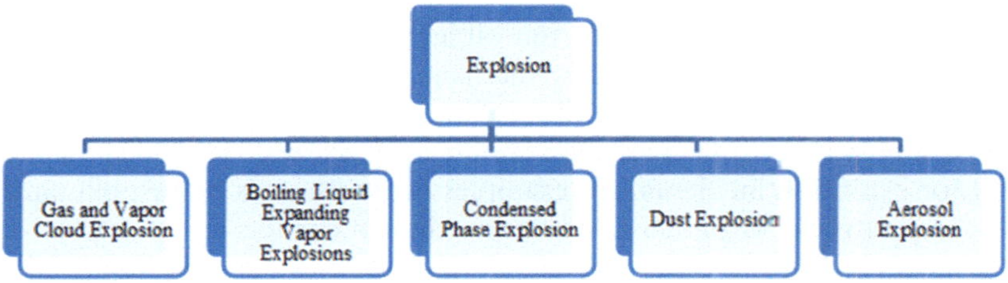


**Fig. 9.1** Major types of explosion events in the oil and gas industry

of Target 6.3 of the UN SDGs (on ensuring water quality through the reduction of hazardous waste release) could be attained by 2030.

As a final point, is it important to discuss the impact of a loss of critical knowledge about sector operations. Over the last decade, the oil and gas sector has had to lay off an unprecedented number of employees to cope with drops in the price of oil. Furthermore, experienced and aged employees have been retiring early, and there is a quick turnover of millennial employees. In the absence of an established process for the retention and transfer of critical knowledge, this loss of a skilled workforce has resulted in a loss of information necessary for the safe operation of processes and execution of activities. According to Marsh (2020):

> The exodus of an aging workforce has created a huge issue around how industry will meet its critical need of process safety knowledge transfer. This issue needs a holistic improvement approach, including enhanced education of process safety in engineering education, effective assimilation of process safety knowledge for early career industry professionals, and ongoing reinforcement of process safety training in the workforce. (p. 1)

### *Geoengineering and Climate Change*

Climate change is one of the significant environmental impacts of the oil and gas industry on a global scale. Scientists have confirmed that GHG emissions are responsible for global warming, and the melting of the arctic sea ice has caused the rising of sea levels in many parts of the world. Carbon dioxide gas and water vapor absorb the outgoing heat of sunlight from the earth's surface and re-emit the heat in all directions in the lower atmosphere which increases the earth's temperature. Global warming and environmental deterioration are also evidenced by increased forest fires and extreme weather events. In the oil and gas sector, the emissions of carbon dioxide, nitrogen oxides, methane, and sulfur oxides from the flaring of natural gases during the drilling stage, in refineries, and other processing centers, and methane venting in processes, or smokes of fire and/or explosion incidents, are examples of the sources of air pollutants that impact the environment and hasten climate change.

To cope with the steady increase of GHG emissions, and in light of the limited results of traditional approaches and technologies, scientists have developed geoengineering technologies as a promising solution. These technologies capture, remove, and sequester carbon dioxide gas, and/or large-scale injections of aerosol particles at the stratosphere layer of the atmosphere, which reflects an important portion of the sun's heat, thus reducing the earth's temperature.

Scientists argue that these technologies could bring down the earth's temperature in a world seemingly unready to cease the extraction and use of fossil fuels as a source of energy in the near future. BP, one of the largest companies in the sector, has been leading and implementing experiments and research projects on capturing millions of tons of carbon dioxide and sequestering it underground in many locations such as Australia, the United Kingdom, and the United States (Ambrose, 2020; Reed, 2021). While projects can yield some encouraging results, none of the above techniques have been tested, so far, on a large scale, verified, and approved as an effective solution to counteract climate change. This chapter does not address the merits and limitations of each of these geoengineering techniques, but we will present the points of views of both the opponents and the supporters of these concepts.

The existing debate among scientists, referred to as *the moral hazard argument*, shifted to one about the morality of using these technologies rather than the existing policies and strategies such as carbon tax trading, cap and trade, and voluntary and regulatory approaches. The supporters of the geoengineering approach think that meeting the Paris Agreement's goal of keeping the global temperature rise below 1.5 degrees Celsius above pre-industrial levels is unachievable. This is mainly because it requires deep and expensive reforms of economic systems about which developed countries are not yet enthusiastic (Geoengineering Monitor, 2022). In view of the drastic impact of climate change, and of the limited results of existing policies and strategies, advocates of geoengineering have recommended that this technological solution might be the only viable way to counteract global warming.

Opponents of geoengineering technologies think that altering solar radiation entails unknown risks to the ecosystem and to human life on earth. Moreover, they claim that these technologies do not address the origins of the climate change issue but deal with its impacts only. This point of view is confirmed by investigations conducted by Corner and Pidgeon (2014) and Cherry et al. (2021) which find that the public endorses existing policies like carbon taxes more than geoengineering. Furthermore, an analysis of the UN SDGs reveals that the actions associated with those goals and their relevant targets rule out geoengineering as a strategy to address climate change. The UN SDGs call for a drastic change in the exiting production processes to be more sustainable, reliable, clean, and environmentally-friendly.

## Risk Controls and Management Strategies

Due to the hazardous nature of activities in the oil and gas sector and following the multiple devastating incidents that have impacted the sector, many countries promulgated acts and regulations to control relevant risks and hazards. In the United States, the Clean Air Act, the Occupational Safety and Health Agency (OSHA), and EPA regulations were passed to manage the permitting process of companies in the sector and ensure that satisfactory risk controls be implemented by companies operating in the United States (Schneider et al., 2013). The European Union enforced the Seveso regulations to oversee the activities of the oil and gas sector among others in Europe (Pasman et al., 2017). Despite the efforts of companies in the sector to comply with the applicable regulations, legal compliance was not enough to prevent accidents from recurring. Moreover, Schneider et al. (2013) find that "significant noncompliance with the EHS laws and regulations is common among the oil companies located in the United States, despite their ongoing efforts" (p. 115).

Oil and gas companies commonly make efforts to adopt voluntary approaches and best practices to: (1) manage the occupational health and safety of employees, (2) ensure the safety of equipment and installation, and (3) manage the environmental performance of companies. National and international standards have been developed and adopted internationally by companies in the sector. The ISO organization, for instance, has developed several international standards such as ISO 45001 on occupational health and safety management, ISO 14001 on environmental management, and ISO 26000 guidelines on social responsibility, all of which are widely accepted and implemented in the sector. Furthermore, the American Petroleum Institute (API) develops and publishes specific standards and specifications for the design, assembly, testing, function, and repair and maintenance of different parts and equipments used in the oil and gas industry. These standards and guidelines enable a systematic approach to managing risks and hazards in the workplace and promote the sustainable efforts of oil and gas companies toward community.

The methods and tools used to identify hazards and to assess risks have matured over the last three decades, as companies have accumulated knowledge and experience from past incidents and from the nuclear sector. These methods also allow for the prediction of causal factors of incidents and for mitigation measures to be implemented. Furthermore, the use of mathematical models and theories such as fuzzy logic and Bayes theory in developing risk assessments enhanced their accuracy, as uncertain and fuzzy data is captured and included in the risk quantification. The digitalization of the sector will further stimulate this trend.

The design of process equipment saw a significant improvement through the integration of automation in the control of activities. Safety instrumented systems, for example, became widely incorporated in the design and safety monitoring of processes (layer of protection). These systems function independently from equipment including the basic process control system, and can detect, alert, and react to various abnormal conditions in the process function in a short time without human intervention. This advancement reduced the likelihood of the occurrence of incidents occurrence and the chance for an escalation of consequences by minimizing the human response time factor. Moreover, ceasing routine natural gas flaring is a measure being increasingly adopted by major companies such as BP to significantly reduce the GHG emissions of oil and gas facilities (Kazi et al., 2019). This measure has been managed through flaring management programs that focus on the inherent safe design of processes and enable a recovery of flared gas The International Association of Oil and Gas Producers (IOGP) adopted a roadmap to decarbonize (eliminate flaring) by 2025 on all upstream activities and reduce methane emission (IOGP, 2022). In fact, new technology also enables spatial methane plume detection over considerable areas, such as refineries or industrial parks.

Finally, in terms of the production of renewable energy, and the elimination of GHG emissions, companies in the sector have increased their investments in the research and deployment of renewable, clean energy technologies such as solar, wind, and hydrogen energies. They have done so to increase the portion of their total produced energy which is. This effort is a sign of a gradual transition from fossil fuel to renewable energy, in order to address the UN's seventh SDG (*Ensuring access to affordable, reliable, sustainable, and modern energy for all.*). In a recent study, Pickl (2019) investigated the strategies and policies of major oil firms with regard to their investment in renewables. He found that five companies (Royal Dutch Shell, Total, BP, Eni, and Equinor) out of the eight covered in the study had already adopted strategies to become renewable energy producers, rather than ones of fossil fuel energy.

Oil and gas companies still have a long journey ahead of them to address their contributions to sustainable development and clean affordable energies. This is partly the case because of the occurrence of devastating incidents in the sector over the last decade along with the environmental performance of companies in the sector in terms of pollution prevention. Thus, the following section discusses some future directions and improvements in the management of environmental health and safety within companies in the sector in an effort to meet the UN SDGs.

## Future Directions and Improvements to Achieve the UN SDGs 2030

It is obvious that companies in the oil and gas sector are far from achieving the relevant UN SDGs by 2030. Although their efforts are yielding positive results, further work is required to mitigate the risks and hazards incurred by the industry's activities, and to effectively counteract climate change.

Such work might include adopting advanced technologies in risk management: First, companies in the oil and gas sector can take advantage of artificial intelligence techniques to analyze big data generated from the operation of petroleum plants (Korotov & Tekic, 2021). To facilitate the adoption of these techniques in industry, the Center for Chemical Process Safety (CCPS) and European Process Safety Centre (EPSC) organize an international conference on big data and process safety on a yearly basis (Aiche, 2022). These conferences are attended by practitioners from large petrochemical companies and researchers in the process safety arena, two areas with similar opportunities, and also challenges, to adopt artificial intelligence techniques. The analysis of big data can help to detect trends in process condition, in forecasting future issues and potential incidents (by generating automated HAZOP or LOPA studies for complex petrochemical processes, e.g.), and making informed-decisions. Thus, these analyses result in better accuracy in the management of the risks and hazards at the plant level, and in the optimization of the maintenance and inspection activities among others. Ultimately, the frequency and severity of incidents in the sector could sharply decrease, thanks to artificial intelligence (Pasman & Rogers, 2016).

Limiting cyber risks, and maintaining control over cybersecurity: The digital transformation in the sector has been accompanied by an emergence of cyber threats and attacks on oil and gas facilities. In the US for example, Colonial Pipeline, announced in May 2021 that it had been subject to a cyber-attack targeting its business systems, which disrupted the distribution of its products to the southeast states of the US (US Government Accountability Office, 2021). Such events can result in a loss of confidential information or in the shutdown or sabotage of plants. Oil and gas companies must therefore consider their vulnerability to cyber-attacks, as these can prove to be devastating to their processes. Although there is no database for cyber incidents in the sector like there is for conventional incidents, it is clear that cyber-attacks on energy facilities become common globally. The development and adoption of international standards and specifications on cybersecurity like ISA/IEC 62,443 standards and ISO/IEC 27,032 demonstrate the significance of cybersecurity on the viability and resilience of oil and gas installations. Since the attackers have different backgrounds and motives and can sometimes even be linked to political conflicts, there is a need to establish a collaborative, multinational strategy among governments and companies in the sector to coordinate cybersecurity measures and protects installations from cyber-attacks.

Implementing climate-friendly process changes: Governments must adopt strict policies banning routine flaring of natural gas and methane venting at oil and gas processing facilities. This approach will drastically reduce the carbon dioxide and methane emissions in the air which exacerbate global warming. In 2015, the World Bank launched an initiative called "Zero Routine Flaring by 2030" which was endorsed by different governments, oil and gas companies, and institutions in the sector. This initiative aims to eliminate greenhouse gas emissions in the sector by ceasing gas flaring from oil and gas operations by 2030 at the latest (World Bank, 2022). This is significant because the initiative involves a commitment from those corporations responsible for 60% of the global flared gas emissions. Yet, this initiative has not been adopted by large natural gas producing countries like China and Iran. Moreover, to be successful, this policy will require the implementation of deep economic changes in gas pricing, incentives for existing investments, and stringent enforcement through national regulations.

Seeking innovative design for climate operation: The designers and manufacturers of oil and gas equipment should enhance the resilience of oil equipment and their capabilities to withstand disruptions throughout their lifecycle through a socio-technical system approach. This enhancement would be reflected on the overall process resilience and its ability to detect, react, and adjust to a sudden malfunction or disruption of the process conditions. We believe also that companies will better control risks like explosion, fire, and accidental release of hydrocarbons through this enhancement of process resilience. This improvement concerns the operating companies and also covers the culture of organizational safety and the human component of the system and its competency: in view of the high turnover of employees in the sector, there is a need for collaboration between academia and companies to address the shortfalls in process safety education among engineering disciplines at higher education levels. Additionally, companies in the sector must develop strategies to ensure the retention of skilled workers and critical knowledge among its key positions. Thus, processes can be adequately operated and safely safeguarded in case of mishaps.

## Conclusion

The oil and gas sector has a major role to play in the global achievement of the UN SDGs. While companies in the sector are directly concerned with the implementation of actions relevant to a set of the UN SDGs, they struggle to meet those goals due to the unique hazards and risks that they face. We therefore recommend that petrochemical companies seek to achieve these goals through the risk management systems they already have in place. Such approaches to risk management vary from the elimination of hazards or risk sources to the substitution of a risk for another and/or the setting up of engineering controls. Although some of these approaches have resulted in positive outcomes, the sector is far from achieving the UN SDGs and more efforts are required.

Future research is needed to benchmark and map the progress of oil and gas companies toward the achievement of UN SDGs. A baseline for benchmarking would be the sustainability metrics in 2015 when the UN SDGs were first established. This assessment will use the published sustainability reports of the major companies in the sector from 2015 up to 2022 which marks the mid of the fifteen-year span of the UN SDGs (2015–2030). As a result, it will be possible to understand where the sector is underperforming and needs more focus to achieve the relevant UN SDGs.

Finally, as previously discussed, the use of artificial intelligence techniques and a systems approach in analyzing and processing big data is another area of research that needs further attention. The outcomes of these studies will enable the prediction of process hazardous conditions and ultimately prevent incidents before their occurrence.

## References

Ambrose, J. (2020). BP leads energy companies preparing two major UK carbon capture projects. *The Guardian*. https://www.theguardian.com/environment/2020/oct/27/bp-leads-energy-companies-preparing-two-major-uk-carbon-capture-projects

BBC. (2016). BP says total Gulf spill bill $61.6bn. *BBC*. https://www.bbc.com/news/36798842

Benson, C., Dimopoulos, C., Argyropoulos, C., Mikellidou, C., & Boustras, G. (2021). Assessing the common occupational health hazards and their health risks among oil and gas workers. *Safety Science*. https://doi.org/10.1016/j.ssci.2021.105284

Canadian Center for Occupational Health and Safety. (2022). *Hazard and risk*. CCOHS. https://www.ccohs.ca/oshanswers/hsprograms/hazard_risk.html

Center for Chemical Process Safety. (2022). *CCPS Process Safety Glossary*. CCPS. https://www.aiche.org/ccps/resources/glossary

Cherry, T., Kallbekken, S., Kroll, S., & McEvoy, D. (2021). Does solar geoengineering crowd out climate change mitigation efforts? Evidence from a stated preference referendum on a carbon tax. *Climatic Change*, *165*(6). https://doi.org/10.1007/s10584-021-03009-z

Corner, A., & Pidgeon, N. (2014). Geoengineering, climate change skepticism and the 'moral hazard' argument: An experimental study of UK public perceptions. *Philosophical Transactions of the Royal A Society*. https://doi.org/10.1098/rsta.2014.0063

Environmental Protection Agency. (2022). *Deepwater horizon—BP Gulf of Mexico oil spill*. https://www.epa.gov/enforcement/deepwater-horizon-bp-gulf-mexico-oil-spill

Geoengineering Monitor. (2022). *Geoengineering supporters plan to set up a new climate overshoot commission*. https://www.geoengineeringmonitor.org/2022/05/geoengineering-supporters-plan-to-set-up-a-new climate-overshoot-commission/

International Association of Oil and Gas Producers. (2022). *Energy transition*. https://www.iogp.org/energy-transition/

International Organization of Standardization. (2018). *ISO 31000:2018(en) Risk management—guidelines.* https://www.iso.org/obp/ui/#iso:std:iso:31000:ed-2:v1:en

Mannan, S., & Lee, F. (2005). *Lee's loss prevention in the process industries: Hazard identification, assessment, and control Volume 1* (3rd ed.). London & Massachusetts: Elsevier.

Marsh. (2020). *100 Largest losses in the hydrocarbon industry 1974–2019.* https://www.marsh.com/us/industries/energy-and-power/insights/100-largest-losses-in-the-hydrocarbon-industry.html

National Commission on the BP Deepwater Horizon oil Spill. (2011). *Deep water: The Gulf oil disaster and the future of offshore drilling: Report to the President*. https://www.govinfo.gov/app/details/GPO-OILCOMMISSION

National Fire Protection Association. (2021). *NFPA Glossary of terms.* https://www.nfpa.org/Codes-and-Standards/Resources/Glossary-of-Terms

Nolan, P. (2011). *Handbook of fire and explosion protection engineering principles for oil, gas, chemical and related facilities* (2nd ed.). Elsevier

Pasman, H. J., Rogers, W. J., & Mannan, M. S. (2017). Risk Assessment: What is it worth? Shall we just do away with it, or can it do a better job? *Safety Science, 99*, 140–155. https://doi.org/10.1016/j.ssci.2017.01.011

Pasman, H., & Rogers, W. (2016). How can we improve HAZOP, our old work horse, and do more with its results? an overview of recent developments. *Chemical Engineering Transactions, 48*. https://doi.org/10.3303/CET1648139

Pickl, M. (2019). The renewable energy strategies of oil majors – From oil to energy? *Energy Strategy Reviews*. https://doi.org/10.1016/j.esr.2019.100370

Kazi, M.-K., Eljack, F., Al-Sobhi, S. A., Kazantzis, N., & Kazantzi, V. (2019). Application of i-SDT for Safer flare management operation. *Process Safety and Environmental Protection, 132*, 249–264. https://doi.org/10.1016/j.psep.2019.10.023

Koroteev, D., & Tekic, Z. (2021). Artificial Intelligence In Oil and Gas Upstream: Trends, challenges, and scenarios for the future. *Energy and AI, 3*, 100041. https://doi.org/10.1016/j.egyai.2020.100041

Reed, S. (2021). Oil giants prepare to put carbon back in the ground. *The New York Times*. https://www.nytimes.com/2021/03/08/business/carbon-capture-bp.html

Schneider, J., Ghettas, S., Merdaci, N., Brown, M., Martyniuk, J., Alshehri, W., & Trojan, A. (2013). Towards sustainability in the oil and gas sector: Benchmarking of environmental, health, and safety efforts. *Journal of Environmental Sustainability*, 3(3). https://scholarworks.rit.edu/jes/vol3/iss3/6/

United Nations. (2022). *Sustainable Development Goals.* https://sdgs.un.org/

US Government Accountability Office. (2021). *Colonial pipeline cyberattack highlights need for better federal and private-Sector preparedness (infographic).* https://www.gao.gov/blog/colonial-pipeline-cyberattack-highlights-need-better-federal-and-private-sector-preparedness-infographic. Accessed on September 31, 2022.

World Bank. (2022). *Zero Routine Flaring by 2030 (ZRF) Initiative*. https://www.worldbank.org/en/programs/zero-routine-flaring-by-2030/about

# Index






T. Walker et al. (eds.), *Sustainability in the Oil and Gas Sector*,
https://doi.org/10.1007/978-3-031-51586-6

SPRINGER NATURE

# GPSR Compliance

*The European Union's (EU) General Product Safety Regulation (GPSR) is a set of rules that requires consumer products to be safe and our obligations to ensure this.*

*If you have any concerns about our products, you can contact us on ProductSafety@springernature.com*

In case Publisher is established outside the EU, the EU authorized representative is:

Springer Nature Customer Service Center GmbH
Europaplatz 3
69115 Heidelberg, Germany

The manufacturer's authorised representative in the EU is Springer Nature Customer Service Centre GmbH, Europaplatz 3, 69115 Heidelberg, Germany. If you have any concerns regarding our products, please contact ProductSafety@springernature.com

Printed and bound by CPI Group (UK) Ltd, Croydon, CR0 4YY
01/10/2026
02225898-0003